TO WHOM DO

Most people believe that parents have rights to direct their children's education and upbringing. But why? What grounds those rights? How broad is their scope? Can we defend parental rights against those who believe we need more extensive state educational control to protect children's autonomy or prepare them for citizenship in a diverse society? Amid heated debates over issues like sexual education, diversity education and vouchers, Moschella cuts to the heart of the matter, explaining why education is primarily the responsibility of parents, not the state. Rigorously argued yet broadly accessible, the book offers a principled case for expanding school choice and granting exemptions when educational programs or regulations threaten parents' ability to raise their children in line with their values. Philosophical argument is complemented with psychological and social scientific research showing that robust parental rights' protections are crucial for the well-being of parents, children and society as a whole.

Melissa Moschella is an Assistant Professor of Philosophy at The Catholic University of America. She speaks and writes for both scholarly and popular audiences on topics including marriage, parental rights, reproductive technologies, and religious freedom.

TO WHOM DO CHILDREN BELONG?

Parental Rights, Civic Education and Children's Autonomy

MELISSA MOSCHELLA

The Catholic University of America

CAMBRIDGE
UNIVERSITY PRESS

CAMBRIDGE
UNIVERSITY PRESS

University Printing House, Cambridge CB2 8BS, United Kingdom

One Liberty Plaza, 20th Floor, New York, NY 10006, USA

477 Williamstown Road, Port Melbourne, VIC 3207, Australia

4843/24, 2nd Floor, Ansari Road, Daryaganj, Delhi - 110002, India

79 Anson Road, #06-04/06, Singapore 079906

Cambridge University Press is part of the University of Cambridge.

It furthers the University's mission by disseminating knowledge in the pursuit of education, learning and research at the highest international levels of excellence.

www.cambridge.org
Information on this title: www.cambridge.org/9781316605004

© Melissa Moschella 2016

First published 2016
First paperback edition 2017

A catalogue record for this publication is available from the British Library

Library of Congress Cataloging in Publication data
Names: Moschella, Melissa, 1979–
Title: To whom do children belong? : parental rights, civic education, and children's autonomy / Melissa Moschella.
Description: New York : Cambridge University Press, 2016. | Includes bibliographical references and index.
Identifiers: LCCN 2015043636 | ISBN 9781107150652 (Hardback)
Subjects: LCSH: Education–Parent participation–United States. | Parent and child (Law)–United States. | Children's rights–United States.
Classification: LCC LC225.3 .M67 2016 | DDC 371.19/2–dc23 LC record available at http://lccn.loc.gov/2015043636

ISBN 978-1-107-15065-2 Hardback
ISBN 978-1-316-60500-4 Paperback

To my family, especially my parents

CONTENTS

ACKNOWLEDGMENTS

This book, which began as my doctoral dissertation, and which I have revised – indeed, for the most part rewritten – over the past several years, would not have been possible without the help of many individuals and institutions. I am pleased to take the opportunity to acknowledge at least some of these debts here.

I am grateful, first of all, to my graduate adviser and dissertation director, Robert P. George. His work and generous dedication to the truth as a scholar, teacher and public intellectual have served as an example and inspiration to me, and his advice during my years of graduate study and in the early years of my academic career has been an invaluable and ongoing source of guidance and encouragement. I am grateful to him, in particular, for challenging me in my intellectual life to plunge without fear into the deep and uncharted waters of philosophical inquiries to which I do not know the answer in advance. This work is, among other things, a response to that challenge.

I owe a special debt of gratitude also to the other two members of my dissertation committee, Melissa Lane and Anna Stilz. Both were extremely generous with their time, providing detailed feedback in person and in writing, and affirming the importance of my work despite their ultimate disagreement with my conclusions. To the extent that this book succeeds in engaging seriously with the best counterarguments to my position, it is due in no small part to their insightful criticisms and suggestions. I also thank Stephen Macedo for serving as the fourth reader of my dissertation, and for the critical feedback which pushed me to make my arguments sharper and more nuanced.

I am grateful to Princeton University for generously supporting my graduate studies, and to the University Center for Human Values for the graduate prize fellowship I received in my final year of graduate school. Mention should also be made of the members of Princeton's political theory community during my time there, especially Daniel Mark, as well as several students and professors in the Philosophy Department, especially Sherif Girgis, who have made a rich contribution to my intellectual life, and from whom I have received helpful feedback on my work.

I am also indebted to the James Madison Program in American Ideals and Institutions for the post-doctoral research fellowship during which I began the long process of revising my dissertation in preparation for publication as a book, as well as the many members of the James Madison Society with whom I coincided while at Princeton, for their insightful and reassuring comments on my work, for their friendship and for their enjoyable and enriching conversation on a variety of subjects. Worthy of particular mention in this regard are Susan Hanssen – whose indomitable spirit, verve, wit and passionate commitment to the truth have reinvigorated and inspired me on many occasions – as well as Sara Henary, Zena Hitz and Gabrielle Girgis. I shared an office with Gabby during my fellowship, and her delightful company, conversation and friendship were – and continue to be – an invaluable source of support and encouragement on many levels.

The Myser Fellowship that I received from the University of Notre Dame's Center for Ethics and Culture afforded me the opportunity to devote much of the 2014–2015 academic year to completing my revisions on the manuscript. I am grateful to all of the faculty and staff associated with the Center during my time there, particularly John Keown, the Center's 2014–2015 Remick Fellow, for his advice, feedback and buoyant company. I am also indebted to many other members of the Notre Dame community, especially Michael Zuckert, who generously took the time to read and offer insightful comments on the penultimate draft of the manuscript, and Mary Keys, who has been an invaluable source of encouragement and advice, both practical and theoretical, since the project's inception.

I am grateful as well to my colleagues at The Catholic University of America's School of Philosophy for creating such a congenial, friendly and supportive working environment, in which I have felt at home since the very beginning of my time here.

Many others both within and beyond the academy have contributed to this project in countless ways. It would be impossible to name them all – and I apologize to anyone whom I have inadvertently neglected to include here – but a few deserve special mention. Esther Hudson, my graduate research assistant, helped me to prepare the final manuscript for publication, and I am grateful for her hard work. Eamonn Callan read an early draft of Chapter 4, and offered a number of helpful suggestions in an enjoyable email exchange. Over the course of several conversations, Sarah-Vaughan Brakman, Elizabeth Kirk and Christopher Tollefsen convinced me of the need to be more sensitive and nuanced in my discussion of adoptive parenthood – I hope that I have been successful in my attempt to heed their advice. Gerard Bradley and John Finnis provided insightful feedback on the draft of an article now published in *The American Journal of Jurisprudence*, parts of which (with permission) have been incorporated into this book. Ana Marta Gonzalez, whom I first got to know many years ago while I was an undergraduate at Harvard and she was a visiting professor, offered me the opportunity to present an overview of my argument for parental rights at a seminar sponsored by the University of Navarre's Institute for Culture and Society; our intermittent contact over the years has profoundly enriched my intellectual life in countless ways.

I am especially thankful to Moira Walsh, whose friendship and guidance on matters both personal and philosophical extend all the way back to my very first foray into philosophical inquiry as a high school senior. Without her prudent advice, sympathetic ear and patient encouragement, together with that of Gabriela Martinez, and, in the project's final stages, Margaret Garvey, I doubt that this project would ever have reached completion.

I owe the greatest debt to my family, especially my parents: it is to them that this work is dedicated, with much love.

~

Introduction

To whom do children "belong"? Political scientist Melissa Harris-Perry sparked heated controversy when she suggested in a 2013 MSNBC commercial that, in order to improve our educational system, "we have to break through our kind of private idea that kids belong to their parents or kids belong to their families and recognize that kids belong to whole communities." Of course, children are not property and do not belong to anyone in that sense. But, like all of us, children belong to – i.e. are members of – various communities, including their families and the larger social and political communities in which their families are embedded. And they also "belong" to others more specifically in the sense of being entrusted to their care and guidance, precisely because as children they are not yet able to care for and guide themselves. When we ask the question, "To whom do children belong?" what we really mean is: Who has primary responsibility for children and decision-making authority over them? Harris-Perry's answer – at least as commonly interpreted – is that the political community, not the family, holds primary responsibility for and authority over children. The furious public discussion that Harris-Perry's comment ignited indicates that the question is far from settled.

To see what is at stake in the answer, consider the case of the Romeike family. Uwe and Hanalore Romeike, along with their five children, lived in a southwest German town called Bietigheim-Bissinge, where their three oldest children attended the public schools. Over time, the parents began to worry that the school curriculum and environment were having a negative impact on their children. They noticed distressing personality changes in their oldest son Daniel, and their oldest daughter started to suffer from frequent headaches and stomach aches.[1] Mr. Romeike was appalled to find that Daniel's health textbook used slang terms, including

---

[1] Jane O'Brien, "German home-school families face US deportation," *BBC News*, November 6, 2013. www.bbc.com/news/business-24804804. Last accessed on: Oct. 22, 2014.

foul language, to refer to sexual acts, and was concerned more generally that the values conveyed in his children's classes and readings conflicted with the Christian moral and religious values he and his wife strove to pass on to their children at home.[2] In 2006, the Romeikes pulled their children out of the public schools and began educating them at home, despite the fact that homeschooling is illegal in Germany. Thus began a long battle with state authorities, which included police attempts to enter the Romeikes' home and bring the children to school by force, and onerous fines adding up to 7,000 Euros.[3] Fearing further legal action, including the possibility of imprisonment and losing custody of the children, the Romeikes moved to the United States where they would be free to educate their children as they thought best. Despite losing their appeal for asylum in 2013,[4] shortly before being deported in 2014 they were granted permission to remain indefinitely in the country. Leaving aside the controversial legal question of whether or not the Romeikes ought to have been granted asylum, what ought we to think of this case? Did the German government violate the Romeikes' rights by forbidding them from homeschooling their children? Or were the Romeikes at fault for failing to recognize the state's legitimate claim to ensure the full integration of future citizens into the broader society through public schooling? The answer to these questions ultimately turns on whether or not Harris-Perry is correct in her claim that children "belong" primarily to the political community rather than to their parents.

The question has been the subject of debate at least since Plato's discussion of communal childrearing in the *Republic*. Throughout the history of the United States, there have been recurring controversies over the relative scope and limits of parental educational authority as against state educational authority, particularly as the state began to take on an increasingly more prominent educational role in the nineteenth and twentieth centuries. These controversies have given rise to famous Supreme Court cases like *Meyers v. Nebraska*[5] and *Pierce v. Society of Sisters*,[6] which proclaimed the existence of a fundamental constitutional right of parents to direct the education and upbringing of their children. Yet, at least from the moral perspective, the Supreme Court's ruling is

---

[2] "German family seeks US asylum to homeschool kids," Associated Press, March 31, 2009. www.foxnews.com/story/2009/03/31/german-family-seeks-us-asylum-to-homeschool-kids. Last accessed on: Oct. 22, 2014.
[3] *Romeike v. Holder*, 718 F.3d 518 (6th Cir. 2013).   [4] *Romeike v. Holder*.
[5] 262 U.S. 390 (1923).   [6] 268 U.S. 510 (1925).

hardly sufficient to ground a moral right, and even if it were, the Court's doctrine still leaves much to be determined in terms of the scope and limits of that right in difficult cases.

Should, for instance, Amish parents be exempted from compulsory education laws and allowed to end their children's formal academic education after eighth grade, in order to teach their children the skills and values they need to carry on the Amish way of life? The United States Supreme Court answered yes to this question as a constitutional matter in *Wisconsin v. Yoder*,[7] but was the decision correct as a matter of moral principle? Or what about cases in which parents find some aspect of the public school curriculum offensive to their religious or moral beliefs? Do they have the right to exempt their children from those classes and offer them alternative instruction? The plaintiffs in *Mozert v. Hawkins*[8] sought, and were denied, just such an exemption from a "diversity-oriented" reading curriculum that conflicted with the beliefs they wanted to pass on to their children. Does this decision of the Sixth Circuit Court amount to a violation of parental rights, or was it a legitimate exercise of state educational authority? And what about homeschooling? Home-schooling is now legal throughout the United States, but for most of the twentieth century homeschooling was considered to be a violation of compulsory education laws, and debates about the practice are ongoing, both in the United States and abroad. In *Konrad v. Germany*[9] the European Court of Human Rights (ECHR) upheld Germany's prohibition on homeschooling, arguing that the state's interest in the integration of children into the broader community outweighs the rights of parents. Was the ECHR correct in its reasoning? Should homeschooling continue to be allowed in the United States? How heavily should it be regulated?

More generally, to what extent should the state be involved in education? Should the state be in the business of running schools at all, or, as John Stuart Mill argued, should the state eschew public provision of education and limit itself to funding private educational institutions? If the state does run its own schools, should those schools enjoy a monopoly on public educational funding, or should the state provide vouchers or scholarships that parents can use to pay for their child's education at any school, private or public? Does the state have the right to regulate private schools and homeschools and, if so, to what extent? Is that

---

[7] 406 U.S. 205 (1972).   [8] 872 F. 2d 1058 (1987).   [9] Appl No 35504/03, 18 Sep 2006.

regulatory power limited to relatively non-controversial academic standards, or does it extend to more controversial areas like sexual education or diversity education?

The dominant view among Rawlsian liberal theorists such as Amy Gutmann, Eamonn Callan and Stephen Macedo is that, when it comes to formal schooling, the state's educational authority is at least equal to, if not superior to, the educational authority of parents. While these theorists do not entirely deny the existence of parental rights to direct the education of their children, they consider those rights to be highly circumscribed by the educational authority of the state. When there is a conflict between parental rights and state educational goals, or when parents and the state disagree over what is in the best interests of the child, most believe that the state has the final say. Most Rawlsian liberal theorists agree, for example, with the circuit court's decision in *Mozert v. Hawkins* denying the parents' exemption request, and disagree with the Supreme Court's accommodation of the Amish in *Wisconsin v. Yoder*. Homeschooling and private schooling are accepted (in some cases grudgingly) by the majority of Rawlsian liberals, but most also call for much heavier regulations to ensure that children receive sufficient exposure to diverse ways of life, both to protect the children's autonomy and to prepare them for citizenship in a pluralistic democratic society.

In the following chapters I seek to challenge this Rawlsian liberal view and provide a robust defense of parental rights in education. Unlike other defenders of parental rights, I do not base my case primarily on the claim that, as a practical matter, parents are the ones who are best placed to make educational decisions in terms of both knowledge of their children's needs and motivation to help their children thrive, although I agree with this claim and think that it is an important one.[10] Nor do I make my case on libertarian grounds, on grounds of economic efficiency,[11] or on constitutional grounds.[12] Rather, I seek to offer a deeper theoretical foundation for parental rights by basing them on the special obligations inherent in the parent–child relationship, and the pre-political parental authority that is the flip side of those obligations.

---

[10] Perhaps the most prominent defense of this claim is that of John E. Coons and Stephen D. Sugarman in *Education by Choice: The Case for Family Control* (Berkeley: University of California Press, 1978).

[11] See John E. Chubb and Terry M. Moe, *Politics, Markets and America's Schools* (Washington, DC: The Brookings Institution, 1990).

[12] See *Pierce v. Society of Sisters* 268 U.S. 510 (1925).

By examining the foundations of parental authority, my approach brings new considerations to the table that require a rethinking of common assumptions underlying Rawlsian liberal approaches to the topic. In her influential book *Democratic Education*, Amy Gutmann asserts that "all significant [education] policy prescriptions presuppose a theory, a political theory, of the proper role of government in educa-tion."[13] Yet in trying to set forth such a theory, she, like other Rawlsian liberal theorists, essentially ends up begging the question in a way that denies the pre-political authority of parents. Gutmann complains about theories that "depoliticize education by placing it as much as possible in the province of parental authority."[14] Such "depoliticization" of educa-tion, however, is only a problem if authority over children belongs primarily to the political community as a whole, rather than to parents. Gutmann makes a valid point when she claims that "because children are members of both families and states, the educational authorities of parents and of polities has to be partial to be justified."[15] The trouble, however, is that she seems to envision authority in a two-dimensional way, like a pie that needs to be divided into pieces, and she assumes that it is the state (via democratic deliberation) that should determine the size of each piece. What if, however, we were to view spheres of authority not as pieces of a pie, but as overlapping or concentric spheres, like trad-itional Russian nesting dolls, in which each sphere has relative autonomy over its internal affairs? This concentric sphere model of authority corresponds to a more nuanced understanding of the difference in kind between children's membership in the family and children's membership in the political community. On this view, which I explain and defend in the course of the book, children belong to – i.e. are members of – their families in a direct and immediate way, whereas (until adulthood) they belong to the political community indirectly, through the mediation of their parents. What this implies is that while parents and the state do both have some educational authority, their authority is not on the same plane or aimed at exactly the same goals. Rather, *parental authority is primary and aims directly at the overall well-being of the child, while the state's authority over education in most respects is indirect and subsidiary to that of parents. Only with respect to specifically civic (rather than child-centered) aims does the state have direct educational authority. With regard to the child-centered aims of education, the state's role is to support*

---

[13] Amy Gutmann, *Democratic Education* (Princeton: Princeton University Press, 1999), 6.
[14] Gutmann, *Democratic Education*, 6.   [15] Gutmann, *Democratic Education*, 30.

parents in carrying out their obligations, rather than to bypass or usurp
parental educational authority, except in cases of abuse or neglect. And
even in pursuing civic educational goals, the state should avoid (when
possible) policies that conflict with parents' rights to educate their children
in accordance with the dictates of their consciences, rights that flow from
parental responsibilities and protect parental authority.

Grappling seriously with this alternative approach to determining the
respective scope and limits of parental and state educational authority –
one grounded in a natural law approach to moral and political thought –
can be beneficial even for those who are ultimately unpersuaded by it, or
whose premises differ from my own. Indeed, most if not all of my
conclusions can be defended in part on liberal grounds, and I draw on
the work of Tocqueville, Mill, Galston and others in support of my
arguments. More generally, I share many of the concerns and values of
the theorists with whose premises and/or conclusions I ultimately disagree, in some cases drawing on the natural law tradition to provide a
deeper grounding for those values than they themselves can. For
instance, Gutmann, Macedo, Callan and others presume, with little or
no explanation, that parents have *some* childrearing authority and that
the state should not be in the business of breaking up biological families,
redistributing children to those who are deemed to be more competent,
or raising children communally in state-run institutions. But why not?
Why presume that parents (biological parents, in the focal case) should
usually be allowed to raise their own children? Why does biological
parenthood have any moral relevance at all? I offer an answer to these
questions in Chapter 1, analyzing the biological relationship between
parent and child in order to establish that that relationship in and of
itself creates personal obligations that are the grounds of parental authority. In doing so, I show that parental authority over children is *natural*
and original, not (as the Rawlsian view seems to imply) *conventional or*
derivative of the authority of the larger political community over its
members. I also explain how the same basic principles about the connec-
tions among personal relationships, special obligations and authority can
be applied to non-biological parent–child relationships as well.

Similarly, in Chapter 2 I develop an account of conscience rights in
dialogue with liberal thinkers such as William Galston and Paul Bou-
Habib. Galston defends conscience rights under the umbrella of "expressive liberty," and Bou-Habib speaks of a "right to integrity" understood
as a right to fulfill one's perceived obligations. Both accounts, however,
have significant weaknesses. Galston's account grounds expressive liberty

on subjective preferences, begging the question of why a preference for maintaining one's integrity should be given more weight than any other preference, and neither account offers much principled guidance on how to balance expressive liberty against competing rights or public interests. Drawing on premises from the natural law tradition, I offer a more robust explanation of why conscience deserves respect, and of the relative weight of conscience rights in cases of conflict. The chapter then goes on to conceptualize parental rights as a sphere of sovereignty that protects parental childrearing authority and safeguards the conscience rights of parents by providing the space within which they can fulfill their child-rearing obligations in accordance with the dictates of their consciences. This view complements – and effectively translates into the language of rights – the conclusions of Chapter 1 regarding the primacy of parental educational authority.

Having established in the first two chapters the foundations for my own view of parental rights in dialogue with liberal theorists, in the following two chapters I consider some of the strongest arguments that have been put forth in favor of more expansive state authority over education than my own account would support. Those arguments can be divided into two distinct but overlapping strands: one focuses on the state's interest in educating children for liberal democratic citizenship, and the other focuses on the need for state regulation of education in order to protect children's future autonomy. I engage with these arguments in Chapters 3 and 4, respectively. In doing so, I seek both to show how Rawlsian liberal arguments rely on premises that are controversial even among liberals, and to show how the interests of children and the concern for the future of the political community figure in my own account. I have grave concerns about general political apathy and lack of informed political participation among citizens, and I recognize that the state has an important interest in educating future citizens. However, I take issue with the controversial Rawlsian ideal of citizenship that is at the heart of Gutmann, Macedo and Callan's educational recommendations, and argue that mandating civic education in line with that ideal goes well beyond the legitimate authority of the state. I argue, instead, that state educational authority justifies the coercive imposition of only a relatively non-controversial civic minimum, and that great respect for the conscientious concerns of parents should be shown in both the crafting and enforcing of that minimum. Likewise, I am sympathetic to liberal theorists' commitment to ensuring that children learn critical thinking skills and are exposed, at the right time and in the right way, to views that challenge their own. Yet I do not think that it is within the proper scope of state authority to coercively enforce any particular educational ideal. Further, an Aristotelian understanding of moral development, corroborated by neurobiological research and empirical research on parenting styles, provides reasons to think that, even in adolescence, fostering a critical attitude toward the values taught by parents may on balance be more harmful than helpful to children.

Given that my approach to the issue of parental rights in education is primarily philosophical in nature, it is beyond the scope of my account to offer detailed, positive policy recommendations. My discussion of education policies is limited to considerations regarding the extent to which parental authority over education sets principled limits on state action in this sphere. There are, of course, other factors that bear upon the justice of educational policies, such as concerns about equality, distributive justice, academic achievement, economic efficiency, and so forth. Any detailed positive policy proposals would have to take all of these relevant factors into account. Here I attempt nothing of the sort. My aim is only to establish some of the moral principles – those related to parental rights and authority – that bear on education policy decisions. These principles, however, do have some specific policy implications insofar as they set a bar that any just education policy must meet. Therefore, while detailed, positive policy recommendations are beyond the scope of this project, the moral principles I establish have specific implications about which policies it would always be unjust to pursue, even in spite of potential advantages with regard to other factors such as academic achievement or economic efficiency. In the final chapter of the book I discuss some of these implications in general terms, addressing debates over whether and to what extent parents have a right to exemptions and accommodations to educational requirements to which they have a conscientious objection, disputes over sexual education and "diversity" or "tolerance" education, and controversies regarding educational funding, particularly voucher programs and other attempts to increase effective school choice especially among those with limited financial means.

It is my hope that this book will offer stimulating and challenging food for thought to those inclined to agree with my conclusions just as much as to those inclined to disagree. For on a subject so crucial to both individual well-being and the good of society as a whole, it is well worth the effort to dig all the way to the foundations in order to find solid principles on which to base our policies.

Foundational premises

Like everyone, I come to the question of parental rights within the context of a more general philosophical perspective that forms the basis for the presuppositions upon which my argument relies, but which are beyond the scope of the current project to defend. While I provide at least a summary defense of my most crucial presuppositions as they come up in the course of the argument, it seems worthwhile at the outset to say a few words about the larger tradition of political and moral thought from which these presuppositions are drawn, and in which they find their full explanation.

Although for the most part I approach the question of parental rights dialectically, in dialogue with contemporary liberal theorists, my foundational premises come from what Isaiah Berlin calls the "central tradition of western thought," and particularly the work of two of its most important and influential figures, Aristotle and Aquinas.[16] From this tradition, I take a number of important metaphysical and ethical presuppositions. The key metaphysical presupposition of my argument is an Aristotelian-Thomistic understanding of the human person in which the body is an essential and intrinsic aspect of personal identity, rather than a mere extrinsic instrument of the conscious, thinking, willing "I" or self. This view of the person is central to my defense of the moral relevance of the biological tie between parent and child, which in turn is central to my view of parental authority as natural and original, rather than conventional and derivative of the authority of the larger political community. Because I discuss this understanding of the person in Chapter 1, there is no need to say more about it here.

The central tradition also provides important ethical presuppositions for my account. I base my view on a general Aristotelian-Thomistic theory of value as interpreted, developed and articulated systematically by contemporary authors such as Germain Grisez, John Finnis, Joseph Boyle and Robert George.[17] The work of these authors is often called

---

[16] Isaiah Berlin, *The Crooked Timber of Humanity: Chapters in the History of Ideas* (New York: Alfred A. Knopf, 1991).

[17] See, for example, John Finnis, *Natural Law and Natural Rights*, Second Edition (New York: Oxford University Press, 2011); John Finnis, Joseph Boyle and Germain Grisez, *Nuclear Deterrence, Morality and Realism* (New York: Oxford University Press, 1987); Robert George, *Making Men Moral* (New York: Oxford University Press, 1993); Germain Grisez, *The Way of the Lord Jesus, Vol. 2: Living a Christian Life* (Quincy, IL: Franciscan Press, 1993); Germain Grisez, Joseph Boyle and John Finnis, "Practical Principles, Moral Truth and Ultimate Ends," *American Journal of Jurisprudence* 32 (1987): 99–151; Patrick

"new natural law theory." However, having clarified that this is the version of natural law theory which I am adopting, I will from this point onward refer simply to "natural law theory," rather than using the more cumbersome and controversial "new natural law" label. In what follows I will offer a brief overview of this theory insofar as it is relevant to my understanding and defense of parental rights.[18]

Theory of value and normative ethics

Central to natural law theory is an account of the basic goods that are constitutive elements of human well-being, and the moral norms that structure and order the pursuit of those goods both individually and as a community.[19] Basic goods are goods that provide intrinsic and not merely instrumental reasons for action, goods that contribute to and constitute human flourishing in its various dimensions – physical, moral and intellectual, as an individual and in relation to other human beings as well as to the divine. These goods include life, health, knowledge, aesthetic appreciation, skillful performance in work and play, friendship, marriage, religion and practical reasonableness.[20] They are basic not only

Lee and Robert George, *Body–Self Dualism in Contemporary Ethics and Politics* (New York: Cambridge University Press, 2008).

[18] I offer a fuller (though still brief) account of natural law theory in Melissa Moschella and Robert George, "Natural Law," *International Encyclopedia of the Social and Behavioral Sciences*, Second Edition (Oxford: Elsevier, 2015).

[19] On the new natural law view, the first principle of practical reason – that "good is to be done and pursued, and evil is to be avoided" (Thomas Aquinas, *Summa Theologiae* I-II, q. 94, a.2) – should be understood as shorthand for multiple principles given the plurality of basic human goods. Thus, the principle really means that life, knowledge, friendship, practical reasonableness, etc. are to be pursued, and their opposites to be avoided.

[20] I believe that, if each of these goods is understood correctly, this is an accurate and complete list of basic human goods, in the sense that any other genuine human good will turn out to be a way of pursuing or realizing one or a combination of these goods. Nonetheless, the theory as a whole does not rely on the accuracy or completeness of this precise list of goods. For an explanation of the basic goods, see Finnis, *Natural Law and Natural Rights*, especially chapters III–IV. The clearest, and most updated succinct articulation of the basic goods is as follows: "(1) *knowledge* (including aesthetic appreciation) of reality; (2) *skillful performance*, in work and play, for its own sake; (3) *bodily life* and the components of its fullness, viz. health, vigour and safety; (4) *friendship* or harmony and association between persons and in its various forms and strengths; (5) the sexual association of a man and a woman which, though it essentially involves both friendship between the partners and the procreation and education of children by them, seems to have a point and shared benefit that is not reducible either to friendship or to life-in-its-transmission and therefore (as comparative anthropology confirms and

in the sense that they provide reasons for action that require no justification in terms of their relation to some other more basic good, but also in
the sense that they *cannot* be justified in terms of some other more basic
good. The intrinsic desirability or goodness of these goods (i.e. that we
grasp these goods as "to-be-pursued") is self-evident; it is the basis of all
practical reasoning and therefore can be defended dialectically but not
demonstrated properly speaking.[21]

These goods are all equally basic insofar as they each provide intelligible reasons for action. Practical reasonableness, however, plays an
architectonic role because it is not only one of the basic goods, but also
the basis for the moral norms that guide morally-significant choice
among the various goods, norms such as the requirement to devise and
follow a rational plan of life, to favor and foster the common good of
one's communities, to respect every basic value in every act, to be
reasonably faithful to one's commitments, to avoid arbitrary preferences
among values or persons, and to follow one's conscience (understood as a
specific judgment of practical reason regarding what one should do or
not do here and now).[22] These norms are not arbitrary, but are simply

---

Aristotle came particularly close to articulating [e.g. Aristotle, *Nicomachean Ethics*
VIII.12:1162a15–29], not to mention the 'third founder' of Stoicism, Musonius Rufus
should be acknowledged to be a distinct basic human good, call it *marriage*; (6) the good
of harmony between one's feelings and one's judgments (inner integrity), and between
one's judgments and one's behavior (authenticity), which we can call *practical reasonableness*; (7) *harmony with* the widest reaches and most *ultimate source* of all reality,
including meaning and value" (Finnis, *Natural Law and Natural Rights*, 448). While not
all natural law theorists agree that practical reasonableness is itself a basic good – Grisez,
for example, does not – all do seem to agree that integrity or inner peace/harmony
(harmony among one's feelings and among one's feelings, judgments and choices) as well
as harmony among one's judgments, choices and behavior (referred to variously as peace
of conscience, consistency or authenticity) are basic human goods (see Grisez, Boyle and
Finnis, "Practical Principles, Moral Truth and Ultimate Ends," 108). Following Finnis'
more recent formulations, in my own account I understand the basic good of practical
reasonableness to consist in a combination of these two goods. My reliance on practical
reasonableness as a basic good in defending the importance of conscience could also be
defended directly with reference to the goods of integrity and authenticity.

[21] For further discussion of the sense in which these goods are self-evident, see Finnis,
Natural Law and Natural Rights, section III.4.

[22] For a complete list and explanation of these moral norms, see Finnis, *Natural Law and
Natural Rights*, chapter V, along with the supplementary notes in the Postscript to the
Second Edition, 450–457. Religion is like practical reasonableness in that, in addition to
being itself a basic good, it is also potentially implicated in all of one's choices and actions,
and plays an architectonic role in the moral life. For more on this point, see Joseph Boyle,
"The Place of Religion in the Practical Reasoning of Individuals and Groups," *American
Journal of Jurisprudence* 43 (1998): 1–24 and Melissa Moschella, "Beyond Equal Liberty:

specifications of what it means to act in a fully reasonable way. Practical reason is concerned with integral human fulfillment, such that a person who lacks practical reasonableness will not flourish with respect to any of the goods for the sake of which he acts because his pursuit of those goods will not be properly structured by norms that distinguish fully reasonable from rationally-based but not fully reasonable options. A morally good action is an action that is fully practically reasonable, an action the willing or choosing of which is compatible with a will toward human well-being integrally conceived – i.e. the well-being of all human beings in all of its dimensions.

Because of the architectonic role that practical reasonableness plays – i.e. because it is integral to all of our practical choosing – there are no circumstances under which one can lay the good of practical reasonableness aside in order to pursue another good. This is why moral norms are second-order reasons, exclusionary reasons that act as decisive reasons against otherwise reasonable courses of action. I may, for example, have a first-order reason to seek the good of aesthetic experience by spending the afternoon at the museum, but my professional commitments might provide a second-order, exclusionary reason against dedicating my time to the pursuit of this and other otherwise reasonable ends. Indeed, to say that the basic goods all provide intrinsically intelligible reasons for action simply means that at any point in time I have a *prima facie* reason to pursue an instantiation of any one of those goods. Determining which of those goods I actually should pursue, and how I should do so, is the task of practical reason. Full practical reasonableness is therefore not only compatible with, but constantly requires, the laying aside of some goods in favor of others.

However, what is never compatible with full practical reasonableness – and therefore never compatible with human well-being integrally conceived – is to lay aside the good of practical reasonableness itself. In a sense this is simply tautological. It is never fully practically reasonable to act against practical reasonableness – i.e. to act in opposition to the considered judgments of practical reason. Therefore, whenever a moral norm, which is simply a requirement of full practical reasonableness, conflicts with the pursuit of a first-order good, the pursuit of that good is immoral, out of line with a will toward integral human fulfillment, and therefore not integrally perfective of the agent or fully respectful of

Religion as a Distinct Human Good and the Implications for Religious Freedom," *Journal of Law and Religion* (forthcoming, 2016).

others' well-being, even though the good pursued is genuinely good. What this implies is that to achieve integral human well-being, to flourish as a human being in the fullest sense, moral goodness (which is essential to practical reasonableness) is central. The person who has bodily health, knowledge, friends and so forth but who lacks a good character is, on this account, importantly worse off than the person who is ill, ignorant and alone, but morally good. In other words, as Plato famously argued in the *Gorgias*, it is better to suffer injustice than to commit it.

This moral theory is similar to Kantian views insofar as morally good action is action in line with a good will, and acting in line with a good will means acting in a fully reasonable way. Nonetheless, it is distinct from Kantian understandings of morality because on this view practical reasonableness is always specified with reference to human goods, and a good will is a will that is in line with human well-being integrally conceived. In other words, on this account acting in a fully reasonable way is not merely a formal requirement but has a necessary connection to the goods that are constitutive of human well-being. For instance, one formulation of Kant's categorical imperative, his basic rule for moral action, is that one should always treat persons (including oneself) as ends in themselves, and never as mere means.[23] Yet without a substantive account of the goods that are constitutive of human well-being, there is no objective standard of what it means to treat a person as an end instead of as a mere means. On the natural law account, one treats persons as ends, rather than as mere means, by respecting their well-being in all of its basic dimensions as specified by the basic goods. Natural law theory therefore gives content to this formal Kantian moral rule.

While this intrinsic connection between morally good action and human well-being may seem to bring the natural law account closer to consequentialist moral theories, which determine the rightness or wrongness of actions based on their consequences, natural law differs importantly from consequentialist theories not only because the moral relevance of consequences is much more limited on the natural law view, but also because human well-being is not understood monistically. Rather, the basic goods are each incommensurably choiceworthy, contributing to human fulfillment in distinct and irreducible ways. This means not that there can be no order of priority among the basic human goods – indeed, forming and pursuing a coherent plan of life demands such

---

[23] Immanuel Kant, *Grounding for the Metaphysics of Morals* (Indianapolis: Hackett Publishing Company, Inc., 1993), Second Section, Ak. 429, 36.

prioritization – but that when action in pursuit of good A is ruled out by a moral norm, or when one reasonably chooses to pursue good B rather than good A, one's reason to pursue A is defeated, but not destroyed. On a consequentialist account, if it is right to pursue B rather than A, then B contains all the good of A, and more. To pursue A in such a case would be unintelligible. According to natural law theory, by contrast, to act for a basic good in a way that is not fully practically reasonable – in a way, for example, that fails to respect the requirements of fairness by giving one person's enjoyment of a good undue weight in comparison to another person's enjoyment of that or another basic good – is still intelligible, even though it is morally wrong. Imagine, for instance, that in order to pay for his daughter's college tuition, a father engages in fraudulent business practices. This action is intelligible – it has a rational basis as directed towards the education of his daughter – even though it is morally wrong (not fully reasonable) because it directly damages the mutual trust that is an essential aspect of the common good.

Obligation

There are three highly interconnected elements within natural law theory that are particularly important for my understanding of parental rights: the notion of obligation, the notion of rights, and the notion of authority. First, on this view, to say that I have an obligation to do or not to do something is equivalent to saying that practical reasonableness requires or forbids it. Moral obligation is not something generated by command or consent, separate from the requirements of practical reasonableness.[24] Rather, moral obligation resides in the moral norms themselves, the force of which is in their reasonableness. One has an obligation to do what reason requires, and an obligation not to do what reason forbids. For example, I have an obligation to refrain from murder because life is a basic good and it is never fully reasonable intentionally to damage or destroy a basic good in oneself or in others. The reason that I have not to murder therefore defeats any alternative reason that I may have in favor of murdering. In general, therefore, in any given situation I have an obligation to act as the practically reasonable person would act (or, in cases where the right action is morally underdetermined – the majority of cases – I have an obligation to act in one of the ways that a practically

---

[24] For a historical discussion distinguishing Aquinas' understanding of obligation from that of voluntarist natural law theories, see Finnis, *Natural Law and Natural Rights*, 44–48.

reasonable person would act). Further, as already indicated, on this account practical reasonableness is not merely procedural or instrumental. It is not simply a matter of acting "rationally" in the sense of choosing means that are well-adapted to some pre-given ends. Practical reasonableness includes a substantive account of human goods that provide basic reasons for action, as well as an account of moral norms that guide deliberation and choice among these goods and the means to pursue them. Since practical reasonableness is itself a basic human good and plays an architectonic role in relation to all aspects of human well-being, it is always morally obligatory to act in accordance with the considered judgments of practical reason – in other words, it is always morally obligatory to act in accordance with the dictates of one's conscience. Put negatively, this means that acting against one's conscience (understood as the considered judgment of practical reason) is never in accordance with human well-being integrally conceived.

The idea, developed in Chapter 2, that parental rights are grounded in conscience rights or a right to integrity, draws on the notion that preserving and developing our practical reasonableness is among the most fundamental interests of human beings, given that flourishing with respect to practical reasonableness has a crucial impact on one's ability to flourish with respect to all of the other aspects of basic human well-being.[25] This point also relates to my argument in Chapter 4 that true education for autonomy requires education for a good moral character. In this context, it is worth emphasizing that there is a crucial difference between actions that practical reason *permits*, and actions that practical reason absolutely *requires* or *forbids*. No harm to one's moral integrity is necessarily involved in omitting an action that practical reason permits (and that one might be strongly inclined to perform), or performing an action that practical reason does not forbid (even though one might strongly prefer not to). Conscience rights protect the agent's ability to act in accordance with what the agent takes to be the requirements and prohibitions of practical reason, not in accordance with the agent's preferences (even perfectly reasonable preferences) in cases where acting

---

[25] When I refer to the good of practical reasonableness, I am referring to the establishment and maintenance of harmony between reason and emotion, and between judgment and action. I often also refer to this good as "integrity." To avoid confusion, I should note that here I use the word "integrity" to encompass *both* harmony between the reasoning and desiring aspects of oneself, *and* harmony between one's judgments and actions, while Finnis distinguishes between the former and the latter, calling them inner integrity and outer authenticity, respectively (See Finnis, *Natural Law and Natural Rights*, 448).

otherwise would still be compatible with practical reasonableness. This is not to say that restrictions on liberty are never unjust except in cases where conscience rights are at stake, since making and following a coherent plan of life and the development of moral maturity more generally require a fairly broad sphere of individual freedom, particularly freedom from coercive state interference in one's choices and actions. Nonetheless, laws which burden conscience rights – laws that require people to perform an action that they believe practical reason *forbids* them from performing, or to omit an action that they believe practical reason *requires* them to perform – directly threaten the moral integrity of citizens in a way that other laws, even if they unreasonably restrict freedom, do not.

Perhaps an example will help to clarify the point. Consider the case of laws prohibiting the use of certain drugs. There are undoubtedly many individuals who sincerely believe that there is nothing wrong with the use of such drugs, and who find their use relaxing, stimulating, exciting or otherwise enjoyable. In requiring such individuals to forego acting on their desire to use drugs (or face legal punishment) the government does not threaten the moral integrity of those individuals, because they do not (let us assume) think that drug use is morally (or religiously) *required*. The case is different, however, for a devout member of the Native American Church whose religion (let us assume) requires him to smoke peyote as part of a religious ritual. The drug law *does* threaten the Native American Church member's integrity, as well as his pursuit of harmony with the divine, giving him a strong claim to an exemption from the law, because his religiously-informed practical reason judges the use of peyote to be morally required.[26] The United States Supreme Court considered such a case in *Employment Division v. Smith*,[27] ruling that there was no

---

[26] Since my aim here is to explain the nature and importance of conscience rights, I do not distinguish conscience rights from the right to free exercise of religion, but I do believe that the distinction matters in other contexts. Any free exercise claim will also necessarily involve a conscience claim, but not vice versa. What distinguishes free exercise claims from conscience claims is that in free exercise claims what is at stake is not only one's integrity (the harmony among one's feelings, beliefs, judgments and actions) but also the good of religion, understood as harmony with the transcendent source of meaning and existence. Due to the uniquely architectonic, pervasive and meaning-giving role of religion in the life of someone aware of its demands, religiously informed conscience claims have even greater weight than non-religious conscience claims, as I argue in "Beyond Equal Liberty: Religion as a Distinct Human Good and the Implications for Religious Freedom."

[27] 494 U.S. 872 (1990).

constitutional right to an exemption, but an exemption was eventually granted through the state legislature. I say nothing here about the constitutional question, but I believe that as a matter of moral principle the legislature was right to grant the exemption. Because of the direct threat to the well-being of the political community's members posed by laws that burden conscience rights, such laws must meet an extremely high bar of justification, such as the one set forth in the Religious Freedom Restoration Act (RFRA), enacted by the federal government in the wake of the *Smith* decision, and later adopted by a number of states as well.[28] RFRA forbids laws that substantially burden the free exercise of religion unless such laws are justified by a compelling state interest and are narrowly tailored to that interest. While the discouragement of substance abuse is arguably a compelling state interest, there was no indication that the controlled use of peyote in Native American Church rituals undermined this interest or otherwise threatened the health and safety of the larger community. Thus the law could be tailored more narrowly so as to exclude the case of ritual peyote use in the Native American Church. There is no unfairness in such an exemption, since the drug law posed a much greater burden (greater in kind, not just in degree) on devout Native American Church members – for whom moral integrity and the good of religion were at stake – than on recreational drug users who were simply restricted in the pursuit of their preferences.

I discuss the nature and importance of conscience rights further in Chapter 2. A full account of conscience rights also presupposes a certain conception of authority and of the common good which authority exists to serve. I will say a few words about these topics in the following sections, and return to them in the context of debates about civic education and other policy issues in Chapters 3 and 5.

Rights

Before turning to a discussion of authority, I should note that on my account, there is nothing magical about the language of "rights." It is simply another way of expressing the requirements of justice in

---

[28] I recognize that RFRA in fact applies only to religious claims, not non-religious conscience claims, but I believe that, for the reasons already stated, similar protections should be granted to non-religious conscience claims as well. Nonetheless, *ceteris paribus*, religiously informed conscience claims are even weightier than non-religious conscience claims, and should be treated as such in law to the extent possible (See footnote 26).

relationships with others as individuals or as groups. Any rights claim
could be translated into a claim about moral obligation, which could also
be translated into a claim about the requirements of practical reasonableness, which could also be translated into a claim about the authority one
rightfully has over oneself or others. For instance, the claim that all
human beings have a fundamental right to life could be translated into
the claim that there is an absolute and universal moral obligation to
refrain from intentional killing, which could in turn be translated into the
claim that intentional destruction of the basic good of life is never fully
reasonable (because practical reason grasps life as something intrinsically
good and to-be-pursued, and its opposite as something bad and to-be-
avoided). Nonetheless, I speak of parental rights not only because the
discourse on this issue is generally carried out using the language of
rights, but also because the language is meaningful as a way of specifying
the obligations of justice with precision. The reason that it makes sense to
talk about parental rights is that parents have authority over their
children, authority which, like all other claims of authority, is vulnerable
to usurpation. Such usurpation is harmful not only to the goods that the
authority is meant to protect, but is also an injustice to the rights-holder.
To speak about parental rights is simply to specify the injustice against
parents that is constituted by the usurpation of their rightful authority.

Authority

My understanding of parental rights also depends on a theory of authority. On my account, claims of authority, like claims of rights, are inextric-
ably connected to claims of obligation, not only insofar as genuine
authority implies an obligation to obey on the part of those subject to
that authority, but, more fundamentally, because genuine authority
derives from one's special obligations with respect to fostering and
preserving the good of the individual or community over which one
has authority. For example, authority over oneself – what we commonly
speak of as autonomy – derives from the obligation to follow one's
conscience, to act in accordance with the considered judgments of one's
practical reason. Each individual (here I am considering only adults in
the full possession of their faculties) is responsible, more than anyone
else, for the achievement of his or her well-being, of which practical
reasonableness is a central and constitutive component. It is precisely for
this reason that each individual has authority over himself or herself.

The focal meaning of authority, however, refers to authority over other people. I mention the individual case only because it is helpful for understanding the relationship among authority, obligation, rights and the well-being of the individual or community. In the case of political authority, those who have a special obligation with respect to solving coordination problems in view of the common good of the political community have authority over that community.[29] Determining how a person or group of persons acquires that special obligation with respect to the political community is an extremely complex question beyond the scope of the current discussion. My point is simply that authority exists in virtue of the common good, and one's authority flows from the nature and content of one's specific obligations to pursue and promote that good. Authority is never just a right to rule, but exists only to serve the good of an individual or group, in cases where the achievement of that good requires the making of decisions by some person or group on behalf of others. That person or group just is the person or group that has the special obligation to make those decisions (because they uniquely have the ability to do so, because they have met certain criteria, or for some other reason). Further, it is important to point out that the common good in view of which authority exists just is the set of conditions that foster and facilitate the pursuit of human flourishing by those individuals and groups. An account of the just exercise of authority, therefore, is inseparable from an account of integral human well-being.

Paternalistic authority – specifically, paternalistic authority over children, the type of authority which will be the focus of this book – differs importantly from political authority in several ways.[30] First, paternalistic authority aims not at the common good, but rather directly seeks the proper good of the child. Second, paternalistic authority is *substitutional*, involving the substitution of one's own judgment for the judgment of another whose decision-making capacity is deficient, unlike political authority which does not indicate any deficiency on the part of the governed. Finally, paternalistic authority is (in the normal case) temporary and largely pedagogical. Aimed at the development of children into mature adults who can make decisions for themselves, paternalistic authority seeks to render itself unnecessary, whereas political authority serves the essential and enduring function of facilitating unified action

---

[29] See Thomas Aquinas, *Summa Theologiae* I, q. 96 a. 4.

[30] Here I rely on Yves Simon's account of paternal authority in *Philosophy of Democratic Government* (Notre Dame: University of Notre Dame Press, 1993), 7–9.

when there are many possible ways of promoting the common good.[31] Nonetheless, despite these differences, the basic point about the relationship among authority, special obligation and human well-being applies to paternalistic authority just as much as to political authority. Indeed, the relationship may be even more straightforward in the case of paternalistic authority, precisely because it directly seeks the well-being of the child, and because (as I will argue in the next chapter), in the focal case the special obligation that grounds it derives from the very nature of the parent–child relationship, rather than from a particular procedure or characteristic determined by custom or convention.

My view of the relationship among authority, obligation, rights and the well-being of individuals and communities is, as the following chapters will make clear, central to my account of the nature, basis and scope of parental rights (and parental authority) to direct the education of their children as against the authority and rights of the state. *Parental rights, on my account, are coextensive with parental authority, which is coextensive with the special obligations that parents have to foster the overall well-being of their children.* This is why, unlike other accounts of parental rights, mine begins by considering the special obligations that parents have toward their children by virtue of the parent–child relationship which is established, in its central case, by the biological bond between parent and child. And that brings us precisely to the subject of the following chapter.

---

[31] Simon, *Philosophy of Democratic Government*, 30.

1

Parent–child bonds, special obligations and parental authority

Maria Lorena Gerbeno and Veronica Tejada began chatting in the waiting room at a doctor's office in San Juan, Argentina. Both were bringing their three-week-old daughters, born on the same day, for their first check-up. As new moms are wont to do, they began comparing baby weights and other details related to their children's births. Maria mentioned that while she had initially been told that her newborn weighed six pounds, eight ounces, when it was time to go home, the clinic staff presented her with a baby that weighed over eight pounds. She had voiced her doubts, but the staff told her she must have misunderstood and insisted that they had given her the right baby. Something similar had happened to Veronica, except that her baby had initially weighed over eight pounds, but the baby she was given to bring home weighed only six pounds, eight ounces. The two moms concluded that their daughters had been accidentally switched at birth. After DNA tests confirmed their conclusion, the newborns were switched back to their rightful mothers.[1]

Upon hearing stories like this one, most people tend to be appalled that a hospital would make such a mistake, but relieved that the error was discovered so quickly and the situation amicably resolved between the mothers. What is striking is the near-universal assumption that such a situation genuinely *requires* resolution, that the biological mothers are the *rightful* mothers. Indeed, almost no one who hears such a story thinks: But why bother to switch the babies back? Each mother had a healthy baby girl, and so far each mother and daughter seem to be getting along fine. Had they not met fortuitously in the clinic waiting room, they might have gone on happily without ever discovering the truth. Why

---

[1] Atkins, Nigel, "Baby girls switched at birth are reunited with mums after chance meeting at blundering hospital," *Mirror*, October 24, 2013, www.mirror.co.uk/news/world-news/baby-girls-switched-birth-reunited-2487370. Last accessed on October 22, 2014.

should they, or anyone, care about the existence or absence of a mere *biological* relationship?

One might argue, as Anca Gheaus does, that an intimate relationship begins to form between mother and child during pregnancy, and that, since intimate relationships are valuable, we should avoid severing that relationship in the absence of strong reasons to the contrary.[2] In the case of Maria and Veronica, it is also true that an intimate relationship was beginning to form between the mothers and the newborn babies that they had been caring for, but three weeks is a relatively short time in comparison to nine months. In baby-switching cases that are not discovered so quickly, however, the situation is more complicated. When Paula Johnson discovered that her three-year-old daughter Callie was in fact not her biological child, she never even considered giving Callie back to her biological family. She was, however, very interested in finding and then developing a relationship with her biological daughter Rebecca, at one point even trying to sue for custody. And Callie, as she grew older, was interested in developing a relationship with her own biological family, although she did not want them to take custody of her despite the fact that their socioeconomic situation was better than Paula's.[3]

Yet psychological bonds developed in utero seem insufficient to explain the interest that people have in biological (specifically genetic) ties. Just imagine how prospective parents who have recourse to in vitro fertilization would feel if another couple's embryo(s) had accidentally been transferred into the woman's uterus instead of their own. If the "embryo switch" were discovered prior to birth, it seems plausible that most couples would want to switch the babies back after birth, although they would have probably been deeply disappointed to have been robbed of the powerful bonding experience with their genetic child that pregnancy affords. While a discussion of the ethical issues related to assisted reproductive technologies is beyond the scope of this book,[4] I bring up this hypothetical case because it lends intuitive plausibility to the claim

---

[2] Anca Gheaus, "The Right to Parent One's Biological Baby," *The Journal of Political Philosophy* (April 2011): 1–24.

[3] "Baby Switch Girls Together Apart," *The Telegraph*, September 17, 2009. www.telegraph .co.uk/news/worldnews/northamerica/usa/6201099/Baby-switch-girls-together-apart.html. Last accessed on October 8, 2014. For the sake of simplicity, I focus only on Paula and Callie's side of the story.

[4] I do, however, discuss these issues elsewhere. See, for instance, Melissa Moschella, "Rethinking the Moral Permissibility of Gamete Donation," *Theoretical Medicine and Bioethics* 35, 6 (2014): 421–440.

that there is something important about biological relationships even in isolation from the psychological ties formed during pregnancy. The practice of gestational surrogacy seems to corroborate this claim as well.

Questions about the moral relevance of the parent–child relationship, which in the focal case involves both biological and psychological ties, are crucial to an analysis of parental rights in education because they strike at the core of the question, "To whom do children 'belong'?" If, (1) as I will argue in this chapter, the bonds between parents and children in themselves give rise to parents' direct and weighty special obligations to care for and educate their children; and if, (2) as everyone recognizes, caring for children requires making decisions on their behalf and thus exercising authority over them; then it follows that parental authority is natural and original, primary to the state's authority over children and in no way derived from it.

Why not raise children communally?

Even those theorists who defend more expansive state educational authority than my own view would permit presume that parents have some degree of legitimate authority over children, rejecting proposals for placing educational authority exclusively in the hands of the state. Gutmann, for instance, strongly opposes Plato's proposal in the *Republic* for creating a perfectly just society by exiling everyone over ten years old and then raising the children communally, so that a new generation of perfect citizens can be created through proper education. Along with most people, Gutmann believes that this "is an exorbitantly high price to pay for realizing a just society."[5] Yet what, precisely, is so problematic about Plato's scheme? Is it the fact of exiling so many people who have done nothing wrong? Is it the separation of parents from their children? Is it the idea of exclusive state educational authority in itself? Gutmann does not specify, but later she does indicate that she thinks one of the problems with Plato's view is that it fails to allow parents to pass on their way of life to their children. She puts the objection as follows: "Don't we also have a claim to try to perpetuate the way of life that seems good to us within our families? After all, an essential part of *our* good life is imparting an understanding of our values to our children."[6] Gutmann never probes further to evaluate this claim or consider its grounds. She

[5] Amy Gutmann, *Democratic Education* (Princeton: Princeton University Press, 1999), 26.
[6] Ibid.

presumes "the legitimacy of the parental impulse to pass values on to children."[7] Yet if in fact the state's values are superior to those of the parents, why should parents have any claim to prevent their children from being educated in accordance with the superior wisdom of the state? Why should parents' desires trump the objective good of children and of society as a whole? One can of course appeal to the value of individual freedom, but again it is unclear why parents' freedom should take precedence over children's well-being, as Gutmann herself later argues in criticizing the views of those who would grant exclusive educational authority to parents.[8]

Gutmann's account lacks the resources to answer these foundational questions. The same is true of the accounts offered by William Galston and Eamonn Callan. Galston believes that "the ability of parents to raise children in a manner consistent with their deepest commitments is an essential element of expressive liberty."[9] To defend this claim, he draws on Eamonn Callan's point that childrearing has a profound expressive significance for parents, as it ranks among the most important meaning-giving tasks in a person's life. Callan argues that a liberal state which recognizes freedom of conscience and association must likewise recognize that "the freedom to rear our children according to the dictates of conscience is for most of us as important as any other expression of conscience, and the freedom to organize and sustain the life of the family in keeping with our own values is as significant as our liberty to associate with others outside the family for any purpose whatsoever."[10] Again, however, it is unclear why parents' expressive liberty or freedom of conscience should give them a claim to make decisions for *others*. Likewise, freedom of association, which protects individuals' freedom to join together freely for common purposes, seems relevantly distinct from the right to form and maintain an association, by virtue of procreation or adoption, with others who are unable to consent. Why, in other words, should we presume that children "belong" to their families at all?

Thus we are brought back to the question with which we began: "To whom do children 'belong'?" And we have seen that theorists like Gutmann, Galston and Callan cannot ground their own, almost universally shared assumption that children "belong" to their families at least to

---

[7] Gutmann, *Democratic Education*, 28.   [8] Gutmann, *Democratic Education*, 29.
[9] William Galston, *Liberal Pluralism* (New York: Cambridge University Press, 2002), 102.
[10] Eamonn Callan, *Creating Citizens: Political Education and Liberal Democracy* (Oxford: Oxford University Press, 1997), 143.

some extent, that upon entering the world they are *already* members of a family community (as well as, in a more indirect way, the political community), and that parents therefore have at least *some* claim to authority over their children (however limited that claim may be by the competing claims of the state).

Insights from Aquinas and Aristotle

Ironically, Gutmann does mention one author whose work offers important, if underdeveloped, insights into this difficult question, when she makes reference to Thomas Aquinas' view that "parents have a natural right to educational authority."[11] Had Gutmann consulted the original text[12] to consider the context of Aquinas' defense of natural parental authority, she might have been intrigued to discover that he offered this defense in response to a controversial question of his time; namely, the question of whether or not it would be legitimate to baptize the children of Jewish parents against the parents' will. His answer is a resounding "no," despite his conviction that Catholicism surpasses Judaism in offering a fuller account of the truth about God, and that knowledge of this truth is crucial for happiness both here and in the hereafter. Thus Aquinas' attempt to respond to this question is analogous in many ways to Gutmann's attempt to respond to Plato's proposal to separate children from their parents so as to be able to instruct them in the objectively best way of life and construct a perfect society. Yet Aquinas' job is made even harder by the fact that he (unlike Gutmann, who is skeptical of Plato's claims regarding the objectively best way of life) actually believes in the objective superiority of the way of life that is on offer. Is Aquinas' response to those in favor of baptizing Jewish children against their parents' will any more satisfying than Gutmann's response to Plato's proposal?

While only a brief sketch, Aquinas' reasoning points us back to the core question of the moral relevance of the parent–child relationship. Aquinas speaks of a child as in some sense "a part" of its parents and as "enfolded in the care of its parents," first physically in the mother's womb, and then in the "spiritual womb" of the family.[13] Aquinas' view here is reminiscent of

---

[11] Gutmann, *Democratic Education*, 28–29.

[12] Gutmann quotes Aquinas not from the original text, but as quoted in the work of another author.

[13] Thomas Aquinas, *Summa Theologiae* II-II, q. 10, a. 12; See also Aquinas, *Summa Theologiae* II-II, q. 57, in which he mentions that "a parent is commensurate with the

Aristotle's claim in the *Nicomachean Ethics* that "parents love their children as being a part of themselves, and children their parents as being something originating from them,"[14] as well as his basic understanding of the conjugal union, and the family[15] which is built upon it, as a "natural community" (literally, "community corresponding to nature").[16]

What do we make of these claims? There are some contemporary theorists who have tried to craft arguments along similar lines. Do any of them succeed? Stephen Gilles, for example, follows Charles Fried in presenting the following case:

> The question "to whom does the child belong" underlies the issue of educational authority over the child. At first cut, the answer seems self-evident: the child belongs to its parents. The child owes its conception to sexual intercourse between its mother and father, and its birth to the reproductive labor of its mother. Every cell of the child's body contains a unique genetic endowment, derived from its mother and father, that determines many of its characteristics and affects most others. As against the rest of the world, the child is its parents' "own." As Charles Fried puts it, to deny that parents have a "special title" to their children is to embrace

offspring to nourish it" (a. 3) and that "a son belongs to his father, since he is part of him somewhat" (a. 4).

[14] Aristotle, *Nicomachean Ethics* VII.12, 1161b16.

[15] Technically Aristotle is referring to the household, grounded in the conjugal union of man and wife, but also, in his time, typically including servants or slaves, since Aristotle seemed to believe that, at least in some cases, the master–slave relationship was natural and mutually beneficial, as those whom he considered to be slaves by nature lacked the full use of reason and thus were unable to rule themselves.

[16] *Politics* I.2, 1252b (my translation). I recognize, of course, that Aristotle's work is frequently cited in support of *more* rather than *less* state educational authority [see Randall Curren, *Aristotle on the Necessity of Public Education* (Lanham, MD: Rowman and Littlefield, 2000)]. Yet there are also elements in Aristotle's work which push in the opposite direction. Aristotle notes, for instance, that children's natural affection for their parents disposes them to obey parents' directives, and that "individual education has an advantage over education in common," insofar as it can be tailored to the specific needs and capacities of each child (*Nicomachean Ethics* X.9, 1180b1-10; see also Moira Walsh, *Freedom and the Legitimacy of Moral Education: Philosophical Reflections on Aristotle and Rousseau*, Dissertation, University of Notre Dame, 1998). Aristotle's comments in Book VIII of the *Politics* about the need for education to be public and the same for all presuppose (1) a small, culturally and ideologically homogeneous political community that is completely at odds with the reality of the modern state, and (2) a subordination of individual well-being to the public good which is out of line with more modern notions of individual rights and limited government. At any rate, here I do not claim to be offering an Aristotelian theory of the respective educational authority of parents and the state. Rather, I am simply drawing on insights from Aristotle, Aquinas and others regarding human nature, the importance of biological ties, and (particularly in Chapter 4) the process of moral development in order to develop my own account.

the untenable proposition that "parents' reproductive functions are only adventitiously their own."[17]

Robert Nozick offers a similar argument:

> There is no bond I know stronger than being a parent. Having children and raising them gives one's life substance. To have done so is at least to have done that. The children themselves form part of one's substance. Without remaining subordinate or serving your purposes, they yet are organs of you. . . . The connection to a child certainly involves the deepest love, sometimes annoyance or anger or hurt, but it does not exist solely at the level of emotion. It is not accurate or illuminating to say that I love my . . . hand.[18]

Niko Kolodny offers a new twist on the attempt to explain the moral relevance of parent–child biological ties, arguing that we are connected to our children in essentially the same way as we are connected to our future selves. He bases this on the claim that a parent's relationship to his child "consists . . . in the fact that the child's creation was, and its biological life has been, later stages of a continuous biological process (i) that began as an episode in the biological life of the parent and (ii) that has been governed throughout, in part, by the parent's genetic code: or, less clinically, by the parent's principle of organization, or specific Aristotelian form."[19]

Though interesting and suggestive, none of these arguments is fully compelling. Gilles and Fried rely on a controversial Lockean theory of ownership as derived from self-ownership, which, even if correct, does not fully apply in this case because the child is also a human being who owns himself.[20] Nozick's view is obviously hyperbolic – children are not "organs of you" or "part of one's substance"; they are themselves individual human organisms, substances in their own right. Kolodny's account likewise suffers from biological and metaphysical inaccuracies, not least of which is his characterization of the child's life as a later stage of a

---

[17] Stephen Gilles, "On Educating Children: A Parentalist Manifesto," *The University of Chicago Law Review* 63, 3 (Summer 1996): 961. Gilles' citation of Charles Fried is from Fried's brief discussion of parental rights in *Right and Wrong* (Cambridge: Harvard University Press, 1978), 153.

[18] Robert Nozick, *The Examined Life* (New York: Simon and Schuster, 1989), 28.

[19] Niko Kolodny, "Why Relationships Justify Partiality? The Case of Parents and Children," *Philosophy and Public Affairs* 38, 1 (2010): 70.

[20] For a critique of the view that the Lockean theory of ownership can be applied to the relationship between parents and children, see Norvin Richards, *The Ethics of Parenthood* (New York: Oxford University Press, 2010), 19–22.

"continuous biological process that began as an episode in the life of the parent," a characterization which masks the crucial *dis*continuity involved in the coming-into-being of a new individual human organism directing its own growth and development. Yet Gilles, Fried, Nozick and Kolodny do seem to be getting at something important in their insistence that the biological connection between parents and children has moral implications.

And what about the relatively undeveloped claims of Aquinas and Aristotle? Although they do refer to children as in some sense "a part" of their parents, their own metaphysics would forbid taking that literally. Their claim is most plausibly interpreted to mean that children are a part of their parents not in the strict metaphysical or biological sense, but in the sense that they are a part of the natural community which is based on and extends from their parents' conjugal union (at least in the focal case, which for Aquinas and Aristotle would also be normative). Aquinas' metaphor of the family as a "spiritual womb" seems to suggest as much. Given Aristotle and Aquinas' understanding of marriage as a conjugal union inherently aimed at procreation and childrearing (though choice-worthy in itself and not merely instrumental to procreation), their view that children are "part" of their parents should therefore be understood to mean that children are part, not of each spouse individually, but of the conjugal union that gives rise to those children. (Thus, though I do not develop this argument here, one could also make a case for parental rights as an aspect of the basic right to marriage – that is, a right of non-interference for capable and consenting parties to enter freely into a conjugal union, and to exercise the rights and responsibilities of married life, including (in most cases) procreation and childrearing.[21]) It is also plausible to interpret Aquinas and Aristotle's reference to children as "part" of their parents to emphasize the permanent and identity-constituting link that children have with their parents (qua joint biological cause of the children's existence and identity). In fact, these two interpretations are interdependent and mutually reinforcing.

Yet the insights offered by Aquinas and Aristotle clearly need further elaboration. In what sense do children have a permanent and identity-constituting link with their biological parents? Why does this link matter? How does the existence of this link connect to the claim that

---

[21] For a fuller explanation and defense of this understanding of marriage as a conjugal union, see Patrick Lee and Robert George, *Conjugal Union: What It Is and Why It Matters* (New York: Cambridge University Press, 2014).

children "belong" to their parents – that is, that they come into the world as members of a family community, in which the parents have primary responsibility for and authority over them? And what about adoptive parents? Do the reasons we have for thinking that the biological parent–child link creates an authoritative community with primary childrearing responsibility apply also (at least analogously) to the adoptive parent–child relationship? Do they explain why Maria Gerbeno and Veronica Tejada were (presumptively) right to switch back their newborn daughters when they discovered the clinic's error, while also explaining why Paula Johnson was (presumptively) right not to exchange her three-year-old (social) daughter Callie for her biological daughter Rebecca? The rest of this chapter will be dedicated to teasing out the answers to these questions. To do so, it is first necessary to step back and consider how, in general, interpersonal ties can give rise to special obligations and authority (when the fulfillment of those obligations requires the exercise of authority). From there I will go on to analyze the parent–child biological relationship to determine the extent to which it, in itself, grounds special obligations and authority. I will also address the case of adoptive parents in the course of the discussion.

Personal relationships and special obligations

We can begin thinking about personal relationships by analyzing a relationship that everyone would agree counts as a genuine personal relationship: the relationship between Paula Johnson and fourteen-year-old Callie, mentioned at the beginning of the chapter. According to a September 17, 2009 article in *The Telegraph*,[22] Paula and Callie have an open, affectionate and trusting relationship, with a deep understanding of each other's strengths and weaknesses and particularly of the psychological difficulties resulting from the baby switch. The article recounts how Paula coached Callie through dealing with her classmates when they discovered that she had been switched at birth, and how Paula has always supported Callie in maintaining her relationship with her biological family. Callie, for her part, considers Paula her best friend and tells her everything. Callie also expresses sympathy for all that Paula has gone through, particularly the fact that Paula's biological daughter Rebecca no longer comes to visit. And

[22] "Baby Switch Girls Together Apart," *The Telegraph*, September 17, 2009. www.telegraph .co.uk/news/worldnews/northamerica/usa/6201099/Baby-switch-girls-together-apart.html .Last accessed on October 8, 2014.

of course the two share fourteen years of memories of the ordinary and extraordinary events that are part and parcel of family life.

As a result of these bonds, Paula and Callie have come to depend on each other in a personal way. When Callie wants to talk to Paula about a hard day at school, she wants to talk to *Paula*, not just to anyone. Paula's sympathetic listening and her words of advice cannot be replaced by anyone else, because the same gestures and words would simply not have the same meaning if coming from someone else with whom she does not have the same shared experiences and memories, and because no one else knows her in quite the same way as Paula. Although of course the relationship is not symmetrical, something similar could be said of the times when Paula seeks the comfort of Callie's companionship, understanding and affection. Their relationship makes them irreplaceable to each other, in the sense that there are things each can "do" for the other (in a broad sense) that no one else can.

Further, as a result of their relationship they expect things of one another that they would not expect from others. When one needs assistance from the other, especially if the assistance is of the sort that *only* the other can provide, there is an assumption that, absent a good excuse (usually a more serious competing obligation), the other will respond obligingly, even if this requires a degree of sacrifice on her part. There is no such general expectation of strangers, beyond the demands of common courtesy or extraordinary situations of dire need in which help can be offered at relatively low personal cost (think, for instance, of a woman who comes across a drowning boy and can save him with relatively little risk to her own welfare).

The same features seem to be true of personal relationships more generally, although what and how much we expect of others varies depending on the nature and closeness of the relationship. Why is this so? We do not make contracts with friends or family members stipulating certain rights and obligations, or otherwise establish expectations through an explicit agreement. Most relationships develop organically without any explicit consent to "enter" or "exit" the relationship, to intensify the relationship, or to allow it to weaken. The obligations involved in relationships vary correspondingly. Those obligations also change in relation to outside circumstances, as when a close friend's illness requires one to dedicate more time and energy to that friend than usual. Certainly culture and convention play a role in our expectations of, and sense of obligation to, others with whom we have a certain type of relationship, but there seems to be more to it than that.

Perhaps a natural law approach can help us to make sense of our common assumptions about the ways in which personal relationships give rise to special obligations. On the natural law view, moral obligation is not something generated by command or consent. Rather, obligations flow from the requirements of practical reasonableness. To say that I have an obligation to do or not to do something is equivalent to saying that practical reason requires or forbids it. Now, the first principle of practical reason indicates that the good is to be pursued and its opposite to be avoided,[23] which, given the complexity of human nature and the correspondingly various, irreducible dimensions of human fulfillment, is best understood to mean that practical reason directs us toward the pursuit of the various basic goods that are constitutive of human well-being, and forbids us from choosing and acting directly against such goods, goods like life, health, friendship, knowledge, performative excellence and so forth.[24] Thus practical reason directs us toward human well-being integrally conceived, and forbids us from choosing and acting in ways that are incompatible with a will toward integral human fulfillment – that is, the well-being in its various dimensions of all human beings.[25] Given that social harmony and cooperation are intrinsically valuable and also instrumentally necessary for human well-being, practical reasonableness requires us to favor and foster the common good of the communities to which we belong, which ultimately means fostering the well-being of the individuals that make up those communities, both directly and indirectly (by fostering the set of conditions within which those individuals, alone or in association with others, can achieve their fulfillment).

Yet as human beings, our time, energy and capacities are necessarily limited. Any resources that we expend to benefit one individual or group are thereby unavailable to benefit another. The time that I spend volunteering at a soup kitchen is time that I will not be able to spend writing my book, helping my daughter with her homework or visiting a friend in the hospital. How do I choose? Thus there needs to be a principled way of prioritizing, of specifying the general obligation to foster the well-being of others which flows from this requirement of practical reasonableness.

[23] Thomas Aquinas, *Summa Theologiae* I-II, q. 94. a. 2
[24] This, at any rate, is the interpretation offered by many contemporary natural law theorists, whose approach to natural law I have outlined in the Introduction. See also Melissa Moschella and Robert George, "Natural Law," *International Encyclopedia of the Social and Behavioral Sciences*, Second Edition, 2015.
[25] For further discussion on this point, see John Finnis, *Natural Law and Natural Rights*, Second Edition (New York: Oxford University Press, 2011), 451–452.

While one way of specifying this general obligation is through the assumption of voluntary commitments (which themselves should be in line with a reasonable order of priorities in accordance with a reasonable overall plan of life), this obligation is also specified by the personal relationships that one has with others, particularly relationships that involve dependence. An insight from Alasdair MacIntyre's book *Dependent Rational Animals* is helpful in this regard. MacIntyre draws on and develops an Aristotelian–Thomistic view of human beings as body–soul unities whose bodiliness, and whose particular mode of exercising rationality as bodily beings, implies vulnerability and dependency at all levels – physical, emotional, moral and intellectual. Based on this understanding of human dependence, he argues that human beings naturally form part of a network of givers and receivers, because we are dependent on the care of others for our ability to flourish as human beings, especially in the early years of life and in periods of sickness or disability. We enter this network as receivers of care, are always in need of at least some sort of care from others, and are aware that at many points in life we are liable once again to find ourselves in a position of complete dependency on others.[26] We can achieve our fulfillment as human beings only by finding our place within a social network of givers and receivers within which what we receive and what we are called upon to give cannot depend on strict reciprocity, but must depend instead in large part on need.[27] While MacIntyre does not spell this out in great detail, his view implies that one's "place" within a network of givers and receivers is determined in large part by the nature of one's relationships with others, both chosen and non-chosen. Thus the strength of one's special obligation for the well-being of another depends on the closeness of one's relationship to that person.

A relationship is a union or interconnection among persons on one or more dimensions of their being – bodily, psychological, intellectual and/or volitional. The closeness of a relationship depends on the intensity (on any one dimension) and the comprehensiveness (across dimensions) of that union. Now, relationships trigger special obligations insofar as they involve actual or potential dependence or interdependence between or among the parties to the relationship. Further, while all relationships among human beings are personal insofar as they are relationships among persons, certain relationships can be qualified as personal in the more specific sense that they are relationships in which the parties relate

---

[26] Alasdair MacIntyre, *Dependent Rational Animals* (Chicago: Open Court, 1999), 108.
[27] Ibid.

as unique and irreplaceable individuals, not merely fulfilling a function or role which anyone with the relevant competencies could fulfill.[28] Thus Paula and Callie's relationship is personal, whereas my relationship with a cashier at the grocery store is not personal as such, insofar as any cashier or even a well-functioning automated check-out machine could fulfill my needs just as well.

Because personal relationships as such are based on unique and irreplaceable characteristics, it is a feature of these relationships that they create personal dependencies. For if two individuals are in a personal relationship, then by definition there are things that each can do for the other (in the broad sense) that no one else can do. This is relevant for practical deliberations about how best to make use of our limited capacities to promote human well-being, because it means that when a need arises out of a personal relationship as such, that need can only be fully met by the person in relation with whom that need arose. Thus if I have a close friendship with someone, I have a specific need for the company and conversation of that particular person, and even if my social calendar is full of interactions with other friends, there is a unique benefit that I am missing when that particular friend becomes absent from my life either permanently or temporarily.

Because they create personal dependencies, personal relationships give rise not only to *special* obligations – i.e. obligations that specify one's general obligation to foster the well-being of others – but also to *non-transferable* or *personal* obligations – that is, obligations that one must carry out *oneself*. When Callie needs Paula's advice on a sensitive matter, Paula cannot just send someone else to listen to and advise Callie in her stead. Of course, Paula's obligation to Callie may be overridden by other, weightier obligations, and in that case Callie may go to someone else for advice. But that does not mean that Paula can transfer her obligation to someone else. The obligation is still *hers*, even if she is excused from fulfilling it. The friend who does take the time to listen to Callie and offer her advice fulfills her *own* personal obligation to Callie, not Paula's, since the need for advice *from Paula* cannot really be fulfilled by anyone else. This point will be particularly important for understanding why the political community cannot just take over parents' obligations for them, since, as I will argue, the parent–child relationship is a personal relationship that gives rise to *non-transferable* obligations.

---

[28] Hugh LaFollette offers a similar characterization of personal relationships in *Personal Relationships: Love, Identity and Morality* (Cambridge: Blackwell, 1996).

The implications of the above discussion on the connection between personal relationships and obligations can be synthesized into three main points:

1. Personal relationships in themselves (independent of consent) ground special obligations.
2. Special obligations vary in weight depending on the closeness of the relationship (from the perspective of the person in need) and the importance of the need in question.
3. Personal dependencies give rise to non-transferable obligations, because, by definition, the need in question cannot be met by anyone else.

While only a sketch, this understanding of special obligations offers a principled way of prioritizing our obligations to others in a way that makes sense of many common intuitions and practices. It explains, for instance, why most people consider it not only acceptable but obligatory to use a greater proportion of their limited resources for the benefit of their family members and close friends than for the benefit of strangers, but also why meeting the dire need of a stranger (stopping to help a child drowning in a lake) can take priority over meeting a less important or urgent need of a family member (as when stopping to help the child makes one arrive late to a son's soccer game). It also explains why it is fine to have someone else grade one's students' multiple choice exams, but not to have someone else read and comment on a draft of a graduate student's dissertation chapter. The differences in the weight and type (transferable or non-transferable) of one's obligations in each of these circumstances is not explainable with reference to voluntary actions and commitments alone, but rather, is based primarily on the closeness of each relationship, the importance of the need in question, and the extent to which that need is one that cannot be met by anyone else.

The biological parent–child relationship as a source of non-transferable obligations

Applying this analysis of the connection between relationships and special obligations to the case of biological[29] parents and their children

---

[29] I use the term biological parents to refer to genetic parents, and the term biological relationships more generally to refer to any relationship in which the individuals have a genetic connection – i.e. a connection with respect to the material and formal cause (in the Aristotelian sense) of their biological existence and identity. Here I leave aside the

can help us to determine the existence, weightiness and content of the obligations triggered by the biological parent–child relationship.[30] (Remember that this is important for the establishment of natural parental authority because the obligation to care for a child implies presumptive authority to make childrearing decisions.) The first question we need to ask is whether or not the biological parent–child relationship is really a relationship in the morally relevant sense. If we understand relationships as a union or interconnection of persons at one or more dimensions of their being, it is clear that the biological parent–child relationship is indeed a relationship. This relationship is based on a bodily relationship – a relationship of biological causality[31] and strong genetic similarity – which, unless truncated, will extend to the psychological and usually also the intellectual and volitional levels. This relationship is also a personal one in the specific sense of the term, because biological parents and their children are related on the basis of unique characteristics. The parents' combined gametes are the biological cause of their child's existence and identity as a human organism, which in turn is the basis of that child's overall continuity of personal identity over time. The child is who he is because of who his parents are; to be begotten by other parents is, simply, to be someone else. Thus biological (i.e. genetic) parents are, and always will be, unique and irreplaceable to their children

difficult question about the nature and closeness of the relationship between a merely gestational surrogate and the child that she carried in her womb. Nonetheless, my conjecture on this matter is that, at least given the way in which I use the term biological, the bond between gestational surrogate and child is psychological rather than biological in nature, because the gestational mother does not determine or change the child's essential metaphysical identity. Gestation does have profound epigenetic effects on the developing human being, but so do a person's environment, relationships and behaviors throughout life. For a discussion of the moral significance of gestation, see Gheaus, "The Right to Parent One's Biological Baby," 1–24.

[30] For a similar defense of the moral relevance of parent–child biological ties in a different context, see Moschella, "Rethinking the Moral Permissibility of Gamete Donation," 421–440.

[31] I use the term "biological cause" to refer to a combination of material and formal causality in the Aristotelian sense. The material elements of the zygote initially are numerically identical to the material elements of the parents' combined gametes, and thus the combined gametes are the material principle of that organism. Further, the material structure of the combined gametes (especially, but not only, the genetic material) contains information which is a formal principle of the new organism constituted by the combined gametes. Of course, if one thinks that the human form or soul is spiritual in nature (because, as the principle of conceptual thought and moral choice, it transcends the limitations of materiality) then that biological information could not be the complete formal cause of a new human being.

even if they have no further interactions with those children beyond conception.

In claiming that the biological relationship is, in itself, a personal relationship, I assume a view of the human person in which the body is an intrinsic and essential aspect of personal identity, not a mere extrinsic instrument of an 'I' or 'self' that is non-bodily in nature. On this view, bodily identity is essential to personal identity, and the continued existence of the same human organism is a necessary and sufficient condition for continuity of personal identity. A defense of this assumption goes beyond the scope of the current project, but this view of the person as a psychophysical substance, a substantial unity of mind and body, is a crucial anthropological premise of natural law thinking within the Aristotelian–Thomistic tradition.[32] Without this premise – amply defended by exponents of the tradition both past and present – even some of the most basic human experiences and moral judgments cannot be explained. Take, for instance, the interrelationship between sense perception (a bodily act) and conceptual thought (an act of the mind understood as relatively independent of the body). When I see a book sitting on my desk and make the simple judgment, "That is a book," I am equating an object of sense perception with an object of conceptual thought. For this to be possible, the subject of sense perception (the sense organs and brain) and the subject of conceptual thought (the mind understood as relatively independent of the brain) must be one and the same being.[33] Human persons, in other words, must be a substantial unity of mind and body. Or consider the common moral judgments that assault is a more serious crime than vandalism (more serious in kind, not just in degree) because it is a crime against one's person, not just one's property, and that rape is a *personal* violation (even if the victim is unconscious and never finds out about it). These judgments are difficult to defend unless we consider the body to be a metaphysically essential and intrinsic part of the human person.

[32] See, for instance, Thomas Aquinas, *Summa Theologiae* I, q. 75–76.
[33] For a more complete version of this argument and for a full defense of the view that the human person is a psychophysical unity, see Patrick Lee and Robert George, *Body–Self Dualism in Contemporary Ethics and Politics* (New York: Cambridge University Press, 2008). Further elaboration of my own position, together with an application of that position to the issue of reproductive technologies, can be found in my "The Wrongness of Third-Party Assisted Reproduction: A Natural Law Account," *Christian Bioethics* (forthcoming) and "Rethinking the Moral Permissibility of Gamete Donation," 421–440, at 424.

Assuming, then, that we are bodily persons and thus that unions or interconnections of persons on the bodily dimension of their being can indeed constitute personal relationships, it is clear that the biological parent–child relationship is itself a personal relationship, because it is a relationship of persons at the bodily level based on unique personal characteristics. The reason why this claim may seem counterintuitive is perhaps that it is rare for human relationships to be based only or even primarily on a bodily connection, since bodily union or interconnection is often just the starting point or one aspect of a more comprehensive union of persons. Indeed, it could even be said that, given the psycho-physical unity of the human person, bodily union or interconnection in some sense calls for a corresponding extension into the psychological, intellectual and volitional aspects of our being. How else can we explain the intelligibility of wanting to know about one's ancestors, of seeking out lost relatives, or of wanting to get to know one particular set of persons rather than another simply because they are one's relatives?

Of course, not all kinship relations are equally strong and thus the strength of the special obligations that they trigger likewise varies. And even among kinship relations the parent–child relationship is unique, because the parent–child relationship is based not only on a shared genetic heritage, but on a relationship of biological causality. Indeed, the event (the union of the parents' gametes) which initially establishes the bio-logical parent–child relationship is the very event by which one of the parties to that relationship – namely, the child – comes into existence. From the child's perspective, therefore, the relationship with his or her biological parents is initially (i.e. at conception) the closest of that child's relationships, and that relationship is permanent by its very nature. It is not the child's only personal relationship, since he or she also has a relationship at the bodily level with siblings and other relatives. But the relationship with parents, as the only one that is the cause of the child's biological existence and identity, is clearly the closest. Thus it is the parents who have the strongest special obligation to foster that child's well-being. Since parents' special obligations are based on a relationship that is permanent, their special obligation for the child's well-being is likewise permanent, although as the child matures the concrete implications of that obligation change significantly. Further, given that adequately meeting the developmental needs of children particularly in the early years has a profound and lasting impact on that child's well-being throughout life, the obligation to care for a child is an extremely weighty and demanding one, perhaps one of the weightiest of a parent's obligations.

Parental obligations as personal obligations
to raise one's children

Now, the fact that children's initial and prolonged state of neediness (together with their existence) flows precisely out of their personal relationship with their biological parents, implies that children are not just needy and dependent in general, but *personally* dependent on their biological parents for the ideal fulfillment of their developmental needs. This means that biological parents cannot fulfill their special obligations to their children without raising those children themselves, which implies exercising decision-making authority over them (except in the case of incompetence, which I will discuss later). Ensuring that some other adequate caregiver(s) take on that role is insufficient. In the earlier discussion of the connection between personal relationships and special obligations, my claim was that personal relationships trigger obligations that must be carried out personally insofar as personal relationships create personal dependencies – i.e. that being in a personal relationship with someone means that there are needs only you are fully competent to fulfill, or benefits that only you are fully competent to provide. This seems obviously true in friendships or romantic relationships – when my boyfriend invites me for a romantic dinner, he cannot just send someone else to buy me dinner in his stead – but is it also true of the biological parent–child relationship? Social science evidence indicates that, in comparison with any other family structure, children do best (all other things being equal) when raised by their own married biological parents in an intact family.[34] Yet though this evidence helps to make plausible my

---

[34] A research brief prepared by Child Trends, for instance, concludes the following: "[R]esearch clearly demonstrates that family structure matters for children, and the family structure that helps children the most is a family headed by two biological parents in a low-conflict marriage. Children in single-parent families, children born to unmarried mothers, and children in stepfamilies or cohabiting relationships face higher risks of poor outcomes." The brief emphasizes that "it is not simply the presence of two parents, . . . but the presence of *two biological parents* that seems to support children's development." (Kristin Anderson Moore et al., *Marriage from a Child's Perspective: How Does Family Structure Affect Children, and What Can We Do About It?* Child Trends Research Brief, June 2002, at 1–2, 6, available at www.childtrends.org/files/MarriageRB602.pdf.) See also Douglas Allen, "High School Graduation Rates among Children of Same-Sex House-holds," *Review of the Economics of the Household* 11, 4 (December 2013): 635–658; Mark Regnerus, "How Different are the Adult Children of Parents Who Have Same-Sex Relationships? Findings from the New Family Structures Study," *Social Science Research* 41, 4 (July 2012): 752–770; D. Paul Sullins, "Emotional Problems among Children with Same-Sex Parents: Difference by Definition," *British Journal of Education, Society and*

claim that there are unique and important benefits to children in being raised by their biological parents, such evidence is inherently limited. It only shows that by and large and in general children do best when their biological parents raise them, and it can only establish correlation, not causation. And if so, what are the unique benefits that biological parents, and only biological parents, can provide for their children?

I think that we can pinpoint at least two unique and important benefits that, regardless of cultural context, biological parents and only biological parents can give to their children. The first is the benefit of being loved in a special way – in a way that takes priority over most other loves – by one's biological parents, by those out of whom one came into existence.[35] This special and high-priority love is called for due to the weightiness of biological parents' special obligations to their children. (Note that, although love usually has a strong emotional component, here I am speaking of love not as an emotion, but primarily as a commitment of the will to another's well-being.) The second benefit is that of knowing one's biological parents (and the larger biological family that one usually has access to via one's parents) as a source of insight into one's own identity.

I begin by considering this second benefit, following an argument offered by David Velleman. Velleman makes an interesting case, based largely on psychological data and phenomenological reflection on that

Behavioural Science 7, 2 (2015): 99–120. Though the studies done by Allen, Regnerus and Sullins focus on evaluating outcomes for children raised by same sex couples, the data compares child outcomes in a wide variety of family structures, and corroborates the earlier research summarized in the Child Trends brief by showing a clear and significant advantage to children raised in intact biological families. Allen's study also shows that even children raised by _married_ same-sex couples in Canada, where same-sex marriage and childrearing is widely culturally accepted, fare worse than those raised by their married biological parents. Sullins' analysis offers especially strong support for the claim that _conjoined biological parenthood_ – being raised jointly by one's own married biological parents – is especially crucial for child well-being.

[35] S. Matthew Liao argues that children have a right to be loved because it is a "primarily essential condition" for children to lead a good life ("The Right of Children to be Loved," _The Journal of Political Philosophy_ 14, 4 (2006): 420–440). He cites several empirical studies to support his claim. Liao does not, however, seriously consider whether there might be a unique benefit to children in being loved _by_ their biological parents. Mhairi Cowden criticizes Liao's view, arguing that love is an emotion that is not under one's volitional control ("What's Love Got to do With It? Why a Child Does Not Have a Right to be Loved," _Critical Review of International Social and Political Philosophy_ 15, 3 (2012): 325–345.) This critique does not apply to my own account, since I do not rely on an emotional understanding of love. Nonetheless, Liao also offers a persuasive rejoinder to Cowden's critique in "Why Children Need to be Loved," _Critical Review of International Social and Political Philosophy_ 15, 3 (2012): 347–358.

data, that the presence of biological parents is irreplaceable in helping a child construct a mature personality out of similar "raw materials."[36] While it is certainly not impossible to develop a mature personality in the absence of relationships with one's kin, being reared by one's own parents, together with one's biological siblings, offers significant and unique advantages, because one can learn from the experiences of others who are similarly situated biologically. Velleman's argument relies on data about the heritability of psychological traits, which suggests that although one's genetic and overall physiological endowment does not determine one's personal characteristics, it does have a profound influence.[37] This accounts for the fact that there is "greater similarity between identical twins than between fraternal twins, or between biological siblings reared apart than between unrelated children reared together," not only with regard to characteristics such as IQ, but also with regard to traits such as conscientiousness, agreeableness, and extraversion, and even inclinations toward conservatism or religiosity.[38] Velleman thinks that even the physical similarities among biological relatives help children to flourish by helping them to become comfortable with their own bodies, something which cannot be taken for granted.[39] Further, the value of knowing one's biological parents and siblings does not depend on the desirability of becoming like them. Indeed, one of the things that children can gain through relationships with their kin is knowledge of the type of person that they do *not* want to become, coupled with an awareness that they will have to take special care to

---

[36] David Velleman, "Persons in Prospect," *Philosophy & Public Affairs* 36 (2008): 221–288, at 258.

[37] Scientists agree that most, if not all, personality traits have some relationship, albeit indirect, complex and non-deterministic, to our genetic endowment. Research has found genetic links for traits and behaviors as diverse as intelligence, risk-aversion, nurturing and alcoholism. The mere possession of the complex pattern of genes linked to these traits in no way indicates that one will necessarily develop or act upon them. Environmental factors and individual choice are also influential. Nonetheless, the possession of the relevant genes does make a difference. For example, someone who has inherited the pattern of genes linked to alcoholism and who falls in with a crowd of heavy drinkers in college is much more likely to develop a strong addiction to alcohol than someone in that same crowd who does not have those genes. On the other hand, someone with the genetic tendency to alcoholism who habitually practices moderation in drinking may never become an alcoholic, while someone without those gene patterns who habitually drinks too much and seeks out alcohol as an escape from life's difficulties may still become an alcoholic despite the absence of a genetic predisposition [Catherine Baker, *Behavioral Genetics* (American Association for the Advancement of Science, 2004)].

[38] Velleman, "Persons in Prospect," 257.   [39] Velleman, "Persons in Prospect," 259–260.

avoid developing those negative traits given their particular genetic endowment.[40]

There is another unique benefit that only biological parents can give to their children which Velleman does not mention, but which seems even more fundamental: the benefit of knowing oneself to be loved *by one's biological parents,* by those out of whose bodies and bodily union one came into existence. No one else can love my biological children for me, or receive their love in my stead. Others can, of course, love those children very deeply, and be loved deeply by them in return. But others' love, no matter how deep, can never replace *my* love for them, and no one, no matter how lovable, can replace *me* as a specific object of my children's love. It is because biological parents stand in a permanent, unique and intimate relationship to their children as the cause of those children's existence and identity, that they are irreplaceable to their children in this way. Of course children can lead a good life without being loved by their biological parents. Yet the absence of biological parents' love is still a significant loss to children, because once children begin to understand the facts of how they came into the world, they can miss the *specific* love of their biological parents, and the absence of that love can harm them. Children do not miss being loved by those with whom they have no intimate relationship, but with their biological parents they do and always will have a unique and intimate relationship, a relationship which is a permanent and identity-defining feature of their existence. Just as being spurned or ignored by a friend can harm me even if I have many other friends who treat me with appropriate affection, children can be hurt by their biological parents' failure to love them, even when they are well-loved by others.

While Velleman's argument for the non-transferability of biological parents' obligations to raise their children focuses primarily on the importance of the self-knowledge that children can gain from knowing their biological parents and relatives, he also makes some interesting observations that support my own claim about the irreplaceability of biological parents' love. He argues that children have a tendency to form attachments even to absent biological parents. Statistics show that about half of adopted children search for their biological parents at some point in their life, that many donor-conceived adults are now likewise expressing a desire to know their biological father, and even that people mourn

---

[40] Velleman, "Persons in Prospect," 260.

the death of biological parents whom they never knew in a way compar-able to the death of the parents who raised them.[41] Velleman attempts to explain this phenomenon by arguing that human beings can form an emotional attachment to someone they do not know by relating to that person as a specific object of thought. Given knowledge of the biological facts of human origins, an adopted or donor-conceived person knows that specific human beings exist who are his or her biological mother and father. Over time a person can develop an intentional relationship with absent biological parents, wondering what they are like – whether or not they too have blond hair and blue eyes, enjoy running, are good at math, have a quick temper, etc. – and whether they care about him.

It will be difficult for a child not being raised by his biological parents to believe that his biological parents really do love him even though they are not raising him, except in cases of incompetence – i.e. cases in which the biological parents (or others on their behalf) could later say honestly to that child, "It was *because* we loved you so much that we let others raise you instead of raising you ourselves" – and to say it with an explanation of why they judged themselves incompetent that can pass muster in the *child's* own mature judgment on the matter. Indeed, research indicates that one of the most important benefits to children of "open adoption" is, aside from the self-knowledge that children gain by being able to know their biological parents, the ability to come to

---

[41] Velleman, "Persons in Prospect," 262–263. A recent extensive study on donor-conceived persons likewise reveals that they seek to know (or at least to receive information about) their biological father in order to gain insight into their own identity. Sixty-five percent of those surveyed agree that "my sperm donor is half of who I am." Consider also the following individual testimonies: "A young woman in Pennsylvania says she wants to meet her donor because she wants to know 'what half of me is, where half of me comes from.'" Another in Britain says, "I want to meet the donor because I want to know the other half of where I'm from." Lindsay Greenawalt in Ohio is seeking any information she can find about her sperm donor. She says, "I feel my right to know who I am and where I come from has been taken away from me." Olivia Pratten, a Canadian donor offspring who recently launched a class-action law suit in British Columbia, has said in interviews: "I think of myself as a puzzle; the only picture I have ever known is half-complete." Danielle Heath of Australia found out when she was nineteen years old that she was donor conceived. She reflected: "I felt like there was a piece missing. It would complete me to know who I am like." Tom Ellis of Britain told a reporter how he felt after submitting a cheek swab with his DNA to the UK Donor Link registry: "It was a huge decision for me to make because it meant admitting that the stranger who helped bring me into the world – and who may never want to meet or know me – is important to me. But he is a part of me and without him, I will never feel completely whole." [Elizabeth Marquardt, Norval D. Glenn, Karen Clark, *My Daddy's Name is Donor: A New Study of Young Adults Conceived Through Sperm Donation* (Institute for American Values, 2010), 21.]

understand that their biological parents do love them and that the decision to give them up for adoption was motivated precisely by love, rather than rejection or indifference.[42]

Sally Haslanger is skeptical of the claim that there are important benefits to children in being raised by their own biological parents. She argues that being raised by one's biological parents is helpful only because it is seen as normal in our particular cultural context. Nonetheless, while she is certainly right that children can develop into mature and healthy adults in the absence of a relationship with their biological parents, she does not give sufficient weight to claims about the *uniqueness* of the kind of help that biological parents can give to children. She specifically dismisses Velleman's claim about the self-knowledge children can gain from their biological family, largely by comparing it to claims that children should not be adopted by those of a different race, but racial bonds are too diffuse to offer any important advantage to children in terms of the self-knowledge that would be helpful for the construction of their own identities. Genetic traits inherited from one's parents, on the other hand, have a direct and powerful (though non-deterministic) effect on one's personality.[43] Haslanger further fails to consider that genetic similarities between parent and child may also provide *parents* with helpful knowledge that will enable them to parent more effectively – knowledge of, say, potential weaknesses to watch out for in their children's temperament, or potential talents to cultivate. Finally, Haslanger's argument completely ignores the fact that, regardless of what is normative in our cultural context, any child with a basic knowledge of reproductive biology will at some point realize that two specific individuals[44] are the cause of her genetic origin, and thus reasonably wonder who

---

[42] For a recent synthesis and overview of the relevant studies, see Deborah H. Siegel and Susan Livingston Smith, "Openness in Adoption," March 2012, The Evan B. Donaldson Adoption Institute. Available online at: www.adoptioninstitute.org/publications/2012_03_OpennessInAdoption.pdf.

[43] See footnote 37.

[44] This is true even in the case of cloning, because biologically speaking the person cloned is the identical twin, not the parent, of his or her clone. Otherwise, in the case of "natural" identical twins (which result from natural cloning of the original embryo through fission) one would have to consider the "elder twin" (the original embryo) the parent of the "younger" one. What is missing in cloning (natural and artificial) which distinguishes it from reproduction is the reshuffling of the genome, usually mixed with the genome of another person. For a full explanation, see Heidi Mertes and Guido Pennings, "Embryonic Stem Cell-Derived Gametes and Genetic Parenthood: A Problematic Relationship," *Cambridge Quarterly of Healthcare Ethics* 17, 1 (Jan 2008): 7–14.

those individuals are, whether or not knowing them might provide her with some insight into who *she* is, and whether or not they love her.

There are, therefore, unique and important benefits to children in being raised by their biological parents – fundamental benefits with regard to self-knowledge and the knowledge of being loved by those out of whom one came into existence. This supports my claim that children really are *personally* dependent on their biological parents for the ideal fulfillment of their developmental needs. What this means is that biological parents have a weighty prima facie obligation to raise their children themselves, based on their absolute obligation to love their children. This obligation flows from the personal relationship that biological parents have with their children, a relationship that begins at the bodily level as a relationship of biological causality and shared genetic heritage. To conceive a child is, in one sense, to already be a parent, but in another very real sense, it is to *begin* to be a parent, and because of children's specific dependency on their biological parents for the ideal fulfillment of their developmental needs, once one *begins* to be a parent one is obligated to continue to act as such unless there are serious child-centered reasons for not doing so. Further, given children's inability to make decisions for themselves, caring for children requires making decisions on their behalf and thus exercising authority over them. *Thus the fact that parents have the strongest and most direct obligation to raise their children to maturity implies that they are the ones with primary paternalistic authority over them.*[45]

The difference between adoptive and biological parents is that the biological parents' biological relationship with their child is what initially grounds their obligation to further develop that relationship at the psychological, intellectual and volitional dimensions through the love and care that they provide, whereas for adoptive parents it is their commitment to take on the parenting role that grounds that obligation. Since, as we have seen, parenthood in the full sense implies permanent obligations to one's children, the commitment of adoptive parents to their children is likewise permanent – this is what distinguishes adoptive

---

[45] Though perhaps obvious, it is worth noting that my view would not imply that someone who conceives a child through rape would have a claim to parental authority. A rapist would still have obligations to the child, and could thus be called upon to pay child support, but conceiving a child through rape itself renders one incompetent to raise that child, in part because it renders the rapist unfit for the close, ongoing cooperation with the child's mother which raising the child would ideally involve.

parents from foster parents or other temporary caregivers. Research regarding children's need to form secure psychological attachments to particular caregivers underscores the importance of the stable bonds between parents (biological or adoptive) and their children, and helps to explain why these bonds entail such weighty special obligations (and corresponding rights to fulfill those obligations).[46] Thus the emphasis on biological parenthood in the foregoing analysis should in no way be taken as a denigration of adoptive parenthood, for parenthood means engendering a new human being not only biologically, but also psychologically, morally and intellectually. Adoptive parents, who accept their adopted children permanently into their family and commit themselves to raising those children, enable and direct their children's development to maturity at all of these levels; they are true parents. The reason I have dwelt primarily on establishing the importance of the *biological* aspect of parenthood is that, while the stable bond between parent and child is widely understood to have moral relevance (and thus to generate obligations and rights), the moral relevance of the biological parent–child relationship as such is not well understood, and has recently been called into question by a number of moral philosophers.[47] Further, since, in the normal case, parenthood begins as biological parenthood, understanding how biological parenthood is in itself a source of parental obligations is important for understanding the family as a pre-political authoritative community.

Conclusion

The account of parental obligations and authority that I have developed in this chapter enables us to resolve our initial questions about the baby-switching cases discussed at the beginning of the chapter. Given the

---

[46] John Bowlby, *A Secure Base* (New York: Basic Book Publishers, 1988); Mary Dozier et al., "Lessons from the Longitudinal Studies of Attachment," in *Attachment from Infancy to Adulthood*, ed. Klaus Grossman et al. (New York: The Guilford Press, 2005), 305–319; R. A. Thompson, "The Legacy of Early Attachments," *Child Development* 71, 1 (2000): 145–152.

[47] See, for example: David Archard, "The Obligations and Responsibilities of Parenthood," in *Procreation and Parenthood*, ed. David Archard and David Benatar (Oxford: Oxford University Press, 2010), 103–127; Michael Austin, *Conceptions of Parenthood* (Burlington, VT: Ashgate, 2007), Tim Bayne, "Gamete Donation and Parental Responsibility," *Journal of Applied Philosophy* 20, 1 (2003): 77–87; Sally Haslanger, "Family, Ancestry and Self: What is the Moral Significance of Biological Ties?" *Adoption and Culture* 2 (2009): 91–122.

permanent interpersonal link between biological parents and their offspring, as well as the psychological ties formed during gestation, it makes
sense that Maria Gerbeno and Veronica Tejada would want their own
biological daughters back, despite the bonds that had already begun to
form between them and the newborns that they had been taking care of
as their own before the switch was discovered. For at this early stage it
seems plausible to claim that the biological moms were still the ones with
the closest personal relationship to each child. On the other hand, after
three years – as in the case of Paula Johnson and Callie – it seems
plausible that Callie's closest personal relationship is with Paula (her
social mom) rather than with her biological parents. Yet understanding
how biological ties give rise to a permanent interpersonal link also helps
us to make sense of Callie's desire to get to know her biological family,
and Paula's desire to get to know her biological daughter Rebecca.

Further, the above explanation of why parents (biological parents, in
the focal case) are the ones with the strongest and most direct special
obligation to care for their children enables us to offer a deeper and more
convincing critique of Plato's communal childrearing proposal than
Gutmann and other liberal theorists. For it shows why and in what sense
children naturally "belong" to their families, why separating children
from their families robs them of important benefits and denies rightful
authority to their parents, and thus why most of us, like Gutmann, balk
at the idea of a "society created out of orphaned infants" and view Plato's
scheme as "an exorbitantly high price to pay for realizing a just society."[48]
Indeed, my account shows why such a society would in fact be *unjust*,
because it fails to respect the intrinsic value of family relationships, as
well as the special obligations and authority that flow from those relationships. Yet while on the one hand this deeper explanation of the
injustice of Plato's proposal explains Gutmann's assumptions better than
she can, it is also the basis for a critique of Gutmann's own claims. For
Gutmann also criticizes those who claim that educational authority rests
"exclusively – or even primarily – in the hand of parents."[49] She is right
to deny that parents have *exclusive* educational authority, since, as I will
argue later, the state also has some authority over education based on its
responsibility to protect and promote the common good of the political
community as a whole. She is wrong, however, to deny the *primacy* of
parental educational authority, since parents, not the state, are the ones

---

[48] Gutmann, *Democratic Education*, 26, 28.   [49] Gutmann, *Democratic Education*, 29.

who have the closest personal relationship to their children and thus the strongest and most direct obligation for the well-being of those children, in part because the intimate relationship that they have with their children makes them uniquely suited to meet their children's developmental needs.

Note, however, that my argument is *not* that we should allow parents to exercise primary educational authority over their children because this will, in every instance, be best for the children. Rather, I am making a principled argument about the locus of primary childrearing authority. Determining who has primary authority over children is a matter of determining who has the strongest and most direct special obligation to care for them until they are able to care for themselves (and to care for them with a view toward enabling them to care for themselves). I have shown that parents are the ones who have that special obligation due to the fact that they have the closest personal relationship to their children. It is also true, as I have argued, that the existence of this intimate relationship makes parents best suited – all other things being equal – to meet their children's developmental needs, because of the unique benefits that they can provide due to their psychological and (in the focal case) biological ties with their children. Thus the well-being of children is part and parcel of my argument for the primacy of parental childrearing authority, but only indirectly. The claim that parents have primary childrearing authority is inseparable from the judgment that according primary childrearing authority to parents promotes the common good, which includes as a constitutive element the well-being of all of the members of the community, including children and parents. It promotes the common good by, as a general matter, fostering the moral, physical and psychological well-being of children and their parents, and, derivatively (particularly as children grow up) that of the whole community, and also by respecting the intrinsic value of intimate relationships which are in themselves a basic and constitutive aspect of human well-being.

Of course, there may be individual cases in which respect for the primacy of parental authority over children is not, all-things-considered, the best thing for those children, their parents or society as a whole. Yet if parents are to exercise their childrearing authority (and if children, parents and society as a whole are to benefit from it) and if the trust and intimacy necessary for healthy family relationships is to be preserved, the state cannot have the authority to supervise and second-guess every non-trivial childrearing decision that is made. For that would be tantamount to eliminating parental authority (and could not be done without destroying family intimacy). Since, like all authority, parental

authority has great instrumental importance for the common good
(including both the proper good of the family community and the
common good of the larger society), preservation of the common good
requires tolerating a great deal of imperfection in the exercise of parental
authority, just as a great deal of imperfection in political authority should
be tolerated before attempting to overthrow the government. The limits
of that tolerance are situations of abuse and neglect, in which parental
authority is clearly and non-controversially failing to fulfill its function,
and also situations in which parents are exercising their authority in a
way that poses a serious threat to the public order, as would be the case if,
for example, parents were training their children to be terrorists, or
refusing to provide their children with a basic level of education that
will enable them to be law-abiding and productive citizens (see
Chapter 3). For the state's role in promoting the well-being of children
is a subsidiary one, secondary to that of parents and aimed at helping
parents fulfill their task, because the obligation to foster the well-being of
children belongs primarily to parents, not to the state. This is why
coercive and direct intervention on behalf of the child is justified only
in cases of abuse and neglect. The state does, however, have the most
direct and primary obligation to preserve the public order, not just in the
present but also into the future. Gutmann and others are therefore right
to claim that parental educational authority is not absolute or exclusive.
However, in regulating education with a view toward the healthy con-
tinuation of society into the future, the state should avoid unnecessary
conflict with parental educational authority. I will further elaborate on
these points in the next chapter when considering parental educational
authority from the perspective of conscience rights, and again in
Chapter 3 when discussing the issue of civic education.

2

Parental rights as conscience rights

Imagine the case of Diana, a conscientious mother struggling to support and raise her twelve-year-old daughter Lia on a meager paycheck, having lost her husband in a tragic car accident several years ago. Diana lives in the Bronx and, given the constraints on her income, has no choice but to send Lia to the public school. One evening she is looking through her daughter's health textbook, and finds a detailed discussion of a variety of solitary and mutual sexual acts, evaluating the relative risk of infection or pregnancy involved in each. This disturbs her deeply. Diana has been open with Lia in talking about issues related to sexuality, while always trying to do so in ways that are appropriate to her age and stage of development. She wants to inculcate in Lia a view of sexuality as a special gift to be saved for the man with whom she chooses to share her life and build a family, and is worried about the trivialization of sex in the broader culture and the resulting physical, psychological and moral harms. The more she reads in her daughter's textbook, the more convinced she becomes that the approach to sexuality presented there is incompatible with the values she is trying so hard to pass on, and that exposing Lia to that approach, particularly at such an impressionable age, could be extremely harmful. The next morning, Diana calls the school expressing her concern, asking if Lia can be exempted from the health class, but, in line with the policy of New York City public schools, officials inform her that the class is mandatory, and that students may only be exempted from the parts of the class that involve graphic descriptions of birth control methods.[1] Distraught and frustrated, she fights to

---

[1] While the case is imaginary, this is a true description of the policy regarding sexual education in the New York City public schools adopted in 2011, and the course content described comes from the recommended middle school textbooks. See Melissa Moschella and Robert George, "Does Sex Ed Undermine Parental Rights?" *New York Times*, October 19, 2011, www.nytimes.com/2011/10/19/opinion/does-sex-ed-undermine-parental-rights .html. For a detailed description of the content of New Jersey's sexual education curriculum, see Cassandra Hough, "Learning About Love: How Sex Ed Programs Undermine

maintain her composure. She has tried so hard to be a good mother, to form Lia's character and teach her self-respect, to equip her to resist peer pressure and the allure of instant gratification. Yet now she has to allow Lia to be exposed to a curriculum that she believes will undermine those efforts on one of the most important battle fronts her daughter will face.

What can she do? Although she believes that, as a parent, she has a serious obligation to prevent Lia from being exposed to this curriculum, she has no choice. Homeschooling is not an option in her circumstances, and she simply does not have the money to send Lia to a private school. What can we say about Diana's plight? Have her rights been violated in some way? If so, how? And what about the competing rights of the state, or the rights of Diana's daughter Lia?

While a full answer to the last question will be developed in subsequent chapters, in this chapter I will begin to answer these questions by explaining what the previous chapter's conclusions about parental obligations imply with regard to parental rights. First, I will discuss the relationship between obligations and rights generally, and then consider the specific case of parental rights. In doing so, I will also explain the relationship among parental obligations, parental rights and parental authority. The conception of parental rights that I will defend is one in which parental rights are understood as a subset of conscience rights, negative rights which provide the moral space necessary to fulfill one's perceived obligations free from undue interference. Translated into the language of authority, this means that, within the sphere marked out by their special obligations and corresponding rights, parents are the ones who have discretionary authority to make controversial decisions regarding what is in the best interests of their children.

The right to integrity

Rights protect basic aspects of human well-being, insofar as they express the requirements of justice from the viewpoint of the person (individual or corporate) to whom something is owed or due. Rights, in the strict sense, consist in either a claim of justice to receive positive assistance for the enjoyment of some good(s), and/or a claim to be free from interference in one's pursuit of some good(s). Rights are intrinsically related to obligations not only because they specify obligations of justice that others owe to the

Healthy Marriage," *The Public Discourse*, October 20, 2014, www.thepublicdiscourse.com/2014/10/13831/.

right-holder, but also because one of the basic aspects of human well-being that rights protect is integrity, which is developed and maintained by the fulfillment of one's perceived moral obligations.[2] To have a duty, therefore, is also to have at least a *prima facie* right to fulfill that duty. The right to fulfill one's perceived obligations is essentially a right to preserve one's practical reasonableness since, in my view, an obligation is simply a dictate of practical reason. This right can also be described as a right to integrity, or a right to follow one's conscience. In my discussion I will treat these and similar phrases as equivalent and use them interchangeably.

While my view about the centrality of integrity to human well-being is based on the natural law theory I outlined in the Introduction, a similar view is also defended by contemporary liberal authors. William Galston, for example, speaks about "expressive liberty" as a core liberal value. He defines expressive liberty as "the absence of constraints, imposed by some individuals on others, that make it impossible (or significantly more difficult) for the affected individuals to live their lives in ways that express their deepest beliefs about what gives meaning or value to life."[3] Expressive liberty is important, on Galston's account, because

> for most people, it is a precondition for leading lives they can experience as complete and satisfying. Part of what it means to have sincere beliefs about how one should live is the desire to live in accordance with them. It is only in rare cases (perhaps certain kinds of stoicism) that constraints imposed by other individuals and social structures do not affect the ability of believers to act on their convictions. For most of us, impediments to acting on our deepest beliefs are experienced as sources of deprivation and unhappiness, resentment and anger. Expressive liberty is a human good because its absence is an occasion for misfortunes that few would willingly endure.[4]

What Galston seems to be saying is that expressive liberty should be protected because acting on one's convictions is, at least for most people,

---

[2] John Finnis distinguishes between inner integrity (harmony between the reasoning and desiring aspects of the self) and outer authenticity (harmony between one's judgments and actions) as distinct elements of the good of practical reasonableness. Since integrity and authenticity are so closely related (one cannot damage authenticity without indirectly damaging integrity, or damage integrity without predisposing oneself to be inauthentic), for the sake of verbal parsimony I do not distinguish between the two, but rather use the term "integrity" in a way that encompasses both integrity *and* authenticity (*Natural Law and Natural Rights*, Second Edition (New York: Oxford University Press, 2011), 448).

[3] William Galston, *Liberal Pluralism* (Cambridge University Press, 2002), 28.

[4] Galston, *Liberal Pluralism*, 29.

central to leading a good life, and the absence of expressive liberty means that one must face the terrible choice between suffering legal punishment (including death) and violating one's integrity.

For Galston, therefore, the maintenance of integrity is an intense preference that most people share. Yet grounding integrity on subjective preferences, no matter how widely shared, is problematic. A robust account of a right to integrity cannot be grounded on an appeal to subjective preferences, for otherwise how do we differentiate a desire for integrity from, say, a strong preference for caviar? Brian Barry actually makes such an argument in *Culture and Equality*, claiming that it would be unfair to give special protection to claims of integrity (or conscience) beyond the protections that are offered for the pursuit of other preferences. I will consider Barry's argument in Chapter 5.

Paul Bou-Habib, who discusses a right to integrity as part of a larger argument for religious accommodations, is likewise skeptical of preference-based accounts. According to Bou-Habib, integrity, defined as "what is maintained when acting in accordance with one's perceived duties," is a basic good that is central to human well-being.[5] Thus, argues Bou-Habib, assuming that each person has a right to an equal opportunity for well-being, it follows that each person has a right to enjoy the basic good of integrity. In characterizing integrity as an objective and intrinsically choiceworthy good, Bou-Habib's account is in agreement with my own natural law view. However, natural law theory provides a better answer to the question of whether integrity is still valuable even when one's perceived duty is, objectively, a morally bad action, such as when a member of a terrorist organization carries out a suicide bombing believing himself to be fulfilling his religious obligations. Bou-Habib argues that in such cases we might reasonably choose a life in which we do not, or are unable to, fulfill such a perceived duty. According to Bou-Habib, this does not undermine the claim that integrity is good in itself. As Bou-Habib explains, "We can hold that perceived duty fulfillment is good *in one respect*, but not necessarily *all things considered*, and that the respect in which perceived duty fulfillment is good can be outweighed by the badness of committing a morally bad act..., so that fulfilling a perceived duty can sometimes make a life worse all things considered."[6] At first glance this analysis seems reasonable. Yet upon further reflection

---

[5] Paul Bou-Habib, "A Theory of Religious Accommodation," *Journal of Applied Philosophy* 23, 1 (2006): 109–126, at 117.

[6] Bou-Habib, "A Theory of Religious Accommodation," 121.

it becomes clear that it ultimately does undermine the claim that integrity is good in itself, or at least makes the right to integrity an extremely weak and easily defeasible one. After all, a right to integrity does not protect much, if it is effectively reducible to the right to act according to one's perceived duties only when those perceived duties are objective, or at least not in conflict with other values held by the larger community. If that is all that the right to integrity amounts to, then it effectively collapses into a right to do the right thing, together with a right to be left alone when one's actions, though wrong, do not sufficiently threaten or offend anyone else's interests or values to warrant intervention.

Bou-Habib's analysis goes astray on this point because it fails to distinguish clearly between the first and third person perspectives in the moral evaluation of an action. Throughout the argument, there is an implicit appeal to an agent-centered perspective, since integrity involves the fulfillment of *perceived* duties – i.e. the performance of actions which the agent *believes* himself to be morally bound to perform, regardless of the truth of this belief. To step outside the first-person perspective, as Bou-Habib does by stipulating that one's perceived duty is in fact morally bad, is to distort the thought experiment, because it imports a third-person judgment into an analysis which is essentially about how obligations are perceived from a first-person perspective. One cannot both perceive something to be a moral obligation and also believe it to be morally bad at the same time and in the same respect. Further, stepping outside the first-person perspective also means stepping outside the only perspective from which an act can be specified morally.[7] It is only possible to know what the agent is doing (in the moral sense) from the perspective of the agent herself, because the moral act is specified by what the will is choosing, not by the physical behavior in which that choice (in the case of external acts) is embodied. Moral acts are not reducible to physical behavior, because the specification of a moral act depends essentially on the agent's intention, on the plan or proposal upon which the agent is choosing to act. What one intends is simply *what one chooses*, as an end or as a means to some further end. Thus the same physical act could embody radically different moral acts, depending on what the agent is choosing to do in performing that physical act. For example,

---

[7] For a full defense of the claim that human action can in fact only be properly specified from the perspective of the agent, see Christopher Tollefsen, "Is a Purely First Person Account of Human Action Defensible?" *Ethical Theory and Moral Practice* 9 (2006): 441–460.

jumping on a grenade could be suicide if done with the intent of killing oneself (even if killing oneself is chosen only as a means to pull one's family out of poverty by enabling them to cash in on one's life insurance), or it could be an act of heroic self-sacrifice if done with the intent of absorbing the impact of the grenade so as to save the lives of one's companions (accepting one's death as a foreseen but unintended side-effect).

A choice not to fulfill a perceived duty implies either (1) a will toward disintegrity or, perhaps more often, (2) acceptance of disintegrity as a side-effect of one's action, as when one judges that one has a duty to speak out against an injustice but maintains silence to avoid offending someone. A choice that directly harms the basic good of integrity (a constitutive aspect of human well-being) – like a choice directly against any of the basic forms of human well-being – is always unreasonable (and thus wrong) because the first principle of practical reason is that the good (in its various, incommensurable forms) is to be pursued and realized, and its opposite to be avoided. But a choice even to accept disintegrity as a side-effect of one's action is also always wrong (unreasonable) due to the architectonic role that practical reason plays in governing and structuring the pursuit of integral human well-being.[8] For what is implicated here is not merely integrity understood as one among many constitutive aspects of human well-being, but also and inseparably the moral requirement to follow one's conscience, one's overall judgment about what should or should not be done, even if that judgment happens to be mistaken.[9] As Finnis explains, "practical reasonableness is not simply a mechanism for producing correct judgments, but an aspect of personal full-being, to be respected (like all other aspects) in every act as well as 'over-all' – whatever the consequences."[10] Disintegrity is therefore *always* worse than integrity, even when, from the third-person perspective, the actions performed by the person who acts against her perceived duties would externally seem to

---

[8] It should be noted, however, that external circumstances (such as the prospect of legal sanction) may alter the requirements of practical reasonableness in a given situation. See footnote 12.

[9] As Finnis states, paraphrasing a position first formulated "in all its unconditional strictness" by Thomas Aquinas: "if one chooses to do what one judges to be in the last analysis unreasonable, or if one chooses not to do what one judges to be in the last analysis required by reason, then one's choice is unreasonable (wrongful), however erroneous one's judgments of conscience happen to be. (A *logically* necessary feature of such a situation is, of course, that one is ignorant of one's mistake.)" (Finnis, *Natural Law and Natural Rights*, 126). See also Thomas Aquinas, *Summa Theologiae*, I-II, q. 19, a. 5–6.

[10] Finnis, *Natural Law and Natural Rights*, 126.

be more in line with objective moral norms. In other words, we would (insofar as we are reasonable) never want to be denied the right to fulfill a perceived duty unless we knew that the perceived duty was false, or that in the future we would come to understand it as false. But in either of those cases we would, for those very reasons, doubt the existence of that duty in the first place.

The reasons grounding a right to integrity – a right to fulfill one's perceived duties – are thus equally present regardless of the objective content of the duty in question. For to respect a person's integrity is ultimately to respect her status as a rational being capable of making free choices for which she is morally responsible, and morally bound to act in accordance with her best judgment of what morality requires in each situation. A judgment of the external action as such enters the analysis only for the purposes of determining the limits to the negative right of non-interference that is the flip side of the positive right to fulfill one's perceived obligations. To return to the case of the would-be suicide bomber, it is clear that the state has a right to prevent him from carrying out his perceived duty.[11] The terrorist's right to integrity is legitimately overruled by the fundamental rights of his potential victims – rights to life, health, safety, and so forth. On the other hand, consider the case that Bou-Habib uses to illustrate the situation of someone who has a perceived duty to do something that is morally bad: the case of a person who believes that she has a moral obligation to engage in animal sacrifice. Unless one thinks that animal life is an inviolable good on a par with human life (in which case eating meat ought to be outlawed as well), there seems to be no sufficiently weighty reason to deprive this person of her right to integrity by, for example, enacting a law against animal sacrifice, unless the practice poses a significant threat to public health or otherwise results in serious public harm.

These modifications to Bou-Habib's account give us a right to integrity, understood as a right to fulfill one's perceived obligations, grounded in a natural law conception of human flourishing, and limited not by the objective accuracy of one's judgments about the content of one's duties,

---

[11] My implicit claim that some terrorists might sincerely believe their actions to be morally right (or even morally required) should not be confused with the claim that such terrorists are not morally blameworthy. For, just as one can be blamed for actions performed while inebriated insofar as one is responsible for being in that state, likewise one can be blamed for having desensitized one's conscience to the point of no longer recognizing the wrongness of killing innocent people. Of course, I make no judgments here about particular cases.

but by the fundamental rights of others and the prerequisites of public order. I will say more in Chapter 3 about why protection of the fundamental rights of others or of the public order itself are the only valid justifications for infringing upon conscience rights.

Integrity and parental rights

My account of the right to integrity explains why, in general, individuals have at least a *prima facie* right to fulfill their perceived obligations free from undue interference. It thus helps us begin to see how the state may be violating Diana's rights in the case introduced earlier, by making it impossible for her to fulfill her perceived obligation to pass on a particular understanding of human sexuality to her daughter. In applying this general view of the right to integrity to the specific case of parental rights, it is important to note that, since the right to integrity simply protects the ability to fulfill one's obligations, knowing the nature of the obligations in question is essential for determining exactly what that right consists in, and what sort of actions would violate it. In this regard, the fact that parental obligations are non-transferable is crucial. For only if I have a non-transferable obligation am I morally bound to fulfill that obligation *personally*. Nothing that anyone else does can fulfill that obligation for me. In other words, if I have a non-transferable obligation, I can participate in the great good of moral integrity – i.e. act in accordance with the requirements of practical reasonableness as I understand them, reinforcing and preserving the harmony among my beliefs, feelings, judgments and actions – only by fulfilling that obligation myself. To bar me from fulfilling such an obligation is either to coerce me to act immorally or to prevent me from pursuing a fundamental aspect of my well-being.[12]

---

[12] The overall morality of one's failure to fulfill a perceived positive obligation despite the state's prohibition will depend on a number of factors, including the severity of the punishment. The prospect of punishment may defeat a positive obligation (though it will never justify transgressing an absolute moral prohibition), as when, for instance, parents choose to send their children to a bad public school in order to avoid losing custody of them and/or being placed in jail. In such a case the parents' choice will not be immoral, but the law in question will nonetheless be seriously unjust insofar as it deprives them (without sufficient justification) of the ability to pursue a great good (namely, to educate their children as they believe that they should) and also of their ability to exercise their legitimate educational authority. [For a helpful related discussion, see Christopher Tollefsen, "Conscience, Religion and the State," *American Journal of Jurisprudence* 54 (2009): 93–115.]

Perhaps a comparison with religious obligations will help to illustrate the point. In most religions the obligation to worship God is considered non-transferable. The religious believer is bound to fulfill that obligation personally. This is true, for example, of the obligation that Catholics have to attend Mass on Sundays. Imagine that government officials enact a law forbidding all Catholics in a certain location from attending Mass, but claim that in doing so they are not preventing those Catholics from fulfilling their religious obligations, because the government has arranged things such that their Sunday worship obligation will be fulfilled by another group of people who will attend Mass in their stead. The Catholics affected by the law would rightly complain that the government has misunderstood the nature of their obligations, because whether or not someone else attends Mass has no relation to their own obligation to do so. Despite the government's claims, such a policy would clearly violate the free exercise rights of those forbidden to attend Mass.

Free exercise rights, like parental rights, can be understood as a subset of the broader category of conscience rights, rights to fulfill one's obligations in accordance with the dictates of one's conscience.[13] Free exercise rights are often given particular importance because of the seriousness and importance of religious obligations for many believers – indeed, many believe that nothing less than eternal salvation or damnation hang in the balance. Yet the obligations of parents toward their children are arguably no less serious – to have the survival and future well-being of another human being on one's shoulders is an enormous responsibility. Fulfilling that responsibility well is a central aspect of their own personal fulfillment. Further, many believers consider parenting obligations to be an important part of their religious obligations more generally.

For the state to tell a parent, "You are forbidden to direct the education of your own child, but consider yourself absolved of your parental educational obligations because I have someone else with greater expertise who will direct your child's education in your stead," is just as much a misunderstanding of the relevant conscience rights as it is for the state to tell Catholics that someone else will attend Sunday Mass for them. In Diana's case, the city's sex education policies are effectively telling

---

[13] Free exercise rights can also be defended with reference to the basic human good of religion, understood as the good of being in harmony with the transcendent, more-than-human source of meaning and value. For further discussion on this point, see my "Beyond Equal Liberty."

her: "We know that you think exposing your daughter Lia to our curriculum is harmful, but we are going to require you to allow us to do so anyway. Don't worry, though; we consider ourselves the ones responsible for Lia's education in this regard, and our curricular experts know better than you do what is good for her." In doing so, the state is failing to recognize that the responsibility to educate Lia (especially, as I will argue later, in moral and religious matters) belongs *personally* to Diana, and that placing obstacles in the way of Diana's ability to educate Lia as she thinks best prevents Diana from fulfilling a very serious obligation, no less serious than a Catholic's obligation to attend Mass, and no less important for her own personal fulfillment and overall well-being. Of course, Diana can seek the help of other individuals and institutions, including the public schools, to fulfill this responsibility, but the responsibility is ultimately *hers*, and fulfilling it is an important aspect of her own good *qua* parent. Diana may also, like many parents, see this responsibility as something with which she has been personally entrusted by God, the conscientious fulfillment of which is central among her religious obligations. If Lia's understanding of important moral truths is seriously distorted by the things that she learns at school, this is not only the school's fault, but also the result of Diana's choice to send her to that school.[14] This is why effective school choice and a generous approach to exemptions (within the limits of feasibility) are so important, for otherwise parents like Diana are effectively faced with the terrible situation of being prevented from fulfilling their perceived obligations in a very serious matter, and of helplessly witnessing the resulting harms to their children. I will discuss these policy implications in greater detail in Chapter 5.

Some might argue that the comparison between religious freedom and parental rights involves a false parallel, since in the parenting case it is

---

[14] In the circumstances of the case as I have described them, Diana would nonetheless not be *culpable* for the resulting harms to Lia. As noted earlier (footnote 10), the presence of state coercion may create circumstances in which a positive obligation is defeated. Diana's choice to send Lia to the public school was right given the circumstances – in particular, the state's monopoly on publicly funded education, her financial inability to pay for a private school, and her financial inability to forego paid work in order to homeschool (here I assume that a reasonable effort was made to explore potential scholarship opportunities or other sources of financial assistance). But the state will nonetheless have done her a serious injustice by preventing her from fulfilling her parental responsibilities as she believes that she should without (as I will argue in subsequent chapters) a sufficiently compelling justification for doing so.

not simply a matter of directing one's own life in accordance with one's beliefs, but of directing someone *else's* life. Nonetheless, from the perspective of the acting agent the situations are essentially the same. In each case, one believes oneself to have a serious and non-transferable obligation – participating in a particular form of worship (and not participating in other forms of worship) or educating one's children in accordance with one's beliefs – and in each case one is being prevented from fulfilling that obligation. To prevent parents from educating their children as they think best, particularly with respect to moral and religious values, is to prevent them from performing a serious moral obligation, which in many instances is viewed as a religious obligation as well. Likewise, using the coercive force of the state to compel parents to teach (or to send their children to a school where they will be taught) certain values which they believe are wrong, effectively prevents parents from fulfilling their obligation to care for their children's moral formation, and thus also from achieving the great personal good that comes from fulfilling one's parental responsibilities.

It might also be objected that there is a difference between teaching one's children something oneself, and allowing others to teach it. While this is true, that difference does not relieve parents of moral responsibility with regard to what others teach their children, insofar as they permit this teaching to occur (either actively or through negligence). Certainly, children will learn many things from others, and from the larger society and culture, of which their parents are simply unaware. It is impossible for parents to control *all* the factors that may influence their children's psychological, moral and intellectual development. Nonetheless, as the ones with primary responsibility for their children's education, parents ought to be aware of the various formative influences on their children, and to try to ensure as much as possible that those influences are, on balance, salutary rather than detrimental. As children grow older, of course, their education begins to depend in part on their own initiative, and a significant portion of parents' task is to foster and direct this initiative, forming their children's judgment with regard to the sorts of influences – friends, clubs, activities, readings, Internet sites, video games, television shows, movies and so forth – to which they expose themselves, and giving them some freedom to make their own choices in this regard within certain limits, and in accordance with each child's level of maturity.

Ultimately, however, parents have primary moral responsibility for all of these aspects of their children's upbringing: for making decisions about the formal educational environment in which they should place their children; for overseeing what their children are taught in that environment and trying to shape that environment as needed or removing their children from it if it seems on balance to be detrimental or inadequate; for surrounding their children, as much as possible, with salutary influences more generally; for forming their children's judgment with regard to what is harmful and helpful to their development; and for making decisions about how much freedom to give their children based on their assessment of the children's maturity. In other words, before the tribunal of their consciences (and, for religious believers, before God), parents may be just as morally responsible for allowing their children to be taught something that is morally harmful to them – by, for instance, sending them to a school where they know that those harmful elements are part of the curriculum, or through negligence in failing to inform themselves about what their children are being taught at school – as they would be for teaching it themselves. Parents, may, of course, make the judgment that a particular school or educational environment is, on balance, the best one for their child, despite having some reservations about it. But in such instances the parents would also have the responsibility to counter any harmful aspects of the curriculum or environment through what they teach their children at home, and/or to supplement anything that they think is lacking in the curriculum.

Perhaps a comparison will help to illustrate the idea. Imagine the following scenario: A mother is aware that the lunches served at her son's school include a substance that she believes is mildly poisonous. Let us assume, to make the scenario more realistic, that the poisonous nature of the substance is a matter of some controversy, and the effects of the poison are only evident in the long term. School regulations require that all students eat the school lunch. If, despite her conviction that the school lunches could have significant negative effects on her child's health, she continued to send her child to that school, she would be just as responsible for the ensuing harm to her child as if she fed him the poisonous substance herself. The same is true for a parent who believes that some aspect of a school curriculum is *morally* poisonous, but does nothing about it. Extending the analogy, we might think that the mother in the imaginary scenario could reasonably decide to send her child to the school if she thought that in all other respects it was the best environment for her son, and that she could neutralize the effects of the poison through what she fed him at home. A similar choice could be reasonably made by parents who think a school is, overall, a good choice for their child, but have reservations with regard to some aspects of the moral or intellectual formation offered at the school.

Parents are the ones with the primary responsibility to provide for their children's physical, psychological, moral and intellectual develop-ment, and this responsibility is in no way mitigated when children walk into the schoolhouse door. The fact that a particular harm – physical, psychological, moral or intellectual – occurs during school does not (insofar as that harm is foreseeable) lessen parents' responsibility for its occurrence. This is why when the state compels parents to allow their children to be taught something that the parents think is harmful, or to place their children in an educational environment that parents believe will be detrimental, the state violates the conscience rights of those parents by preventing them from fulfilling their perceived parental responsibilities. Though the specifics will be discussed at greater length in subsequent chapters, such a violation of parental rights arguably occurs when, for example, financial strictures leave parents with practic-ally no option but to send their children to public schools, and parents object to some aspect of the public school curriculum. In such cases I believe that parents would have a right to exempt their children from the offensive aspect of the curriculum, to educate them at home, and/or to receive some sort of a voucher which would enable them to send their children to a school whose curriculum better conveys the values that they believe themselves to be morally (and perhaps also religiously) bound to pass along to their children.[15]

Rights as spheres of authority

How does this account of parental rights as conscience rights connect to the previous chapter's defense of parental authority as primary and pre-political? Parental rights, like all conscience rights, are discretionary by their very nature, because they are rights to fulfill perceived obligations. Such rights, therefore, carve out a sphere of authority within which one can make judgments and act in accordance with one's judgments free from

---

[15] I realize that what I have said thus far is insufficient to ground these policy claims. It is also necessary to consider the potential counterclaims based on the rights of children or the rights of the state to educate children for democratic citizenship, which I do in the following two chapters. In Chapter 5, after having considered these other claims, I return to a fuller discussion of the policy implications of my view. Here I only mention possible policy implications in order to give the reader a preliminary sense of what my under-standing of parental rights might mean in practice.

external interference, even when those decisions are objectively wrong. A helpful conceptual tool for articulating this point can be found in Gerald Gaus' characterization of rights as establishing spheres of sovereignty by distributing discretionary authority in a community.[16] A rights-holder is like an umpire whose directives, within the proper sphere, provide what Joseph Raz refers to as exclusionary reasons for action – i.e. reasons to exclude our own first-order moral considerations from our deliberation, within certain limits.[17] An umpire is necessary precisely for those moments in which there is disagreement about the correct course of action.[18] Thus, acceptance of the practical authority of the umpire constitutes an exclusionary reason, a reason not to act on one's own best judgment of the matter at hand, even while continuing to consider one's own judgment to be true. However, as Gaus points out, there are limits to players' deference to the umpire's authority. If the umpire's calls seem consistently outside the range of what most players consider reasonable, the umpire's authority itself is called into question. There is a "range of justifiable decisions" within which players will accept the umpire's practical authority; outside that range the exclusionary reason no longer applies, and players fall back on their own first-order judgments.[19]

To claim that parents have a right to raise their children as they think best is to claim that parents have a sphere of sovereignty within which they have the authority to make controversial child-care decisions. Even if the community disagrees with parents' decisions, the parents' right provides the community with an exclusionary reason to accept those decisions as practically authoritative. Of course, there are limits to the range of justifiable decisions that parents can make. How do we determine that range? For an umpire, the reasonable range of decisions is determined by the rules of the game. As long as the umpire's calls seem explicable as an application of the rules of the game, the umpire is acting within her proper sphere of authority and players have an exclusionary reason to accept her judgments as a practical resolution to their disputes. For parents, those rules of the game are their parental obligations. Since parental rights are grounded in obligations to care for the child, those rights are also limited by those obligations. Parents do not have the right to harm their children, because they have no obligation to do so, and they

---

[16] Gerald Gaus, *Justificatory Liberalism* (New York: Oxford University Press, 1996), 200–201.
[17] Joseph Raz, *Practical Reason and Norms* (London: Hutchinson, 1975), 35.
[18] Gaus, *Justificatory Liberalism*, 188.   [19] Gaus, *Justificatory Liberalism*, 189.

only have the right to fulfill their obligations. While in some instances what parents consider to be good for the child may in fact be harmful, as long as parents' decisions can be understood as a fulfillment of their obligations to their children, are not tantamount to abuse or neglect, and do not pose a serious threat to the public order, we have reason to respect those judgments even if we disagree with them, just as we have reason to respect an umpire's judgments as long as those judgments can reasonably be understood as an application of the rules of the game.[20]

Scope and limits of parental rights

Since parental rights are based on parental obligations, the sphere of parental authority that those rights protect depends on the content of parental obligations. When it comes to determining the content of parental obligations, we need to consider that parenting in general (including adoptive parenting) is about bringing a new human person into the world. And human persons have a very long period of gestation. Physical birth only ends the first and shortest period of human gestation, but the gestation of a human person is not over just because that person can exist outside the womb. The gestation of a person requires bringing that person not only to a state of relative physical independence, but also to the point of relative psychological and rational independence. Thus parents' obligations are extensive in both scope and duration. From the moral perspective, parents are obligated to care for their children until those children are capable of caring for themselves and directing their own lives, and with a view toward enabling them to do so. While caring for children requires making decisions on their behalf, it also requires progressively training children to make decisions for themselves (and to take responsibility for the consequences), beginning with relatively trivial matters and then building toward matters of greater importance. Once children are independent and mature enough to govern their own lives, parents continue to have special obligations to their children, but the fulfillment of those obligations no longer involves the exercise of paternalistic authority over their children (although if adult

---

[20] We have reasons to accord authority to make judgments about what is best for children to the parents, not only because of the unique bond between parents and children and the moral obligations which flow from that bond, but also because coercive state intervention may often be worse than the harm of tolerating imperfect parenting in individual cases, and a societal pattern of overzealous government intrusion into family life may undermine parental authority and expectations of family stability, both of which are important for the well-being of parents and children alike.

children continue to live at home the parents still have authority as heads of the household to establish guidelines for living together harmoniously). Parents' obligations are also drastically diminished when their children achieve maturity because adult children's objective need for their parents' care is much less, and also because the children develop close relationships with others (particularly if they marry) who may have stronger special obligations for their well-being. Here we are interested in parental obligations only insofar as they imply decision-making authority over children.

Parental authority over moral and religious education

The sphere within which parents exercise discretionary authority may be extensive because of the extensiveness of parental obligations, but it is not entirely impermeable, nor is it equally impermeable in all areas. It is in determining the content – particularly the moral and religious content – of education that parents should have the highest degree of discretionary authority. In other words, the impermeability of parents' sphere of authority should be strongest in the area of moral and religious education. This is because to flourish humanly is, most centrally, to flourish morally. For the goods of integrity and religion play an architectonic role in human flourishing, governing and ordering one's pursuit of all of the other goods that are constitutive of and instrumental to human well-being. When we call someone a "good person," we are referring not to the person's state of health, expertise in mathematics or overflowing bank account, but to that person's moral character. Although goods like health, knowledge, professional success and wealth contribute to a good life, the achievement of such goods is to a significant extent outside our direct control, and it is possible to enjoy all of these goods and yet be a very bad person. On the contrary, as Aristotle notes, if one has a virtuous character, not even the greatest misfortunes will make one miserable, as a good character equips one to make the best of any circumstance.[21] I will develop this idea further in Chapter 4. For now, my point is that if parents are charged with continuing the task of creating a flourishing human being, and if moral flourishing is the central aspect of human flourishing as such, then providing moral and religious education are among parents' most serious obligations.

---

[21] Aristotle, *Nicomachean Ethics*, I.10, 1101a6–7

Moral and religious education also seem to be among the most personal aspects of the overall care which parents are obligated to give their children. For moral education is not just a matter of learning certain technical skills which can be taught by anyone with the relevant competency; it is a matter of learning a certain way of life, and it is taught in large part through the example of others who have thoroughly incorporated that way of life into their habitual mode of being, whose actions are permeated by its underlying principles. Further, learning to be moral means learning how to be a good person given one's specific temperament, personality traits, tendencies and predispositions. Parents are uniquely placed to help children in their moral development, not only because they are in a better position to know the characteristic strengths and weaknesses of their children, but also because, in the central case of biological parents, they themselves are likely to have had the experience of forging a mature moral character out of similar raw materials. Further, because human beings are a psychophysical unity, there is a complex interrelationship among the various levels of human development – physical, psychological and rational – such that what happens at one level prepares for and is in turn influenced by what happens at another. Parents' physical proximity and the physical care that they provide enables children to form healthy psychological bonds with their parents, which in turn fosters the trust in and affection for parents that facilitates education (especially moral education) – in part by motivating the obedience to parents' directives that is essential for helping children to overcome the tyranny of sub-rational desire and thus become capable of practical reasoning about the good at a distinctively human level, and in part by grounding a sense of security that enables children to experiment with and develop their independence in the knowledge that someone will be there to pick them up and take care of them when they fall, literally or metaphorically.[22]

Thus while parents have a serious obligation to provide for all of their children's needs, care for the moral development of children is the need that parents have the strongest obligation to attend to *personally*, and to oversee with the greatest care. The particularly weighty and personal nature of parents' obligation to educate their children morally and religiously implies that respecting parents' right to integrity requires

---

[22] For a more detailed analysis of what children need to learn to develop successfully into independent practical reasoners, see MacIntyre, *Dependent Rational Animals*, chapters 7 and 8.

granting them a highly protected sphere of authority to make decisions about the moral and religious content of education. Further, the centrality of moral and religious education to parenting means that the parents' own moral, religious and overall personal fulfillment are deeply implicated in how they carry out this task.

The authority of parents is, however, not without limits, precisely because parental authority, like all authority, is intrinsically connected to the promotion of integral human well-being. Further, unlike political authority which aims directly at the common good and only indirectly at the proper good of the members of the political community, parental authority aims directly at the well-being of children, and the responsible exercise of that authority is also central to the well-being of the parents themselves and to the common good of the family unit. The good of children (a crucial aspect of the common good of the family as a whole) is therefore the primary justification for parental childrearing authority, and the reason why parents have authority to make controversial childcare decisions is that they are the ones who have the strongest and most direct special obligation to care for those children. Like all authority, the authority of parents ceases to merit respect to the extent that it fails to promote the good which it exists to serve.

The family as analogous to a sovereign state

Within the larger political community, the family is in some ways analogous to an individual sovereign state within the larger international community. Although the analogy is imperfect, it can nonetheless shed light on the scope and limits of parental authority with respect to the authority of the state. Like parental authority, political authority exists to favor and foster the good of the community, including the good of the individuals and groups that make up that community. The political authority (regardless of its form) has the right to make controversial decisions regarding the means to pursue the common good, within the limits of natural and positive law, because those in authority are the ones who have the special obligation to foster the common good of the political community as such, which includes an obligation (though a subsidiary and indirect one) to foster the good of each of the community's members.

At the same time, by virtue of the general obligation to foster the good of every human being, and also to some extent by virtue of positive law, the international community as a whole is legitimately concerned with the well-being of the individuals and societies within it. The international community has an obligation to respect the proper spheres of authority of the sovereign states within it, and also has an obligation to assist other states and their people when they are in need.[23] Usually that assistance is offered in a subsidiary way, respecting the proper channels of authority and working through (or with the permission of) the government of the state whose people another state or international organization is trying to assist. Coercive interference, however, requires extremely strong justification, such as the presence of serious and widespread human rights abuses, and, more controversially, the request of insurgents for outside assistance in cases of legitimate rebellion. The international community is also justified in intervening coercively when a state engages in activity that directly threatens the peace, security or fundamental human rights of other sovereign states or the individuals within those states.

Likewise, every political community is composed of numerous families, communities which, as I have argued, have their own natural authority structure and sphere of competence with respect to the common good proper to them, which includes the overall organization of family life with a view toward the flourishing of the family community and of all of the persons within it. Parental authority extends as far as the proper ends of that community, among which the upbringing and education of children, particularly their moral and religious formation, are primary. Of course, the international relations analogy has limits. Even in our globalized world, a sovereign state is more self-sufficient than a family, because it has the resources within itself to meet a much fuller array of human needs, whereas a family does not offer the full range of resources necessary for children to reach personal maturity beyond a certain stage, nor does it offer the full range of resources necessary for the flourishing of the parents or other adult members of the family. Nonetheless, in the areas which form part of the proper competency of the family – again, a primary one being the education of children – the state has a general obligation to assist, but to do so in a way that respects rather than usurps or contradicts the authority of parents. The state may also have an obligation to intervene coercively on children's behalf,

---

[23] Norms regarding state sovereignty and international intervention are of course a matter of lively debate. Here I present what I take to be a mainstream view reflecting norms widely accepted by the international community and by prominent scholars. See, for example, Michael Walzer, *Just and Unjust Wars* (New York: Basic Books, 2000) and John Rawls, *The Law of Peoples* (Cambridge, MA: Harvard University Press, 2001).

but only in cases parallel to the international intervention cases: cases of abuse and neglect, and perhaps cases in which children who are still minors but old enough to think and speak for themselves bring a serious complaint to state authorities of their own volition.[24] Finally, completing the parallel with norms for the use of coercive force in international relations, the state has an obligation and a right to intervene for civic reasons in cases where the parents' mode of raising their children constitutes a serious threat to public order – for example, a case in which parents set up a school to teach their children to be terrorists, or, less dramatically, a case in which parents fail to provide the minimal level of education required for the child to be a productive and law-abiding citizen in the future.[25]

When should the state intervene?

Deciding what counts as abuse or neglect, or determining when the state has an interest strong enough to trump the rights of parents, is admittedly not a simple matter, nor is it a matter about which moral principles yield clear-cut rules applicable to all cases. As Aristotle pointed out, morality is not like mathematics in which there is a clear and precise answer to every problem.[26] While the political community ultimately has to decide where the line should be drawn, and there is room for

---

[24] There should be a strong presumption in favor of the parents even in the latter scenario, however, particularly given the neurobiological evidence (presented in Chapter 4) indicating that, despite their ability to engage in sophisticated reasoning, adolescent children's decision-making capacity remains immature.

[25] Obviously, the threat in the latter case lacks the immediacy and seriousness of the sort of threat that would justify coercive international intervention. However, as pointed out earlier, the family's self-sufficiency with respect to the larger political community is much more limited than that of the state with respect to the larger international community. Thus, while the grounds justifying coercive intervention in each case remain essentially the same (human rights abuses and protection of public order), the abuse or threat to public order need not be as serious or immediate to justify state intervention into the family sphere as to justify international intervention.

[26] "Our discussion will be adequate if it has as much clearness as the subject-matter admits of; for precision is not to be sought for alike in all discussions. . .. Now fine and just actions, which political science investigates, exhibit much variety and fluctuation. . .. And goods also exhibit a similar fluctuation because they bring harm to many people. . .. We must be content, then, in speaking of such subjects and with such premises to indicate the truth roughly and in outline, and in speaking about things which are only for the most part true and with premises of the same kind to reach conclusions that are no better. . .. For it is the mark of an educated man to look for precision in each class of things just so far as the nature of the subject admits: it is evidently equally foolish to accept probable

prudential judgment in borderline cases, my argument gives reasons for drawing that line in a way that gives substantial deference to parental authority. Even in cases where that line has clearly been crossed, efforts should be made to alleviate the abuse or neglect with as little intervention as possible, only removing children from their parents' care in the most extreme cases where the child faces grave danger, or where less invasive means of intervention such as mandatory parenting classes or counseling sessions, supervision from social workers, etc. have proved ineffective. It is true that a policy of deference to parents' judgments and of trying to avoid removing children from their parents' care (as well as, when removal is necessary, of trying to return them to their parents' care as soon as possible, when there are reasonable assurances that the problematic situation has been overcome) might occasionally leave children vulnerable to harm that could have been avoided by intervening sooner or more aggressively. Yet overzealous intrusion also harms children by breaking up the family unnecessarily, undermining parental authority and family intimacy, preventing parents from achieving their own good *qua* parents, and tearing children away from caregivers (however imperfect) to whom they have formed attachments that are important for their psychological well-being.

A counterargument

One counterargument to my view is offered by James Dwyer. Dwyer would deny the claim that the state has any obligation to respect the childrearing decisions of parents, as part of his larger argument that "the very notion of parental rights is illegitimate" because the only relevant consideration is children's well-being.[27] While Dwyer's argument focuses primarily on religiously-based child-care decisions, it applies much more broadly. Dwyer implicitly assumes that we should generally trust the state (rather than parents) to judge what children's welfare interests actually are, and which ones are more important in case of conflict. Though he does not actually make this point himself, Dwyer could perhaps even use my own arguments against me in the following manner: If the state is capable of recognizing the natural rights of parents, then why isn't the

---

reasoning from a mathematician and to demand from a rhetorician demonstrative proofs." (Aristotle, *Nicomachean Ethics*, I.3, 1094b13–25)

[27] James Dwyer, *Religious Schools v. Children's Rights* (Ithaca: Cornell University Press, 1998), 63.

state capable of correctly judging what the requirements of *children's* rights are? And since parents' rights really are in the service of children's well-being, why should the state respect parents' rights when it judges that children's well-being would be better promoted by raising and educating a child in a way that goes against the will of the parents?

One way of responding to this line of questioning is to return to the comparison between the family and the sovereign state. For the norm of non-interference in the internal affairs of sovereign states is perfectly compatible with the claim that in some instances the international community or another state's government might have a better proposal for promoting the well-being of the members of a particular state than that state's own government. The underlying reason for this norm of non-interference is that, by and large (but not necessarily in every single case taken in isolation), it best promotes human well-being. Thus my claim is not that in every case parents will be correct (and the state will be wrong) about what is actually in the best interests of a child,[28] nor that the state may never intervene (at the child or parents' request) in an intra-familial dispute,[29] nor that parents' rights are more important than children's rights, but rather that respecting a broad sphere of parental authority over childrearing decisions is, for all of the reasons mentioned above and in the previous chapter about the general characteristics and developmental needs of children, by and large the best way to protect and promote children's well-being.

Dwyer also bases his case against parental rights on concerns about liberal neutrality. He argues that "the state should no more allow parents to balance their child's spiritual and temporal interests and decide that they will sacrifice the latter than it should allow me to do this in relation to my neighbor."[30] In explaining his view, Dwyer points out that the liberal state's commitment to religious neutrality leaves individuals free

---

[28] There is, however, a strong case to be made that (1) because of their intimate knowledge of their child, parents are usually in the best position to know what is in their child's best interest, and (2) because of the strong bonds of affection that usually characterize the parent–child relationship, parents are also the most motivated to promote the well-being of their child. For more detailed arguments and evidence along these lines, see John E. Coons and Stephen D. Sugarman, *Education by Choice: The Case for Family Control* (Berkeley: University of California Press, 1978).

[29] The state, however, should not intervene in intra-familial disputes (excluding cases of abuse, neglect or threat to the public order) unless the child and/or parents *request* such intervention.

[30] Dwyer, *Religious Schools v. Children's Rights*, 83.

to balance their secular and religious concerns as they see fit, but only when the temporal interests of others are not implicated. At the same time, the state has the role of protecting individual rights from usurpation by others. For these reasons, Dwyer believes that "the state should protect the child's temporal interests no matter what the parents believe until the child becomes an adult capable of making his own self-determining choices."[31] Dwyer goes on to clarify that the state can only take parents' beliefs into account "insofar as the parents' adherence to those beliefs affects the temporal well-being of the child – for example, if psychological harm might befall a child as a result of his parents' belief that they and the child are damned to an eternity in hell."[32]

What Dwyer fails to recognize is that his approach is not neutral at all. By making the state the ultimate arbiter of children's best interests, and claiming that it is not the state's role to determine the plausibility of religious beliefs about the spiritual interests of the child, he is effectively forcing upon children a way of life that prioritizes non-religiously-based interests over religiously-based ones, perhaps even a way of life that does not recognize the existence of religiously-based interests at all. To impose that way of life upon a child before she can make the decision for herself is not neutral between religion and non-religion, but is tantamount to choosing a non-religious life for the child. Would this be in the best interests of children? If it were true that religiously-based interests actually do not exist, or that non-religiously based interests are always more important than religiously-based ones, then Dwyer's proposal would in fact be in the best interests of children. Dwyer offers no argument, however, to support such a controversial claim. Further, even if it were objectively true that non-religiously-based interests trump religiously-based ones, in proposing that the state take on a role which effectively enforces this controversial view upon children, Dwyer also seems inadvertently to run afoul of his own commitment to state religious neutrality. Unlike Dwyer's view, which begs the question in favor of privileging non-religious interests over religious ones, my view simply leaves the authority to make these controversial judgments in the hands of parents, rather than giving that authority to the state. Dwyer's concerns about neutrality would therefore actually support my view that parental judgments about the best interests of children should be respected except in extreme cases.

[31] Ibid.   [32] Ibid.

Conclusion

In this chapter, I have argued that parental rights follow from parental obligations, and can be understood as an aspect of the general right to fulfill one's perceived duties without undue interference. This right is based on the basic human good of integrity. The right to integrity creates a moral space within which one can fulfill one's perceived obligations without undue interference. This moral space can be conceptualized as a sphere of authority. The extensiveness of the sphere depends on the extensiveness of the duties in question. The impermeability of the sphere – i.e. the seriousness of the reasons that would be required to justify interference – depends on the weight and non-transferability of the duties in question. Because parents have weighty and extensive non-transferable obligations to their children, respecting parents' right to integrity requires according them an extensive sphere of discretionary authority over childrearing decisions. The aspect of parental obligation which is weightiest and most inherently non-transferable is the duty to provide moral and religious education. It follows that in the area of moral and religious education the impermeability of parents' sphere of authority is strongest. In this realm, therefore, the state should almost always refrain from coercive intervention absent extremely serious reasons.

Returning to the case introduced at the beginning of this chapter, we can now articulate how exemption-less sexual education policies like New York City's 2011 sexual education mandate violate the rights of conscientious parents like Diana. For, given compulsory education laws and the public schools' monopoly on public funding, such laws force parents to allow their children to be taught material that the parents consider potentially harmful, and thus violate parents' conscience rights by preventing them from fulfilling their perceived educational obligations. Such policies also fail to respect the primacy of parental educational authority and rob parents of the deep personal good involved in fulfilling their own parental responsibilities.[33] Yet, as objectors will certainly point out, there is more to the story. After all, the objection might go, parents like Diana are not the only ones whose interests are at stake. What about Diana's daughter Lia? What if she disagrees with her

---

[33] I would say the same thing if the tables were turned, ideologically speaking – i.e. if the state were imposing abstinence-only education and Diana sincerely believed that such an education was not only insufficient (since she would of course be free to supplement it at home), but could also be positively harmful to Lia by, for instance, fostering a repressive attitude toward sexuality.

mother's values regarding appropriate sexual behavior? And even if she does not, shouldn't she at least be exposed to a different approach so that she can choose her values on this intimate matter for herself? What about the state's interest in preventing teenage pregnancy and sexually transmitted infections, or in fostering tolerance and understanding of those who identify as gay or lesbian? The next two chapters will help to answer these questions by considering the arguments of liberal theorists who claim that the state has an obligation to promote children's autonomy even when this means going against parents' educational preferences, and/or that the state's interest in civic education outweighs parents' interests in passing on their own values to their children. In the final chapter I will return to the issue of sex education as I consider some of the policy implications of my view in greater detail.

3

Parental rights and education for liberal democratic citizenship

Even the strongest defenders of parental rights admit that the state has some legitimate role to play in the education of children. The health and survival of the political community depends on its ability to reproduce itself over time, which requires not only that people have children and that most of those children survive to adulthood, but also that those children receive an upbringing which will enable them to be productive and law-abiding members of society. The maintenance of democratic political institutions over the long term also requires that each generation receive a civic education that will inform them of their rights and duties as citizens, and enable them to participate meaningfully in political life. Further, although parents are the ones with the primary obligation to care for their children, the larger community also has a subsidiary obligation to ensure that children (and all of those members of society who are unable to care for themselves) receive what is necessary to meet their basic needs.

The latter concern – in particular, the concern for children's development into autonomous adults – is the subject of the next chapter. In this chapter, I will consider some of the arguments for mandatory civic education advanced by Rawlsian liberal theorists such as Stephen Macedo, Eamonn Callan and Amy Gutmann. From the perspective of a concern for parental rights, Rawlsian civic education is problematic only insofar as it is made mandatory. My aim here, therefore, is quite limited. All I need to show is that Rawlsian civic education does not serve a state interest that is serious enough to justify usurping parental authority or infringing upon the conscience rights of parents with regard to the upbringing of their children. My position does not imply, as will become clear in the course of the argument, that the state lacks a grave interest in providing all citizens with *some* form of civic education, only that there is no grave interest in the particular *type* of civic education proposed by Rawlsian liberals. I will argue that their recommendations rest on a flawed view of liberalism and an implausible understanding of what good citizenship in a pluralistic liberal democracy entails. However, my goal is not to persuade the reader fully of these claims – that goes well beyond the scope of the current project. Rather, I simply want to provide enough evidence for these alternative views to show that the necessity of Rawlsian civic education for the future health of liberal democracy is dubious at best.

When pursuing an important state goal involves infringing on the conscience rights of citizens and stepping into the domain of parental authority, respect for individual rights and parental authority requires thoughtful consideration of whether that goal is really important enough to justify such infringement, and in the case that it is, whether there might be a means of achieving that goal that eliminates or minimizes the potential conflict with individual rights. The formation of good citizens is indeed an important goal of the political community. However, given that there is reasonable doubt regarding Rawlsian civic education's suit-ability for advancing that goal, and that mandating this type of civic education conflicts with individual rights significantly more than other means for attempting to do so, pursuing it is not justifiable.

The standard I offer is much like the "strict scrutiny" standard used by the Supreme Court in cases where a law conflicts with the fundamental rights of individuals. In these cases, the burden of proof is on the state to show that the law in question serves a compelling interest, and that the law is narrowly tailored to achieve that interest – in particular, that there is no other means to achieve that interest without an infringement of individual rights. As mentioned in the Introduction, the Religious Free-dom Restoration Act (RFRA) sets forth essentially the same standard for the legality of legislation that substantially burdens the free exercise of religion. While there is controversy regarding the legitimacy of the strict scrutiny standard and its application as a matter of constitutional juris-prudence, and also regarding the application of RFRA, as a matter of moral principle (rather than constitutional interpretation) this standard of justification for laws that burden fundamental rights (including par-ental rights and conscience rights more generally) seems exactly right. Of course, there is still plenty of room for controversy over what qualifies as a compelling state interest, and what qualifies as a fundamental right or a "substantial burden" to the exercise of that right. For the purposes of this chapter, I will assume that the state has a compelling interest in some form of basic citizenship education – what I mean by that will be clarified in the course of the argument – and that parents have a fundamental right to raise their children in accordance with the dictates of their consciences, whether that right is conceptualized as flowing directly from parental childrearing authority, or as a subset of the more general right to fulfill one's perceived obligations. I therefore take for granted here my earlier defense of parental rights and of the primacy of parental education authority.

My argument in this chapter will proceed as follows. First, I will offer a brief summary of the defenses of Rawlsian civic education offered by Stephen Macedo, Eamonn Callan, and Amy Gutmann. Next, I will argue, following William Galston, that the views of these theorists conflict with the fundamental liberal commitment to respect for diversity. Then I will turn to the question of good citizenship itself, arguing that the Rawlsian understanding shared broadly by Macedo, Callan, Gutmann and others is, at best, overly demanding and highly controversial even among liberals, and, at worst, fundamentally mistaken and unjustly intolerant toward non-liberal ways of life. Finally, I will lay out what I consider to be the proper scope and limits of the state's authority with regard to civic education.

Three arguments for mandatory Rawlsian civic education

Three of the most sophisticated defenses of mandatory civic education are provided by Stephen Macedo, Eamonn Callan, and Amy Gutmann. All of them argue within a broadly Rawlsian framework. Macedo offers an account based explicitly on Rawls' political liberalism, Callan draws from both comprehensive and political liberalism (claiming that in practice political liberalism collapses into comprehensive liberalism), and Gutmann's approach is based on her theory of deliberative democracy. I will outline each of their views in turn. Given the significant overlap among the three authors' views, to avoid repetitiveness I will describe Macedo's account in the most detail, and then consider the others more briefly, highlighting their distinctive elements.

Stephen Macedo's civic liberalism

Stephen Macedo's argument for mandatory civic education, and his views about the essential content of that education, are based on the principles of Rawlsian political liberalism. Following Rawls, Macedo is concerned about how to justify political coercion in a way that is consistent with the freedom and equality of individuals. The solution, he thinks, is to limit the grounds of coercion to principles and values accessible to all reasonable persons – in other words, to justify coercion based on reasons and arguments that all reasonable people can reasonably be expected to understand. We can do this, on the Rawlsian view, by eschewing an appeal to controversial comprehensive conceptions of the good life – about which reasonable people can reasonably disagree – and appealing only to widely-shared "public ideals and principles that have emerged in and around liberal democratic institutions" when justifying constitutional essentials and matters of basic justice.[1] To be committed to this ideal of justifying political coercion only on the basis of reasons that others can reasonably be expected to accept is to be committed to what Rawls calls public reasonableness.

This view forms the backdrop of Macedo's claims about the requirements of civic education in a liberal state. If respect for the freedom and equality of all requires a commitment to public reasonableness on the part of citizens, then inculcating that commitment is an essential aspect of civic education. Indeed, for Rawlsians what is at stake here is the very legitimacy of the state, for political coercion is only legitimate on this view to the extent that it is based on principles that all reasonable people would accept. This is what Rawlsians call the liberal principle of legitimacy.[2] In order to understand what the requirements of Rawlsian civic education are, therefore, it is necessary to understand the requirements of public reasonableness.

Public reasonableness entails, first, seeking to establish and follow "fair terms of cooperation" in political and social life.[3] This means, effectively, abiding by norms of reciprocity, proposing laws and policies that other reasonable people can reasonably accept, even if they have different comprehensive views. Second, the good citizen acknowledges the "burdens of judgment"[4] and the consequent "fact of reasonable

---

[1] Stephen Macedo, *Diversity and Distrust* (Cambridge: Harvard University Press, 2003), 169.

[2] As John Rawls puts it, "Our exercise of political power is fully proper only when it is exercised in accordance with a constitution the essentials of which all citizens as free and equal may reasonably be expected to endorse in the light of principles and ideals acceptable to their common human reason." [*Political Liberalism* (New York: Columbia University Press, 1993), 137].

[3] Macedo, *Diversity and Distrust*, 171.

[4] Rawls' own non-exhaustive list of the burdens of judgment, with which Macedo agrees, is the following: "(a) The evidence — empirical and scientific — bearing on the case is conflicting and complex, and thus hard to assess and evaluate. (b) Even were we to agree fully about the kinds of considerations that are relevant, we may disagree about their weight, and so arrive at different judgments. (c) To some extent all our concepts, and not

pluralism," the fact that reasonable people reasonably disagree about many things, especially questions of ultimate truth and meaning.[5] Recognition of the burdens of judgment is, in itself, a condition of reasonableness. Given the fact of reasonable pluralism and a commitment to fair terms of cooperation, in public life (when exercising political power directly or indirectly, or when advocating the exercise of political power) the good citizen will act in accordance with the "duty of civility" – that is, he or she will refrain from appeals to "*any* authority impervious to critical assessment from a variety of reasonable points of view."[6]

Macedo's claim that "grounds for a range of public authority with respect to public education are furnished by our desire to shape future citizens" needs to be read in the context of his larger commitment to the liberal principle of legitimacy.[7] Macedo wants to defend a "tough-minded version of liberalism"[8] that is willing to engage in a "positive, transformative enterprise that aims to shape normative diversity in a basic way, to foster a civic life supportive of liberal citizenship."[9] He calls this view "civic liberalism."[10] Because a commitment to public reasonableness does not arise spontaneously, the state, according to Macedo, has to take positive measures to try to form citizens who will endorse basic liberal principles of justice and who will show their respect for diversity by their commitment to public reasonableness, acting in the political sphere in

---

only moral and political concepts, are vague and subject to hard cases; and this indeterminacy means that we must rely on judgment and interpretation (and on judgments about interpretations) within some range (not sharply specifiable) where reasonable persons may differ. (d) To some extent (how great we cannot tell) the way we assess evidence and weigh moral and political values is shaped by our total experience, our whole course of life up to now; and our total experiences must always differ. Thus, in a modern society with its numerous offices and positions, its various divisions of labor, its many social groups and their ethnic variety, citizens' total experiences are disparate enough for their judgments to diverge, at least to some degree, on many if not most, cases of any significant complexity. (e) Often there are different kinds of normative considerations of different force on both sides of an issue and it is difficult to make an overall assessment. (f) Finally, as we note in referring to Berlin's view (V: 6.2), any system of social institutions is limited in the values it can admit so that some selection must be made from the full range of moral and political values that might be realized." (Rawls, *Political Liberalism*, 56–57).

[5] Macedo, *Diversity and Distrust*, 172.
[6] Ibid. In other words, "when it comes to justifying basic rights and principles of justice, good liberal citizens leave aside their conceptions of the truth as a whole" [Stephen Macedo, "Multiculturalism for the Religious Right? Defending Liberal Civic Education" in *Democratic Education in a Multicultural State*, ed. Yael Tamir (Oxford: Blackwell Publishers, 1995), 71].
[7] Macedo, *Diversity and Distrust*, 243.   [8] Macedo, *Diversity and Distrust*, 5.
[9] Macedo, *Diversity and Distrust*, 10.   [10] Macedo, *Diversity and Distrust*, 169.

ways that do not rely solely on their religious beliefs or comprehensive philosophical commitments. Public schooling is one of the primary means that the government has for this task, and therefore the state has a right to ensure that schools foster these values through their curricula, even if some families would prefer not to expose their children to beliefs in tension with their own. Macedo recognizes that this transformative enterprise may be in conflict with parents' educational goals for their children, and will make it difficult to sustain and pass on some traditional ways of life.[11] However, he believes that state authority trumps parental authority in these cases: "Each of us can reasonably be asked to surrender some control over our own children for the sake of reasonable common efforts to ensure that all future citizens learn the minimal prerequisites of citizenship. There is no right to be exempted from measures necessary to secure the freedom of all."[12]

Macedo's position would justify extensive state powers to determine the content of education, even in private schools and homeschools. He argues that all schools should be forced to inculcate the values of tolerance and mutual respect that he believes are a necessary aspect of civic education. For Macedo, tolerance requires developing an appreciation of the burdens of judgment through even-handed exposure to diverse conceptions of the good life that will help children see the reasonableness of different views. And mutual respect requires honoring the Rawlsian duty of civility by refraining from making political decisions or advancing political agendas that are based on any comprehensive religious or philosophical framework. While Macedo concedes that parents have the right to send their children to private schools or educate them at home, he believes that right is "conditioned by a public authority to regulate private schools to ensure that civic values are satisfied and the child's right to freedom is preserved."[13] When combined with Macedo's demanding view of what it means "to ensure that civic values are satisfied," this claim justifies very expansive state intervention in private education.[14] Macedo observes that usually regulation of private education is minimal, and that civic education is often barely regulated at all.

---

[11] "To accept the liberal settlement is to accept institutions, ideas and practices whose influence over our lives and our children's lives will be broad, deep and relentless: family life, religious life and all paradigmatically private associations take on the color of liberal values" [Stephen Macedo, *Liberal Virtues* (New York: Oxford University Press, 1990), 62].

[12] Macedo, *Diversity and Distrust*, 202.   [13] Ibid.

[14] See the discussion in Macedo, *Diversity and Distrust*, 165, 180.

He insists, however, that states have the authority to do much more. There is no right, he asserts, "to opt selectively out of those basic civic exercises that the state may reasonably require for all children." Likewise, "private schools have no right to resist reasonable measures to ensure that all children learn about the many ways of life that coexist in our polity."[15]

Eamonn Callan on creating citizens

Callan's proposal for mandatory civic education is similarly based on the goal of building and sustaining a society that satisfies the liberal principle of legitimacy. His account, however, places much more emphasis on the centrality of the burdens of judgment to the Rawlsian ideal of the reasonable citizen.[16] The stringent notion of reasonableness at the heart of political liberalism, argues Callan, makes it just as controversial (and comprehensive) as comprehensive liberalism. This means that in a regime regulated by a conception of justice in line with the ideals of political liberalism, the liberal principle of legitimacy will be satisfied only by severely restricting the audience to whom we think justification is owed. In other words, to all who do not accept the burdens of judgment, the ideal of public reason will itself seem an arbitrary and unjustifiable "restriction on appeals to the truth on matters of the highest moral significance."[17] Callan explains:

> Rawls's conception of public reason cannot be free-standing relative to an audience as inclusive as the one to which his argument is explicitly tied. That is so because the ideal of civic virtue latent in that conception cannot fit appropriately as a 'module' within all comprehensive doctrines that are reasonable in the minimal sense. Rawlsian public reason is only free-standing relative to a much more restricted range of persons – namely, those who adhere to the strenuous ideal of the reasonable contained in his political conception of the person.[18]

Callan does not take this to be a critique of political liberalism, or a reason for abandoning the goal of liberal legitimacy. Rather, he argues that achieving legitimacy requires a much more demanding program of civic education than Rawls himself recognized. For it seems unsatisfying

---

[15] Macedo, *Diversity and Distrust*, 203.
[16] Eamonn Callan, *Creating Citizens* (New York: Oxford University Press, 1997), 30. See Rawls' list of the burdens of judgment in footnote 4.
[17] Callan, *Creating Citizens*, 32.   [18] Callan, *Creating Citizens*, 33.

to claim that liberal legitimacy has been achieved when all reasonable citizens accept the principles of justice upon which the regime is based, if large swathes of the population fail to count as reasonable citizens. After all, liberal legitimacy is ultimately about justifying coercion in a way that respects the freedom and equality of individual citizens. If Rawls is right that this is only possible when citizens are reasonable in his sense of the word, then the only way to achieve this goal is through civic education that will ensure, as much as possible, the reasonableness of future citizens. For Callan, the goal of education is to create citizens who are reasonable in the Rawlsian sense, citizens who can accept the society's underlying principles of justice. In other words, legitimacy "presupposes a civic education which instills acceptance of the burdens of judgment."[19]

Acceptance of the burdens of judgment, however, is no simple or innocuous task. It requires engaging sympathetically with reasonable views that differ from one's own, recognizing that our own view of the good is but one among many reasonable options, and that in many instances others hold their views just as reasonably as we hold ours. It also implies agreeing to live by political principles that are reasonably acceptable to all reasonable people who hold a variety of reasonable comprehensive views.[20] When Callan speaks of sympathetic engagement with diverse views, he means an imaginative engagement in which "the beliefs and values by which others live are entertained not merely as sources of meaning in *their* lives; they are instead addressed as potential elements within the conceptions of the good and the right one will create for oneself as an adult."[21] An acceptable political education in a society marked by reasonable pluralism "will teach the young the virtues and abilities they need in order to participate competently in reciprocity-governed political dialogue and to abide by the deliverances of such dialogue in their conduct as citizens."[22] Concretely, this means teaching children that treating others with respect and civility in public life requires refraining from voting or advocating a particular policy or candidate based on reasons that cannot be supported without reference to their own comprehensive view – i.e. reasons that are not sufficiently *public* in nature.

Callan, like Macedo, is clear that his recommendations for political education "will be far less banal, and much more corrosive of some powerful and long-entrenched sources of diversity, than many would

[19] Ibid. [20] Callan, *Creating Citizens*, 43. [21] Callan, *Creating Citizens*, 133.
[22] Callan, *Creating Citizens*, 28.

like."[23] Though the aims of such education are political, it will unavoidably have a profound effect on the person's overall comprehensive understanding of the good, because "to understand the reasonableness of beliefs that initially seem wrong or even repellent I must imaginatively entertain the perspective those very beliefs furnish, and from that perspective my own way of life will look worse, or at least no better, than what that perspective affirms."[24] He is aware that for this reason Rawlsian civic education will indeed interfere with many parents' ability to pass on their values and way of life to their children.[25] Religious ways of life will be the most frequent casualty of such an education, because maintaining religious belief while being a good Rawlsian citizen is, in Callan's words, a "high-wire act. One falls off it if adherence to a comprehensive doctrine influences (perhaps unconsciously) political judgment.... One also falls if acceptance of the burdens of judgment eats away at the creed that public reason pushes outside its boundaries. This would be an acute worry for many religious families regarding the kind of education political liberalism implies."[26] Likewise, Callan admits that acceptance of the burdens of judgment is not only difficult, but actually incompatible with at least many, if not all, totalistic belief systems.[27]

Amy Gutmann on education for conscious social reproduction

Amy Gutmann argues that the goal of education should be to facilitate "conscious social reproduction," which requires educating "all educable

---

[23] Callan, *Creating Citizens*, 13.   [24] Callan, *Creating Citizens*, 36.

[25] He thinks, however, that this is a necessary interference because the partiality of the family is "a threat to political liberalism so far as doctrines learned in the family press outside the boundaries of a reasonable pluralism. That outcome is avoided only so far as future citizens learn at some stage to accept the burdens of judgment in other institutional settings, and the school is an obvious candidate for that role" (*Creating Citizens*, 35).

[26] Callan, *Creating Citizens*, 37.

[27] "If acceptance [of the burdens of judgment] is compatible with some kinds of fundamentalism, these will have to be very different from many that are currently familiar, and the religious education intended to sustain them would have to depart drastically from the insular and dogmatic education that characterizes garden-variety fundamentalism" (*Creating Citizens*, 38). To bring their faith within the boundaries of the reasonable, for example, Catholics would have to depart from official magisterial positions on a number of issues: "In contemporary liberal democracies, a great many Catholics have combined their faith with a steadfast disregard of official church teachings on issues such as birth control. No doubt many are also capable of a similar accomplishment in reconciling their faith with the acceptance of the burdens of judgment." (39).

children to be capable of participating collectively in shaping their society."[28] Her underlying concerns are quite similar to those of Macedo and Callan, for ultimately her goal is to educate future citizens such that they will affirm the basic liberal democratic principles of justice upon which our society is based, and actively contribute to the perpetuation of a regime that respects the freedom and equality of all by satisfying the liberal principle of legitimacy.[29] Critical thinking skills, exposure to diverse ways of life and the inculcation of tolerance and respect for different viewpoints are all necessary to achieve conscious social repro-duction in a pluralistic liberal democracy like ours.[30] On Gutmann's view, there are two principles that place limits on permissible education schemes: the principle of non-repression and the principle of non-discrimination. According to the non-repression principle, neither the state nor any group within it may use "education to restrict rational deliberation of competing conceptions of the good life and the good society."[31] Non-repression is an essential requirement of *conscious* social reproduction, for without it, Gutmann claims, children will lack the critical thinking skills and respect for other ways of life that are essential for productive political participation and conscious affirmation of core liberal democratic values. The principle of non-discrimination extends the principle of non-repression to all children, requiring that *every* educable child receive "an education adequate to participating in the political processes that structure choice among good lives."[32] This principle implies that parents have no right to exclude their children from autonomy education or civic education, even if they fear that such an education will undermine the values they are trying to pass on to their children.[33] Gutmann thinks that private schooling is permissible, though she denies that there is a principled case against prohibiting it. Rather, she argues that from an empirical perspective a mixed system which

---

[28] Amy Gutmann, *Democratic Education* (Princeton: Princeton University Press, 1999), 39.

[29] See Amy Gutmann and Dennis Thompson, *Democracy and Disagreement* (Cambridge, MA: Belknap Press, 1996) and Amy Gutmann and Dennis Thompson, *Why Deliberative Democracy?* (Princeton: Princeton University Press, 2004) for a fuller account of the ideal of democracy that underlies her recommendations for political education.

[30] Gutmann, *Democratic Education*, 41.   [31] Gutmann, *Democratic Education*, 44.

[32] Gutmann, *Democratic Education*, 45.

[33] For Gutmann, civic education is inseparable from some sort of autonomy education (which she also believes is valuable in itself), but she justifies it not primarily with reference to children's interests, but rather with reference to the interests of society as a whole in reproducing itself over time.

accommodates private schools on the condition that they "teach the common set of democratic values" would fulfill democratic purposes better than a purely public system.[34] Determining the content and extensiveness of that set of democratic values is a matter for collective democratic decision-making. Likewise, in the case where certain values conflict with the religious or moral convictions of parents or educators, Gutmann argues that it is permissible for legislatures to make exemptions, though certainly not required.[35] The bottom line, for Gutmann, is that educational authority over children is shared among parents, teachers, and the larger democratic community, and it is the community which has the ultimate authority to determine the relative size of each share.[36]

Liberalism and the protection of diversity

Macedo, Callan, Gutmann and other defenders of robust mandatory civic education are right to point out that children do not spontaneously grow up to be good citizens. Some form of civic education is indeed necessary, and the state has an obligation and a right to foster such an education. However, they go too far in claiming that *only* an education for Rawlsian liberal citizenship will do, and that such an education is crucial enough to the health of the polity that it ought to be mandated even against the

---

[34] Gutmann, *Democratic Education*, 117.   [35] Gutmann, *Democratic Education*, 120.

[36] Another distinctive feature of Gutmann's view is her emphasis on the need to achieve a proper balance of democratic authority over education at the local, federal and state levels, and also to accord a certain degree of autonomy to teachers in order to uphold "the principle of nonrepression *against* democratic authority" (*Democratic Education*, 76, emphasis mine). "The professional responsibility of teachers," she goes on to explain, "is to uphold the principle of nonrepression by cultivating the capacity for democratic deliberation" (76). Gutmann suggests that, to this end, reforms should be made to raise teaching, in terms of its status and rewards, to a degree of professionalism similar to that of other major professions in our society like law and medicine. She points out rightly that teachers' relatively low salaries, heavy workload and lack of autonomy within the institutional structure of most schools "make it all but impossible for teachers to develop a positive sense of professionalism," to the detriment of educational quality (78). I agree with Gutmann's call for change in this regard, but do not emphasize it in my account of her theory simply because it does not affect the larger source of disagreement as indicated in the Introduction and Chapter 1 – namely, that, on my view, parents have primary authority over their children's education *even within school*, while on her view, once children reach the age of formal schooling parents' educational authority is largely limited to their interactions with their children *outside of school*. For further discussion on this point, see the second to last section in this chapter.

reasonable concerns of some parents that it will erode the particular religious or moral values that they consider themselves obligated to pass on to their children. In fact, their lack of respect for ways of life that they consider to be "unreasonable" may even be illiberal, at least on some versions of liberalism.

Defenders of Rawlsian civic education are well aware that it will favor certain ways of life over others, and thus make those other ways of life less accessible in practice than those which are more in consonance with comprehensive liberal values.[37] As we have seen, promoters of Rawlsian civic education unapologetically defend this foreseeable effect of their educational policy recommendations. Macedo, for example, writes that "we should not aim to create a level playing field in which no special burdens are placed on some religious people."[38]

This attitude toward the place of non-liberal ways of life in a liberal polity, however, is in tension with another value that is also central to liberalism: respect for diversity. William Galston criticizes Rawlsian liberalism, with its emphasis on autonomy over diversity, on precisely these grounds. Instead, he advocates a liberalism which focuses on "the protection of diversity, not the valorization of choice."[39] Galston argues that Rawlsians' emphasis on autonomy – either as a direct goal or as a necessary and desirable side-effect of Rawlsian civic education – leads to an illiberal pressure toward social uniformity: "In the guise of protecting the capacity for diversity the autonomy principle in fact represents a kind of uniformity that exerts pressure on ways of life that do not embrace autonomy."[40] Galston's concern is precisely for ways of life based

---

[37] "Liberal political principles do not 'stay on the surface' and their consequences cannot be confined to a particular sphere of our lives." Radically illiberal associations and commitments, such as Nazism or communism, are ruled out by liberal political principles, and "many other interests and commitments, while not strictly ruled out, are bound to be discouraged by the free, open, pluralistic, progressive and (arguably) commercialistic nature of a liberal society" (Macedo, *Liberal Virtues*, 53–54). He makes a similar point later in the book as well: "Liberalism embodies a set of substantive moral values, positive values that should secure the highest allegiance of liberal citizens, values that override or preclude many commitments, require some, and condition all other goals and projects, positive values that penetrate and pervasively shape the lives and characters of liberal citizens. . . . Liberal public norms have a private life" (264–265).

[38] Stephen Macedo, "Transformative Constitutionalism and the Case of Religion: Defending the Moderate Hegemony of Liberalism," *Political Theory* 26, 1 (February 1998): 73.

[39] William Galston, "Two Concepts of Liberalism," *Ethics* 105, 3 (April 1995): 516–534, at 523.

[40] Galston, "Two Concepts of Liberalism." Though political liberals like Macedo do not base their views on a comprehensive commitment to autonomy, they nonetheless recognize

primarily on tradition or revealed faith, which will be threatened by the kind of civic education programs that Rawlsians like Gutmann, Callan and Macedo advocate. Following Mill, Galston warns that overweening state intervention in education can produce uniformity, and that such uniformity is unhealthy for a liberal society. Yet at times such uniformity seems to be precisely what liberals like Macedo – who "aim at a 'moderate hegemony' of liberal public values" – are seeking.[41]

By contrast with the approach adopted by Gutmann, Callan and Macedo, Galston advocates a "diversity state," that seeks to respect the freedom of association of its members and to avoid disadvantaging groups that do not share the liberal prioritization of autonomy. However, Galston does recognize that there are limits on diversity, precisely to maintain the minimal requirements of citizenship. Further, he admits that a liberal society will inevitably exert some pressure toward liberal values on the individuals and groups that encompass it. He outlines three types of liberalizing pressures. The first, which he calls "membership effects," are "the formal requirements of shared citizenship that must be accepted by all associations and enforced if need be by the larger society." The second are "regime effects," which involve the "informal consequences of public principles for private groups." To explain this concept, he compares a society governed by liberal principles to a "rapidly flowing river":

> A few vessels may be strong enough to head upstream. Most, however, will be carried along by the current. But they can still choose where in the river to sail and where along the shore to moor. The mistake is to think of the liberal regime's public principles as constituting either a placid lake or an irresistible undertow.[42]

Importantly, however, Galston thinks that where feasible and not excessively costly, the state should mitigate these regime effects in order to facilitate the survival of diverse ways of life by protecting non-liberal ways of life at least partially from the pull of the liberal current. For instance, regime effects could be mitigated through exemptions and accommodations, as when members of the Native American Church in Oregon were granted an exemption from drug laws for the sacramental

---

that "explicitly or not, liberal regimes promote autonomy" (*Liberal Virtues*, 253) and affirm that "for liberals, the capacity to choose is more basic than what is chosen" (*Liberal Virtues*, 239).

[41] Macedo, "Transformative Constitutionalism," 77.

[42] Galston, "Two Concepts of Liberalism," 531.

use of peyote. Further, the state should, as far as possible, avoid the third type of liberalizing pressure, which he calls "colonization effects." Colonization occurs when, "above and beyond the requirements of citizenship, subcommunities and associations (including intimate associations) are expected or compelled to conform to public principles."[43] Macedo and others would welcome "regime effects," and perhaps "colonization effects" as well. Indeed, it may be hard to distinguish the regime effects from the colonization effects of Rawlsian liberal education proposals, given the particularly demanding Rawlsian view of what citizenship requires. Galston's understanding of liberalism as aimed at enabling the existence of diverse ways of life, however, leads him to seek to mitigate or eschew such effects as an unnecessary threat to legitimate diversity.

Respect for individual freedom of conscience and the fear of an overweening state, both central aspects of the liberal tradition, powerfully support Galston's approach to liberalism. These considerations alone, however, might be satisfied by a grudging toleration of "illiberal" ways of life, or ways of life that would be "unreasonable" in the Rawlsian sense, such as the stricter or more totalistic versions of most major world religions. There are, however, reasons to think that the presence of these alternative ways of life, precisely insofar as they present a serious challenge to the liberal worldview, is actually good for a liberal society.

The first set of reasons is given by John Stuart Mill, in his famous defense of "liberty of thought and discussion" in Chapter 2 of *On Liberty*. Mill argues that the presence of diverse viewpoints – even viewpoints that one thinks are clearly unreasonable – is essential to the health of society. He points out, first of all, that it just might be possible that a view one thinks is entirely unreasonable may actually turn out to be true, or at least partially true.[44] Rawlsians like Gutmann, Macedo and Callan presume that totalistic faiths, such as some versions of Protestantism, Catholicism, Judaism and Islam, are false, and that the ways of life they foster are inferior to lives lived in accordance with comprehensive liberalism. Recognizing that "a measure of alienation from any and all associations goes with modern freedom," and that the education programs he wants to mandate will make it much more difficult to live without such alienation, Macedo writes: "It would be truly unfortunate if many people had psychological needs that could only be satisfied by all-encompassing associations. Then we would have to radically rethink the value of the

---

[43] Ibid.   [44] J. S. Mill, *On Liberty* (Cambridge: Cambridge University Press, 1997), 20–21.

liberal civic order explored here."[45] Yet without ever seriously entertaining this possibility, Macedo and others accept the fact that the policies they propose will make such totalistic ways of life less available in our society.

Second, even if the views in question are indeed wrong, their presence is nonetheless helpful to prevent intellectual stagnation and superficiality. On Mill's view, the presence of genuinely opposing ideas is so crucial that "if opponents of all important truths do not exist, it is indispensable to imagine them, and supply them with the strongest arguments which the most skillful devil's advocate can conjure up."[46] The ideal, however, is to hear arguments "from persons who actually believe them; who defend them in earnest, and do their very utmost for them."[47] The hegemony of liberalism that Macedo and others seek to establish might therefore lead to the enervation of liberalism itself by robbing it of sincere critics.

Defenders of Rawlsian civic education might object, however, that their proposed policies are unlikely to result in the complete *extinction* of illiberal or non-liberal ways of life, only in their decreased availability. Further, they might argue that the strictures of public reason apply only in certain specific public contexts, not in the larger background culture, and that, at any rate, freedom of speech still protects the right of the unreasonable to run foul of the duty of civility. However, even though unreasonable ways of life and the introduction of comprehensive doctrines into debates on basic principles of political justice will be legally tolerated in the ideal Rawlsian polity, mandatory Rawlsian civic education, if successful, will create a climate in which such behaviors will receive significant social disapprobation. This sort of "social intolerance" is also a deep worry for Mill:

---

[45] Macedo, *Democracy and Distrust*, 251. Similarly, Macedo writes in *Liberal Virtues* that "liberals forsake all-enveloping memberships in particular, homogeneous local communities for memberships in many overlapping communities, and a regulating membership in an overarching, abstract, universalistic community of all persons – the Great Open Society. ... Central to both liberal justice and liberal autonomy is the capacity to reflect upon, criticize and shape our identity-defining projects and commitments. ... The common perspective of tolerant liberal citizenship is a platform from which we can recognize the reasonableness of many choices we have not made, many options we have forgone. The consciousness and inner experience of value conflict is conducive to critical reflectiveness but also, perhaps, productive of a certain uneasiness of alienation from our own ends and purposes" (239–240).
[46] Mill, *On Liberty*, 39.   [47] Mill, *On Liberty*, 38.

A state of things in which a large portion of the most active and inquiring intellects find it advisable to keep the general principles and grounds of their convictions within their own breasts, and attempt, in what they address to the public, to fit as much as they can of their own conclusions to the premises which they have internally renounced, cannot send forth the open, fearless characters, and logical, consistent intellects who once adorned the thinking world.[48]

It is precisely to protect genuine diversity of thought that Mill speaks strongly against state provision of education or direction of education either in whole or part. "A general State education," he writes, "is a mere contrivance for molding people to be exactly like one another."[49] At most, state-controlled education should be "one among many competing experiments, carried on for the purpose of example and stimulus, to keep the others up to a certain standard of excellence."[50] However, Mill thinks the state ought to require that each child receive an education, and fund that education when the parents are not able to. This requirement would be enforced through a system of public examinations. Mill is clear, moreover, that the state should not be in the business of requiring children to be taught certain values, even civic values; the examinations should involve only knowledge of "facts and positive science."[51] This is not because Mill does not think values ought to be taught to children at all, or that virtuous citizens are unnecessary for the health of society, but rather because of the homogenizing effects of state-run or state-mandated values education.[52]

It would be unfair, of course, to suppose that Macedo, Gutmann, Callan and other defenders of Rawlsian civic education are unaware of or unsympathetic to these concerns. Nonetheless, they believe that fostering the skills and dispositions of good liberal citizenship is so crucial to the health of liberal democracy that it is worth the risk of sacrificing some degree of diversity, because it ensures that the preconditions for freedom and diversity will continue to exist into the future.[53] In

---

[48] Mill, *On Liberty*, 35.   [49] Mill, *On Liberty*, 106.   [50] Ibid.

[51] Mill, *On Liberty*, 107.   [52] Mill, *On Liberty*, 76.

[53] They would be likely to argue, further, that Rawlsian civic education is actually in line with Mill's recommendations, because it promotes critical thinking and provides exposure to diverse views (even if that set of views is limited to those that are "reasonable"). However, Mill's recommendations are for adults, not children, and he would arguably be sympathetic to the view that such exposure to diversity might not be helpful for children in their formative years (Mill, *On Liberty*, 13). Further, Mill clearly thinks that the value of diversity extends beyond "reasonable" doctrines and ways of life.

other words, according to Rawlsian civic education's advocates, mandating that children receive an education that exposes them to diverse ways of life and teaches them to think critically about their own beliefs – even against the protests of parents who think that such an education will undermine the values they are trying to pass on to their children – does not imply mandating anything beyond the basic requirements of citizenship. It is this claim that I will call into question in the next section.

The requirements of citizenship

As we have seen already, defenders of Rawlsian civic education ground their notion of good citizenship on a Rawlsian understanding of political justification. While they offer slightly different underlying arguments in defense of mandatory Rawlsian civic education, they all agree that good citizenship requires tolerance based on acknowledgment of the burdens of judgment, as well as a commitment to public reasonableness or its equivalent.[54] In this section I will analyze Macedo's discussion of *Mozert v. Hawkins*, as a means of shedding light on what these requirements of civic education might mean in practice.

In *Mozert*, fundamentalist Christian families in Hawkins County, Tennessee, objected to the local public schools' use of a reading textbook series that aimed – aside from teaching the relevant academic skills – to expose children to diverse religious and cultural viewpoints. The parents complained that the reading curriculum interfered with their right to raise their children in accordance with their religious beliefs. The readers, they claimed, were unbalanced, lacked favorable portrayals of Protestant Christianity and portrayed relativistic viewpoints and non-Christian views too sympathetically.[55] The *Mozert* parents did not want their

---

[54] Theoretically, Macedo's reliance on political liberalism rather than comprehensive liberalism implies greater accommodation for ways of life not in sync with comprehensive liberal values (*Democracy and Distrust*, 169–170). As Gutmann points out, however, in practice political liberals do not differ from comprehensive liberals in their notion of what good citizenship requires and are no more accommodating when it comes to their recommendations for civic education. [Amy Gutmann, "Civic Education and Social Diversity," *Ethics* 105, 3 (April 1995): 557–579].

[55] "Of 47 stories referring to, or growing out of, Religions (including Islam, Buddhism, American Indian religion and nature worship), only 3 were Christian, and none Protestant." [Danny J. Boggs, Circuit Judge, concurring opinion in *Mozert v. Hawkins County Public Schools* 827 F.2d. 1080–1081, fn. 13 (6th Cir. 1987)].

children to be exposed to conflicting moral and religious viewpoints unless those viewpoints were presented as erroneous.[56]

Macedo lauds the reasoning of the federal appeals court in denying the plaintiffs' request for a religious accommodation that would allow them to exempt their children from the school's reading curriculum and teach their children an alternative, academically equivalent reading program on their own. The Court was correct, argues Macedo, in judging that "mere exposure to diversity" – as opposed to promotion of a particular view – does not constitute state establishment of religion or violate free exercise.[57] Macedo, however, takes the complaints of the *Mozert* parents more seriously than Judge Lively does in his majority opinion. He agrees, instead, with Judge Boggs in conceding that the policy is a substantial burden on the free exercise of religion, because "the *Mozert* families can take advantage of the important benefit of public schooling only if they do things that they view as at odds with salvation."[58] While the parents could choose to send their children to Christian schools or to school them at home, taking either of these courses of action would involve a significant personal expense over and above the mandatory contribution that they make to public schools through their state and local taxes.

Despite the recognition that "the mandatory reading program interferes with the *Mozert* parents' ability to teach their children their particular religious views," Judge Boggs nonetheless concurs with the majority opinion on the grounds of judicial restraint. Macedo, however, agrees with the Court's decision because he thinks that the state's interest in educating for liberal citizenship justifies the burden to free exercise that the reading program imposes. On Macedo's view, no parents have the right to prevent their children from receiving an education that will prepare them for good citizenship, because "a liberal democratic polity cannot endure without citizens willing to support its fundamental institutions and principles and to take part in defining those principles"[59] Those fundamental principles include a commitment to public reasonableness as understood in Rawlsian political liberalism. Such a commitment, together with a recognition of the fact of reasonable pluralism that underlies that commitment, cannot be inculcated in children without some sort of exposure to diversity along the lines of the

---

[56] Opinion of Judge Lively, *Mozert v. Hawkins County Public Schools*, 827 F.2d. 1062 (6th Cir. 1987).
[57] Macedo, *Democracy and Distrust*, 161.   [58] Macedo, *Diversity and Distrust*, 161.
[59] Macedo, *Diversity and Distrust*, 164.

mandatory reading program at issue in *Mozert*. Macedo emphasizes that
it would be inappropriate, from the perspective of political liberalism, for
schools to go beyond teaching *civic* toleration, teaching children "to
acknowledge *for civic purposes* the authority of public reasonableness"
while "avoiding taking a stand, as a political matter, on the question of
religious truth."[60] He realizes that the boundaries between *civic* toleration
and a more comprehensive, relativistic approach to religious toleration
like that of John Dewey can sometimes be fuzzy in practice, and that
"civic liberals must walk a tightrope, emphasizing the great weight of
shared political aims but, so far as possible, avoiding taking sides on the
wider religious dimensions of political matters and allowing that reasonable citizens may disagree about their religious and some of their basic
philosophical views."[61] He accepts, nonetheless, that "a public school
program that teaches civil tolerance will have the effect of indirectly
promoting religious tolerance."[62] Still, the fact that an education for
liberal citizenship "is bound to have the effect of favoring some ways of
life or religious convictions over others" does not imply that those whose
way of life is disfavored have the right to an exemption, because "there is
no moral right to opt selectively out of those basic civic exercises that the
state may reasonably require for all children."[63] Indeed, as a general
matter there is not even a right to shelter one's children from diversity
through private schooling or homeschooling, since the state has the
authority to regulate private education "to ensure that civic values are
satisfied and the child's right to freedom is preserved."[64]

Stated in its most basic form, the argument against accommodation in
cases like *Mozert* seems to run as follows:

Premise I. The government has an obligation to support the preservation
of the liberal democratic order which, in case of serious conflict, can
outweigh its obligation to make accommodations for the free exercise
of religion (or respect parental authority).

Premise II. The preservation of the liberal democratic order requires
teaching children the virtues necessary for good citizenship.

Premise III. The virtues necessary for good citizenship in a pluralistic
liberal democracy include, centrally, tolerance of diverse ways of life
based on acceptance of the fact of reasonable pluralism, and a

[60] Macedo, *Diversity and Distrust*, 175.   [61] Macedo, *Diversity and Distrust*, 175.
[62] Macedo, *Diversity and Distrust*, 176.   [63] Macedo, *Diversity and Distrust*, 203.
[64] Macedo, *Diversity and Distrust*, 202.

commitment to public reasonableness – i.e. to acting in public life (when it comes to determining constitutional essentials and matters of basic justice, and of voting for or advocating laws and policies that will be imposed upon all) in ways that can be justified by public reason rather than (only) by reliance on one's comprehensive vision of the good.

Premise IV. Even-handed exposure to diverse ways of life is essential to the inculcation of these virtues in future citizens.[65]

Conclusion. The state should make education for liberal citizenship, including even-handed exposure to diverse ways of life, mandatory – even in private schools and homeschools. There is no principled reason to exempt those who think that such a requirement burdens their free exercise of religion or violates their parental authority, though there may be prudential reasons to do so.

I concede that the first two premises of the argument, if properly understood, are correct. Of course, as argued in the previous section, proper understanding of these premises means, in my view, understanding liberalism more as Galston does than as Macedo and other Rawlsians do. The key problem with the argument, however, lies in Premise III. While Macedo and others, following Rawls, seems to treat this premise as non-controversial, this view of what good citizenship entails is highly questionable, especially considering that Macedo considers these qualities not as defining the exceptional, heroic practice of citizenship, but as defining "the *minimal* prerequisites of citizenship."[66] It seems implausible on its face to claim that the minimal prerequisites of citizenship include things like abstaining from appeals to one's comprehensive beliefs in the public square, or thinking that one's religious beliefs (for political purposes) constitute one reasonable worldview among many.[67]

---

[65] By "even-handed" I mean exposure that simply presents diverse ways of life and diverse philosophical and religious worldviews "for what they are worth," neither affirming nor denying their plausibility. For example, the district court decided that the reader at issue in the *Mozert* case was acceptable – despite its inclusion of a poem that could reasonably be understood "to assert as a religious matter that anyone who thinks they have religious truth is really in ignorance" – precisely because the poem is simply presented "for what it is worth." Macedo agrees with the court's judgment (*Diversity and Distrust*, 177).

[66] Macedo, *Diversity and Distrust*, 202, emphasis added.

[67] While Macedo emphasizes that good citizens need only consider their comprehensive beliefs as one reasonable worldview among many as a *political* matter, rather than as a matter of truth, he and Callan nonetheless recognize that it will be difficult, in practice, for this not to influence one's overall comprehensive views. On this point, see footnotes

I do not think it is reasonable to set the bar so high. In fact, I do not think that these qualities constitute good citizenship at all.[68]

Consider, for example, someone like Mother Teresa of Calcutta. Given her upbringing and education, it is likely that her exposure to other ways of life in conflict with the teachings of Catholicism was limited and always involved a presentation of those ways of life as erroneous in some way. In other words, her education was probably in this sense equivalent to (and probably significantly more restrictive than) the type of education that the *Mozert* parents wanted to give their children. She had great compassion and respect for those who held other beliefs, as evidenced in her ministry to the sick and dying of Calcutta, yet she did not think that those other beliefs were just as reasonable as her own, or that those who held those beliefs held them just as reasonably as she held her own beliefs. Indeed, she thought that those who did not hold to the tenets of Catholicism were in error, and tried to convince them (more through her actions than through her words) to embrace what she believed to be the true faith. In public life, she did not hesitate to advocate controversial policies – such as laws against abortion, or an end to the state promotion of artificial contraception – with reference to her own comprehensive views, and in many cases without ever providing an alternative "public" justification. She failed miserably, it seems, in living the Rawlsian duty of civility, and she taught many others to do the same. According to Macedo's criteria, therefore, Mother Teresa counts as a bad liberal citizen, as someone who failed in the minimal prerequisites of citizenship, as someone whose way of life constituted a threat to the preservation of the liberal democratic order.

Of course, few – probably not even Macedo himself – would dispute that Mother Teresa contributed greatly to the common good of her country, and many other countries as well. Furthermore, it is arguably the case that Mother Teresa was able to make such an exceptional contribution to the common good precisely *because* of her strong (and, from Macedo's perspective, illiberal) convictions regarding the truth of her Catholic faith, and the (illiberal) education that facilitated the formation of those convictions. In other words, Rawlsian civic education, insofar as it

---

37 and 47, as well as the discussion of Callan earlier in the chapter and in the beginning of Chapter 4.

[68] James Bohman likewise calls into question whether insistence on public reasonableness is actually good for a liberal democracy. ["Deliberative Toleration," *Political Theory* 31, 6 (December 2003): 757–779.]

achieves its objectives, would actually prevent the development of future citizens like Mother Teresa. One need not agree that Mother Teresa was a good citizen in all respects in order to see the implausibility of any account of citizenship on which people like Mother Teresa do not even meet the minimum bar, or to see that preventing the development of future citizens like her would be a great loss to society.

The problem with Macedo's understanding of the minimal prerequisites of citizenship seems to be that he assumes that those who lack a commitment to Rawlsian public reasonableness will, for that reason, be unable to engage in a civil manner with other citizens whose views differ significantly from their own. For example, Macedo defends Rawlsian civic education against critics like Stephen Arons – who argues that it will unfairly burden religious believers such as Protestant Fundamentalists – by claiming that such education is necessary for the survival of the "liberal political project." We cannot take for granted, he goes on to say, "a mutually respectful desire to live in peace with those one believes to be damned.... We need to avoid making the mistake of assuming that liberal citizens – self-restrained, moderate, and reasonable – spring full-blown from the soil of private freedom."[69] Likewise Callan, in trying to explain why acceptance of the burdens of judgment is a necessary condition for respectful political dialogue in line with the value of reciprocity, offers the following hypothetical scenario:

> Suppose I am deeply convinced of the truth of atheism and think that human life is wasted by the illusion of religious belief. You believe with a passion that matches my own that life can have no meaning without belief in God. We want to engage in reciprocity-governed dialogue about the role of the state in regulating our children's education. But we get nowhere so long as either of us insists that the religious beliefs of the other deserve no respect in the making of policy.[70]

Yet, as the example of Mother Teresa indicates, it is perfectly possible to consider others to be gravely in error about fundamental moral and religious questions, yet to have a deep respect and even love for them, and also to defend their freedom of conscience. What Callan and Macedo overlook is the possibility that one can deny that others' *beliefs* are worthy of respect, without denying that the *persons* who hold those beliefs are worthy of respect, and that respecting persons involves

---

[69] Macedo, "Transformative Constitutionalism," 59.
[70] Callan, *Creating Citizens*, 31–32.

respecting their right to live in accordance with their beliefs (within the limits of the common good) even if those beliefs are wrong.

A more ordinary example of "intolerant" or "illiberal" citizens who pose no threat to the liberal democratic order can be found in the *Mozert* case itself. The plaintiffs are clearly not good citizens in the Rawlsian sense, nor, it seems, are any fundamentalist Protestants, because the all-encompassing nature of their belief system makes them unwilling to abide by the strictures of public reason, which would require them to set aside their religious beliefs in at least some aspects of public life. Yet do we have any evidence that fundamentalist Protestants are, as such, more likely to act violently or hatefully toward those who disagree with them than anyone else passionately committed to a particular cause, be that cause "liberal" or "conservative"?[71] In support of his view that "we should not bend over backwards to accommodate such people, or cry crocodile tears over forms of non-neutrality that make life hard on the intolerant," Macedo argues that "we need to remember how such people would behave if they had political power."[72] Yet some of these people do have political power, and in some states or districts, especially in the South, they make up the majority of the population. There is no evidence – at least Macedo has not provided any – to indicate that basic civic freedoms are being threatened in those locations. On the other hand, there is clear evidence that these "intolerant" people can and do live and work peacefully side-by-side with non-believers, and that their beliefs often lead them to sponsor and participate in community service organizations to help those in need, believers and non-believers alike.[73]

In fact, recent studies of conservative religious political activists have found that they exemplify many important democratic political virtues. Jon Shields, for example, has shown that leaders of the Christian Right teach the values of democratic deliberation based on Biblical norms.[74] In another study, Kimberly Conger and Bryan McGraw conducted interviews with fifty religious conservative activists, leaders of groups such as

---

[71] Just think, for instance, of the now unfortunately common phenomenon of Internet trolls' posting hateful or inflammatory comments or reviews on the Internet in response to articles, books, videos, etc. with which they disagree. Such incivility comes at least as frequently from defenders of "liberal" causes as from defenders of "conservative" ones.

[72] Macedo, *Diversity and Distrust*, 197.

[73] See Sidney Verba, Kay Lehman Schlozman and Henry E. Brady, *Voice and Equality: Civic Volunteerism in American Politics* (Cambridge: Harvard University Press, 1995).

[74] Jon Shields, "Between Passion and Deliberation: The Christian Right and Democratic Ideals," *Political Science Quarterly* 122, 1 (2007): 89–113.

the Christian Coalition, the Family Research Council and Right to Life. The interviews revealed the activists' "commitment to what they see as the common (democratic) good," as well as their "technical political sophistication," their "strong attachment to the American political system and the procedural and substantive requirements of representative democracy," their firm support for "the American system's focus on individual rights and responsibilities," their affirmation of "the idea that politics has a limited scope," and their recognition of "the distinction between politics and religion."[75] Far from seeking to undermine liberal democracy, these activists "all agree that, whatever its faults, our democracy is the best political system available," a view that is strengthened by the fact that many "attribute America's stable form of government and prosperity to divine intervention, thus giving extra weight to their democratic commitments."[76] Further, though they run afoul of the Rawlsian duty of civility because of their unwillingness to set aside their religious convictions in politics, they do try to defend their views in ways that are as widely accessible as possible, and "recognize that there exist legitimate differences of opinion over what the common good should look like. They all acknowledge that people cannot be forced to agree with their policy stands, regardless of the issue, and pursue political ends that they think can find reasonably wide agreement."[77] One activist, for example, made the follow comment:

> The Christian's responsibility is to show love to others and treat all people fairly and equitably . . . That responsibility goes for the unborn child who needs to be protected from having his life taken by someone else, and that goes for the unbeliever who should be free not to believe. We can't force others to serve God. God himself gives each of us the freedom to choose to serve Him or not.[78]

Are these the people to whom Macedo is referring when he states that "we should not bend over backwards to accommodate such people, or cry crocodile tears over forms of non-neutrality that make life hard on the

[75] Kimberly Conger and Bryan McGraw, "Religious Conservatives and the Requirements of Citizenship: Political Autonomy," *Perspectives on Politics* 6, 2 (June 2008): 259. See also Alan Wolfe, *One Nation, After All* (New York: Viking, 1998).
[76] Conger and McGraw, "Religious Conservatives and the Requirements of Citizenship," 259.
[77] Conger and McGraw, "Religious Conservatives and the Requirements of Citizenship," 259, 261.
[78] Conger and McGraw, "Religious Conservatives and the Requirements of Citizenship," 259.

intolerant," because "we need to remember how such people would behave if they had political power"?[79]

Public reason and liberal legitimacy

Macedo might concede that religious fundamentalists and others unwilling to abide by the strictures of public reason are unlikely to use violent means to achieve their ends, and are committed to many core liberal democratic values. Nonetheless, his larger point is that to coerce others (even through procedurally-legitimate democratic means) based on principles that they cannot be reasonably expected to accept – i.e. principles that are not sufficiently public in nature – is in itself a violation of their freedom and equality. In other words, Macedo's claim that the freedom of all is endangered by fundamentalist citizens sounds more plausible in the context of his commitment to the liberal principle of legitimacy. Of course, if we translate all of Macedo's warnings about the dangers to our freedom that come from the likes of the *Mozert* plaintiffs into warnings about living in a society that does not fulfill the demands of liberal legitimacy as Rawls understands it, the prospect seems a lot less scary. If the threat to our freedom that Macedo refers to really comes down to living in a society in which citizens are not committed to the Rawlsian ideal of public reasonableness, there are many, including many liberals, who would welcome that "threat."

There are many who, like Callan, recognize that public reasonableness relies on a controversial and comprehensive view of the good life, but who, unlike Callan, do not think that it is a necessary basis for liberal legitimacy. In other words, there is considerable dissension even among liberals regarding the claim that liberal legitimacy requires limiting the grounds of political coercion to public reasons in the Rawlsian sense.[80] James Bohman and Henry Richardson offer a particularly powerful critique of the role that public reasons play in Rawls' theory of legitimacy.

---

[79] Macedo, *Democracy and Distrust*, 197.

[80] See, for example, Gerald Gaus and Kevin Vallier, "The Roles of Religious Conviction in a Publicly Justified Polity: The Implications of Convergence, Asymmetry and Political Institutions," *Philosophy and Social Criticism* 35 (2009): 51–57; Jeffrey Stout, *Democracy and Tradition* (Princeton: Princeton University Press, 2004); Christopher Eberle, *Religious Conviction in Liberal Politics* (New York: Cambridge University Press, 2002); William Galston, *Liberal Purposes* (New York: Cambridge University Press, 1991); Jeremy Waldron, "Public Reason and 'Justification'," *Journal of Law, Philosophy and Culture* 119 (2007): 107–134.

They argue that the notion of "reasons that all can accept" (RACAs) is both ambiguous and inherently problematic:

> If the notion of RACAs is to do serious theoretical work, it must sort reasons into two classes: those that all can accept and those that not all can accept. It turns out, however, to be surprisingly hard to come up with a sensible interpretation of the "can accept" aspect of the idea of RACAs that meets this elementary desideratum. Interpretations of "can accept" (or "could accept") might be essentially empirical or essentially normative. Empirical interpretations, we will argue, are deeply indeterminate. Hence, some normative constraint is needed. When normative constraint is imported, however, it will turn out that all the important sorting work is done, not by the idea of reasons that all "can accept," but rather by the relevant normative notion, such as consistency with the requirements of reasonableness.[81]

In other words, Bohman and Richardson argue that the Rawlsian notion of public reason effectively "stacks the deck" in favor of a comprehensive liberal understanding of reasonableness: "Rawls's reliance . . . on a theory of the reasonable allows substituting a substantive standard in the indicative for the problematic idea of RACAs [reasons that all can accept]. Our reasonable expectations about either will be governed by whether a given reason coheres well with the constitutive commitments of reasonableness, and by nothing else."[82]

Thus the Rawlsian ideal of public reason, precisely by narrowing the terms of public justification, is unfair to those who do not hold a liberal comprehensive view, because it implies that only those positions in line with comprehensive liberalism can constitute legitimate grounds for legal coercion. Consider, for example, how Rawls deals with the "rationalist believer" whose understanding of the requirements of basic justice is shaped by her beliefs, who claims that her views are at least in principle accessible to anyone who will consider the evidence with an open mind, and who is more than happy to explain the reasons for those views to fellow citizens.[83] Rawls thinks that such a person is wrong to try to shape

---

[81] James Bohman and Henry Richardson, "Liberalism, Deliberative Democracy, and 'Reasons that All Can Accept'," *The Journal of Political Philosophy* 17, 3 (2009): 257.

[82] Bohman and Richardson, "Liberalism, Deliberative Democracy, and 'Reasons that All Can Accept'," 260.

[83] Rawls, *Political Liberalism*, 152–153. For a more detailed critique of Rawls' view on this point, see Robert George and Christopher Wolfe, "Natural Law and Public Reason," in *Natural Law and Public Reason*, ed. Robert George and Christopher Wolfe (Washington, DC: Georgetown University Press, 2000).

public policy in line with her comprehensive understanding of what justice requires, because she ignores the fact of reasonable pluralism. This charge is true if you take the limitations of public reason to be based on a prediction of behavior, of what people right now are likely to accept. But this is not what the rationalist believer is claiming. She is claiming that, in principle, others can reasonably accept her view – in other words, that her view is in fact reasonable. Rawls might disagree with this substantive assessment of the reasonableness of the view, but he would have to do so from the perspective of his own comprehensive liberal view. What it means to be reasonable, what the bounds of human reason are, whether or not reason is capable of knowing true moral norms, or whether or not there are true moral norms that transcend human history and culture, are all highly controversial questions, which only a comprehensive view can address.

Interestingly, in his discussion of the *Mozert* case Macedo considers the objection that religious reasons might in principle be just as accessible to people – i.e. just as public – as are the reasons that justify the values of political liberalism. Macedo dismisses the point, however, citing Gutmann and Thompson's argument that "'any claim fails to respect reciprocity if it imposes a requirement on other citizens to adopt one's sectarian way of life as a condition of gaining access to the moral understanding that is essential to judging the validity of one's moral claims.'"[84] In other words, if gaining access to a point of view would require, for example, learning to live according to certain moral standards or receiving an education that promotes certain values, that point of view is not "public" in the way that Rawlsian public reasonableness demands. Yet is it not true that learning to appreciate the values of political liberalism requires a similar training? If not, what is left of Macedo, Callan and Gutmann's defenses of mandatory Rawlsian civic education? Macedo's entire argument focuses on the need to inculcate certain civic virtues beginning at a young age, indirectly through political institutions, and directly through schools. Indeed, Macedo's account is premised on the view that coming to appreciate any set of values requires exposure to those values and the acquisition of certain habits of character that open one to appreciate those values. Religious values or other values based on non-liberal comprehensive understandings of the good life seem to be no different than politically liberal values in this sense.

---

[84] Macedo, *Democracy and Distrust*, 172.

Macedo, Callan and others are therefore importantly right in their arguments that robust Rawlsian civic education would be necessary to make a Rawlsian liberal regime one which most citizens can understand and accept as just. They recognize, in ways that Rawls himself did not, that much of the work required for liberal legitimacy lies in creating citizens who are reasonable and virtuous enough (on what Callan himself admits to be a comprehensive liberal account of reasonableness and virtue) to recognize and accept just laws and institutions (and to propose such laws when they themselves have power). Yet it is inconsistent with a liberal commitment to individual rights and respect for legitimate plur- alism to use coercive state power to promote adherence to a comprehen- sive liberal understanding of justice, at least when doing so would violate the rights of some citizens (such as the rights of parents who believe themselves obligated to teach their children a non-liberal comprehensive view of the good life).[85]

Ironically, my own natural law account of legitimate authority, as sketched in the Introduction, actually brooks much greater diversity of belief than the Rawlsian account, at least as interpreted by advocates of mandatory Rawlsian civic education. On my view, a law, constitution or regime is legitimate to the extent that it is actually just – i.e. to the extent that it advances the common good understood as the set of conditions that foster and make possible the pursuit of overall human well-being by the community's members.[86] It is morally desirable (intrinsically[87] as well as instrumentally for the survival of the political community) that as

---

[85] Criticizing the views of Rawlsians like Macedo, Gutmann and Callan on citizenship and civic education, Melissa Williams writes, "I think it likely that the ends of toleration and civil cooperation are better served by an openness to accommodation than by the conscious marginalization of the 'unreasonable' and 'illiberal.' The project of a civic education aimed at citizenship as identity seeks a security for liberal democracy in the content of the individual soul. I have suggested above that this is a security that we do not need, and that it is dangerous to seek." ["Citizenship as Identity, Citizenship as Shared Fate, and the Functions of Multicultural Education," in *Citizenship and Education in Liberal Democratic Societies*, ed. Kevin McDonough and Walter Feinberg (New York: Oxford University Press, 2003): 224].

[86] See my discussion in the Introduction regarding the common good and the larger theory of value on which my view of the common good is based. See also John Finnis, *Natural Law and Natural Rights* (Oxford: Oxford University Press, 1980), especially chapter 6.

[87] It is intrinsically morally desirable for citizens to recognize just laws as such and follow them for that reason because to follow a just law for the right reasons is better (more morally perfective of the agent) than to follow a just law based on sub-rational or imperfectly rational motivations (i.e. fear of punishment or a desire to avoid social disapprobation).

many citizens as possible actually recognize the laws under which they live – or at least the vast majority of those laws – as just. Determination of whether or not a proposed law would actually promote the common good therefore requires not only an abstract evaluation of whether or not that law is in accordance with moral norms more generally, but also a consideration, among other things, of what current citizens are actually likely to be able to accept and recognize as just.[88] The legitimacy of the law, however, depends not on the *fact* of its acceptance as just by all or most citizens, but on whether or not it actually fosters the common good. In other words, the likelihood that most citizens will accept a law as just factors into a determination of whether or not the law will genuinely promote the common good, but it is not the only or most important factor.

Much more would need to be said in order to flesh out this account adequately, but that task goes well beyond the scope of this project.[89] My point here is simply to explain why, on my view, it is possible to tolerate a broad range of approaches to civic education based on diverse comprehensive understandings of the good life without endangering the legitimacy of the regime.[90] Further, though the above argument certainly does not amount to a full-fledged critique of the liberal principle of legitimacy, it does present important problems for the liberal account which cast doubt on the possibility or desirability of liberal legitimacy, at least as some Rawlsians understand it. For if, as many liberals themselves have pointed out, liberal legitimacy rests on a substantive and comprehensive understanding of what is reasonable, then it is the substantive reasonableness of any particular law, policy or constitution, and not the fact that citizens can or could or would accept it, that is doing all of the normative work. But if that is the case, then the liberal view actually turns out not to be so different from my alternative account, because for both accounts the legitimacy of a law or constitution depends ultimately on a comprehensive understanding of what is reasonable or just.

---

[88] Thomas Aquinas makes a similar argument in the *Summa Theologiae* I-II, q.96, a.2.

[89] For a fuller account of a view along these lines, see Finnis, *Natural Law*.

[90] On my view civic education is nonetheless important, however, not only for straightforwardly perfectionist reasons – i.e. for the well-being of the citizens themselves – but also because the survival of the regime requires that at least a critical mass of citizens recognize it to be just. However, as I argue below, the survival of the regime requires a relatively minimal civic education, and there are reasons to pursue the perfectionist elements of civic education only in ways that are non-coercive and that respect the primacy of parental educational authority.

Tolerating diverse understandings of citizenship

The controversy over public reasonableness is simply one slice of a larger disagreement over the nature of good citizenship, and more fundamentally, the conditions of justice and legitimacy. There are a wide variety of views, both within and outside of liberalism, regarding the qualities of good citizens and how to foster them. As the public reason debate indicates, the Rawlsian duty of civility or its equivalent holds a prominent place only among Rawlsian liberals, but holds a secondary place or no place at all in others.[91] Some views focus more on tolerance and respectfulness of diversity, others on qualities like law-abidingness, honesty or industriousness. Some think active, participatory citizenship is crucial; others consider that more passive forms of citizenship are also acceptable.[92]

Even where there is agreement on the importance of one particular aspect of citizenship, such as tolerance, such agreement masks even greater disagreement about what that value actually means, and how to go about fostering it. As David Kahane points out:

> Depending on one's understanding of tolerance, there will be quite different stories about the proper boundaries of tolerance; or about whether tolerance entails embracing difference, prescinding from judgment, or simple forbearance when it comes to legal sanctions. Depending upon one's understanding of toleration, an adequately virtuous citizen may be one who can give a tight-lipped smile to those of different faiths and persuasions; one who enjoys the strangeness of various Others; one who has a positive regard for others regardless of their difference; or one who recognizes her own way of life as contingently constituted by the differences of others. Each of these versions of tolerant citizenship gives rise to its own account of how individuals come by their tolerant characters: an awareness of legal prohibitions and sanctions may be enough; religious teachings may play a role; the prohibition of hate speech might be important, but so might an uncensored public debate over who and what deserves to be tolerated. . . . People who agree that toleration is a key liberal virtue can disagree on all of these things, and more. Favoring one

---

[91] Stout, *Democracy and Tradition*; Eberle, *Religious Conviction in Liberal Politics*; Galston, *Liberal Purposes*; Conger and McGraw, "Religious Conservatives and the Requirements of Citizenship: Political Autonomy;" Michael Perry, *Love and Power: The Role of Religion and Morality in American Politics* (New York: Oxford University Press, 1991).

[92] See Kathleen Knight Abowitz and Jason Harrish, "Contemporary Discourses of Citizenship," *Review of Educational Research* 76, 4 (Winter, 2006): 653–690; and Joel Westheimer and Joseph Kahne, "What Kind of Citizen? The Politics of Educating for Democracy," *American Educational Research Journal* 41, 2 (Summer 2004): 237–269.

version of liberal tolerance or one story about how to cultivate it is
partisan, not between liberalism and something else but between different
forms of liberalism. To the extent that liberals favor letting different ways
of life be, they should hesitate to impose some single account of liberal
virtues on other liberal citizens.[93]

Mandatory Rawlsian civic education effectively amounts to imposing one
controversial account of liberal virtues on all citizens through the coercive power of the state, and to do so even at the cost of violating parental
rights.

Further, while discussions of civic education tend to focus on the
distinctively political virtues, it is worth remembering that general moral
virtues, such as justice, self-mastery, honesty and courage are no less
important – and on some accounts (like my own) more fundamental –
for good citizenship than the virtues that Macedo and other Rawlsians
emphasize. If my argument in the following chapter is correct, respect for
the discretionary rights of parents especially in moral and religious
education favors the development of moral virtue in children, because
it allows them to be brought up within a coherent moral framework that
facilitates the development of self-mastery. On the contrary, as I will also
argue in the next chapter, education aimed at fostering autonomy or an
appreciation of the burdens of judgment is likely to undermine parental
authority and create moral confusion by introducing conflicting moral
views before children have sufficient moral maturity to make reasoned
moral judgments. Such education could, therefore, be an obstacle to the
consolidation of an upright moral character especially in situations where
the views parents are trying to pass on conflict with those implicit in
Rawlsian civic education.

While the sort of education that traditionalist parents like the plaintiffs
in *Mozert* want to provide for their children may not score highly in terms
of its ability to produce citizens committed to public reasonableness, it is
arguably more likely to produce citizens of strong moral character. Indeed,
it is often a desire to foster good character in their children that leads
parents to object to many aspects of autonomy or diversity education. As
Shelley Burtt points out, religious parents and schools are not inimical to
rational inquiry or to tolerance correctly understood. Rather, they "desire
to provide and then preserve, in the face of an aggressively materialistic

[93] David Kahane, "Liberal Virtues and Citizen Education," in *Citizenship After Liberalism*,
ed. Karen Slawner and Mark Denham (New York: Peter Lang Publishing, 1998): 117–
118.

culture, a sense of the transcendent in human life," and they aim "to supply the child with the resources necessary to live a righteous life, to prevent as far as possible the corruption that can follow from too early or too overwhelming temptation to sin."[94] Supporting Burtt's characterization, Paul Kienel, speaking as executive director of the Association of Christian Schools International, described Christian schools as akin to hothouses in which children are sheltered from temptations until they have developed a moral character that is strong enough to withstand them:

> A hothouse is designed to protect young, tender plants during their growing years so they can be transplanted in the real world later on and be ahead of plants that didn't have the opportunity. I grew up in Oregon, and we had a hothouse nearby to grow tomatoes during the winter months. Outside the door were scrawny, gnarled plants that didn't make it inside the hothouse. They were handicapped. Inside, the tomatoes were healthy and strong. The Christian school movement performs that function.[95]

Perhaps these efforts may actually do a greater service to the preservation of democracy than the sort of education promoted by Rawlsian liberals.

Tocqueville famously and powerfully noted the particular importance that religion has for the health of liberal democracies, precisely because of its unique ability to foster certain qualities of character. A serious problem that liberal democracies face, according to Tocqueville, is that they tend to foster individualism. Counteracting this trend is crucial, given that individualism goes hand in hand with political apathy and civic disengagement, the symptoms of which are clearly present in contemporary society.[96] Religion helps to counteract this individualistic tendency because there is no religion "that does not impose on each some duties toward the human species or in common with it, and that does not thus draw him, from time to time, away from contemplation of himself. . . . Religious peoples are therefore naturally strong in precisely the spot where democratic peoples are weak."[97] Furthermore, because religion

---

[94] Shelley Burtt, "Religious Parents, Secular Schools: A Liberal Defense of an Illiberal Education," *The Review of Politics* 56, 1 (Winter 1994): 63.

[95] Paul F. Parsons, *Inside America's Christian Schools* (Macon, GA: Mercer University Press, 1987), 13–14.

[96] See, for example, Robert Putnam, *Bowling Alone* (New York: Simon and Schuster, 2000). And for evidence that religion helps to combat this individualism, see Robert Putnam, *American Grace* (New York: Simon and Schuster, 2010).

[97] Alexis de Tocqueville, *Democracy in America*, trans. Harvey C. Mansfield and Delba Winthrop (Chicago: University of Chicago Press, 2000), 419.

also helps to counteract the tendency of freedom to degenerate into license, Tocqueville makes the rather bold claim that religion "should therefore be considered as the first of [the Americans'] political institutions, for although it does not give them the taste for freedom, it singularly facilitates their use of it."[98] According to Tocqueville, the need for religion to instruct people on how to use their freedom well is particularly crucial in democracies: "How could society fail to perish if, while the political bond is relaxed, the moral bond were not tightened? And what makes a people master of itself if it has not submitted to God?"[99] Moreover, Burtt's comment that religious families often want to foster and preserve "a sense of the transcendent" in an "aggressively materialistic culture" resonates perfectly with Tocqueville's observation that materialism and an excessive drive for physical pleasures are great dangers to democracy. Precisely for this reason, he writes:

> Legislators of democracies and all honest and enlightened men who live in them must therefore apply themselves relentlessly to raising up souls and keeping them turned toward Heaven. It is necessary for all those who are interested in the future of democratic societies to unite, and for all in concert to make continuous efforts to spread within those societies a taste for the infinite, a sentiment of greatness, and a love of immaterial pleasures.[100]

Likewise, it is crucial in a society where the political realm is in a perpetual state of flux that moral ideas remain steady and tied to a force more stable and lasting than the government. In Tocqueville's estimation, the principal source for morality must be religion. The reason for this view is that

> There is almost no human action ... that does not arise from a very general idea that men have conceived of God, or of his relations with the human race, of the nature of their souls, and of their duties toward those like them... Men therefore have an immense interest in making very fixed ideas for themselves about God, their souls, their general duties toward their Creator and those like them; for doubt about these first points would deliver all their actions to chance and condemn them to a sort of disorder and impotence.[101]

One need not agree completely with all of Tocqueville's claims to appreciate that parents who provide an "illiberal" education for their children

---

[98] Tocqueville, *Democracy in America*, 280.
[99] Tocqueville, *Democracy in America*, 282.
[100] Tocqueville, *Democracy in America*, 519.
[101] Tocqueville, *Democracy in America*, 417.

may actually, at least in some cases, be offering a crucial service to the health and maintenance of liberal democracy.

Nothing that I have said, however, implies that there should be no requirements at all with regard to civic education. Rather, my point is that such requirements should be broad and general enough that they allow for a legitimate diversity of views regarding the appropriate content and methods of civic education. To return to the example of tolerance, the state might require that tolerance be a component of all civic education programs, in public, private and homeschools. If pressed by the state, the school or the parents would have to give some account of how they are complying with that mandate. Perhaps one school will teach about tolerance in a broadly Rawlsian way, exposing children sympathetically to diverse ways of life, helping them to understand the reasonableness of different comprehensive views and those who hold them, and encouraging them to practice the duty of civility in public life. Yet another might teach that tolerance involves eschewing violent or disrespectful treatment of those with whom you disagree, while not requiring that you consider them reasonable or have any sympathy for their views. The families in the *Mozert* case might teach a religiously-based understanding of tolerance, grounded in Biblical notions such as the view that all human beings are made in the image and likeness of God, the Golden Rule, Jesus' example of mercy toward sinners, or even the injunction to love one's enemies. Perhaps Macedo is right that the willingness to live in peace with those one believes to be damned ought not to be taken for granted, but there is a huge logical leap between recognizing the legitimacy of this concern and concluding that Rawlsian civic education should be mandatory for all.[102] The state has an obligation to make sure that all citizens receive an education that will foster the disposition to live in peace with those one believes to be in error, but it can do so in ways that accommodate the values and beliefs of the vast majority of citizens.

It is also likely that heavy-handed state measures to impose a particular mode of civic education even when it conflicts with the values that parents want to pass on to their children will be counterproductive. As Galston argues, "Genuine civic unity rests on unforced consent. States that permit their citizens to live in ways that express their values are likely to enjoy widespread support, even gratitude. By contrast, state coercion is

[102] Kenneth Strike makes a similar point in "Must Liberal Citizens Be Reasonable?" *The Review of Politics* 58, 1 (Winter 1996): 41–48.

likely to produce dissent, resistance, and withdrawal."[103] Such coercion may even push otherwise peaceful people to react violently if they see no other way to protect the values they hold most dear. As shown in a recent international study, religious conflict usually results not from the inherent intolerance of any particular religious creed, but in response to denials or restrictions on free exercise.[104]

Defining the boundaries of tolerance

I have argued so far for maximal tolerance of diversity with regard to the content and methods of civic education. Yet this tolerance is not without limits. To understand the limits of tolerance with regard to the debate about mandatory civic education, it is important to distinguish between minimally decent citizenship and good citizenship. Roughly speaking, minimally decent citizenship means abiding by just laws, working to support oneself provided that one is capable of doing so, and having a basic knowledge of one's civic rights and duties (though not necessarily exercising all of those rights or fulfilling all of those duties).[105] Good citizenship, on the other hand, involves not only following the law and supporting oneself to the extent that one is able, but having a genuine concern for the well-being of one's fellow citizens, making a positive contribution toward one's community through one's work and other activities, actively contributing to civic and political life in accordance with one's capacities, responsibly exercising one's civic rights and fulfilling one's civic duties even at the cost of personal sacrifice. On my view, good citizenship certainly involves tolerance in the sense of treating those who hold different views with respect, but need not involve thinking that those with whom one disagrees are fully reasonable in their beliefs. Nor need it involve eschewing reliance on one's comprehensive moral or religious views in public life.[106]

---

[103] William Galston, "Parents, Government and Children," in *Child Family and State*, ed. Stephen Macedo and Iris Marion Young (New York: New York University Press, 2003), 211–233.

[104] Brian Grim and Roger Finke, *The Price of Freedom Denied: Religious Persecution and Conflict in the 21st Century* (New York: Cambridge University Press, 2011).

[105] Kahane likewise points out that Macedo and others exaggerate what is required of citizens in order to avoid social breakdown ("Liberal Virtues and Citizen Education," 108).

[106] For a similar, but more detailed account of good citizenship, see Galston, *Liberal Pluralism*, 221–224.

The exact content of minimally decent and good citizenship does not really matter here. What matters is the recognition that there is a level of citizenship which the vast majority of citizens must live up to if we are to maintain a liberal democratic order, and that that level is significantly less demanding than a full-fledged notion of good citizenship. In other words, the survival of a liberal democratic order requires that most citizens be minimally decent, but only that a relatively small minority of citizens be actually *good*, with the majority of people falling somewhere in between. In terms of education, therefore, the state has grave reasons to compel all educable children to receive an education that will enable them to be minimally decent citizens, reasons that are serious enough to trump even the rights of parents with regard to the education of their children, in cases of conflict. On the other hand, the state's interest in education for good citizenship is strong enough to justify *encouraging* such an education, but not *compelling* parents to provide it or to allow the state to provide it for their children. As Galston puts it, "the state must be parsimonious in defining the realm in which uniformity must be secured through coercion. An educational program based on an expansive and contestable definition of good citizenship or civic unity will not ordinarily justify the forcible suppression of expressive liberty," which Galston considers to be the primary ground of parental rights.[107]

The state's interest in fostering good citizenship is, in this sense, akin to – and in some ways inseparable from – the state's interest in fostering moral excellence. At least on a perfectionist account, the state has an obligation to foster moral excellence in all members of society. This obligation stems both from the recognition that many of society's problems – violence, economic injustice, racism, fraud – would be mitigated if more people were morally virtuous, and from the concern that the state (in a subsidiary way) has for the well-being of every individual as such. However, even strong perfectionists like Thomas Aquinas agree that the government should only use coercive force to prevent the gravest forms of immorality which result in serious harm to others or to society as a whole.[108] This, in fact, is what tolerance means in its classical sense: refraining from impeding a harm which one has the legitimate authority to impede, because doing so would result in an even greater harm to the individuals involved and/or to the relevant

---

[107] Galston, *Liberal Pluralism*, 109.
[108] See, for instance, *Summa Theologiae* I-II, q.96, a.2–3.

community as a whole.[109] For example, while undoubtedly we would all be better off individually and as a community if people avoided dishonesty in their private relationships, the intrusion into private life that would be involved in enforcing a law against dishonesty would do more damage to relationships than legal toleration of dishonesty in private matters. Lying, therefore, is (and ought to be) illegal only when it is sufficiently public in its nature and consequences – that is, only when it amounts to something like fraud, perjury, calumny or libel.

As critics of Mill's harm principle never tire of pointing out, the relevant distinction here is not between behaviors that harm others and behaviors that harm no one. Arguably, any immoral behavior, no matter how seemingly private, at least indirectly has a negative impact on others, especially when considering the aggregate social impact when that behavior is practiced by many individuals.[110] As already mentioned, few would disagree that all would be better off, both individually and as a society, if people were always honest in their private relationships. Instead, determining which immoral behaviors should be legally proscribed or required, and which should be legally tolerated or left to the free initiative of citizens, involves a complex prudential judgment that takes into account such factors as how direct and serious the harm in question is, whether the measures that would be necessary to impede the harmful behavior would damage other important goods, whether those other goods are more or less important than the goods threatened by the harmful behavior, and so forth.

The most important goods that political authorities are obliged to protect are human rights, including, crucially, parental rights, the free exercise of religion and freedom of conscience more broadly. These rights place limits on the means by which the government can foster or prevent certain behaviors, unless the good sought is more fundamental than the right that will be infringed, and there are no other feasible, less burdensome means by which that good can be achieved.[111] Applying these considerations to the state's interest in educating for citizenship, we can

---

[109] Jeremy Waldron and Melissa Williams, "Introduction," *Toleration and its Limits*, ed. Jeremy Walrdron and Melissa Williams (New York: New York University Press, 2008), 4

[110] See Robert George, "The Concept of Public Morality," *American Journal of Jurisprudence* 45, 1 (2000): 17–31.

[111] Callan points out that "an important point of agreement in recent discussion of rights is that they provide a framework of moral constraints within which a politics of the common good can be practiced" (*Creating Citizens*, 135). I would not phrase the matter in exactly these terms, because I think that the protection of rights is itself a crucial element of the common good, but the basic idea is the same. See also Ronald Dworkin,

now see more clearly why the distinction between minimally decent citizenship and good citizenship is essential. Unless the vast majority of citizens are minimally decent, the political community will literally fall apart (at least in the long run), and all human rights will be endangered.[112] For this reason, the state rightfully uses coercive power, for example, to force people to obey the laws. For the same reason, the state also rightfully uses coercive power to ensure that all children receive an education that will foster law-abiding behavior, enable them to earn their own living as adults, and provide them with at least basic knowledge of civic rights and responsibilities. Thus the state can reasonably require that all schools (including homeschools) teach the basic academic and practical skills necessary for obtaining future employment or pursuing post-secondary education, as well as instruction regarding civic rights and duties and the laws, governmental structure and history of the country. Such an education for minimally decent citizenship, therefore, can rightfully be mandated and coercively enforced by the state.

While conflicts with such a minimal regulatory scheme are unlikely to be frequent, they are far from unthinkable. Imagine, for example, that radical Muslim parents, who sincerely believe that the use of violence against non-Muslims is not only justified but necessary, want to set up schools (or school their children at home) in order to shield their children from contact with non-Muslims that might make them sympathetic to them, as well as to pass on their beliefs to their children, encourage them to join terrorist groups, and teach them terrorist tactics.[113] Though it would be an infringement of the parents' freedom of conscience and free exercise of religion, such an infringement would be justified in this case. The government could rightly shut down such a school. In the case of children schooled at home, if the government had evidence that the children were indeed being taught criminal behavior,

---

Taking Rights Seriously (Cambridge: Harvard University Press, 1978), especially 184–205.

[112] William Galston offers a similar justification for limiting toleration of diversity when it threatens the minimal conditions of public order (*Liberal Pluralism*, 64–66).

[113] Allow me to emphasize that this case is purely hypothetical, chosen simply because it is an example often offered as a potential objection to my robust view of parental rights in education. Research on Muslim schools in the United States and Canada actually indicates that these schools neither isolate students from the diversity of the larger society nor breed intolerance, but actually foster civic engagement and interfaith dialogue. See, for example, Louis Cristillo, "The Case for the Muslim School as a Civil Society Actor," in *Educating the Muslims of America*, ed. Yvonne Haddad, Farid Senzai and Jane I. Smith (New York: Oxford University Press, 2009), 67–84.

they could force the parents to send their children to a school which does provide an education for minimally decent citizenship.

Wisconsin v. Yoder may also seem to offer an example of a situation in which the parents were unwilling to provide their children with an education for minimally decent citizenship. In this case, Old Order Amish parents wanted a religious accommodation that would allow them to remove their children from school at age 14, though compulsory education laws in Wisconsin require schooling until age 16. While there is certainly room for debate about exactly how long children should be in school in order to receive an education for minimally decent citizenship, the Wisconsin law does not seem unreasonable. Was the Supreme Court wrong, then, to exempt the Amish from this reasonable requirement? Two facts are key to correctly understanding this case. The first is that while the Amish wanted to remove their children from public schools at age 14, they did not want to stop educating their children, only to continue their children's education at home.[114] The second is that the Amish community has proven itself exemplary in its ability to educate its children to become peaceful, law-abiding, productive citizens. It is clear, therefore, that the Amish parents were not running afoul of their obligation to provide their children with an education for minimally decent citizenship. In this case, as opposed to the hypothetical Muslim fundamentalist case, the conscience rights of parents could be protected without seriously endangering public order or public peace. As a matter of moral principle – here I make no claims about the matter from a constitutional perspective – the Court was therefore right to decide that the state exceeded its legitimate authority by requiring Amish parents to send their children to public school despite their religious objections.

Of course, the state has an interest not only in the formation of minimally decent citizens, but also in the formation of *good* citizens, just as the state has an interest not only in fostering lawfulness, but also in fostering moral excellence. Since, however, good citizenship – as opposed to minimally decent citizenship – need not be widespread for the political order to survive, and since the protection of parental rights is an

---

[114] Classroom-based schooling ends at age 14 for the Amish, after which point children receive a vocational education at home from their parents. After Amish fathers in Pennsylvania were jailed for failing to send their children to high school, the Amish community came to an agreement with the state by formalizing its vocational schooling plan, including a requirement that children write journal entries detailing the skills that they learned each day [Mark Dewalt, *Amish Education in the United States and Canada* (Lanham, MD: Rowman and Littlefield Publishers, Inc., 2006), 88–89].

important element of the common good, the state ought to tolerate those who want to educate their children in ways that are likely to foster something less than fully good citizenship. To tolerate, however, means only to refrain from the use of coercion, not to refrain from all measures to foster desirable behavior or discourage undesirable behavior. The state might, therefore, legitimately use a number of non-coercive means to foster good citizenship, such as publicly honoring exemplary individuals, providing incentives to engage in a desirable behavior like contributing to charity, sponsoring advertisements that encourage behaviors like informed voting and community service, or offering more robust citizenship education in public schools, provided that parents who object can exempt their children from the classes, and/or that the government does not have a monopoly on publicly-funded education.

Some might worry that my view rests on two unsubstantiated empirical assumptions: (1) that a liberal regime can survive in the long run even if a significant majority of citizens are only minimally decent and a small minority are actually good, and (2) private initiative coupled with non-coercive state measures will be sufficient to produce a critical mass of good citizens. While precise empirical verification of these claims is impossible, nonetheless the history of the United States and of many European liberal democracies seems to support them. We have long had a society in which a majority of citizens are generally law-abiding and productive, have only basic knowledge of their civic rights and duties, and rarely (if ever) participate in politics (at least if voter turnout is any indication of general political participation). Further, for most of our nation's history we did not have compulsory education laws at all, and even now most government regulations regarding civic education in schools are fairly minimal.[115] Yet while our nation is far from perfect, we have nonetheless managed to preserve and even extend basic liberal freedoms over the course of almost 250 years. This is not to deny that more should be done to encourage informed and active participation in public life. Rather, my point is simply that the situation is far from being so dire as to justify the violation of parental rights.

Further, the burden of proof in this matter ought to lie with those who *do* think that a robust civic education program (like the one Macedo, Gutmann and Callan defend) is so essential for the survival of liberal

---

[115] See Kenneth W. Tolo, *The Civic Education of American Youth: From State Policies to School District Practices*, Lyndon B. Johnson School of Public Affairs Policy Research Project Report, Volume 133 (Austin: Lyndon B. Johnson School of Public Affairs, 1999).

democracy that it should be mandatory for all children, even in cases where parents have conscientious objections to the content of that education. In the absence of clear evidence indicating the need for such coercive state action, we should err on the side of safeguarding the rights of parents and respecting the relative autonomy of the family regarding its own internal affairs.

Aside from concerns about the use of coercive state power in ways that threaten parental rights and family autonomy, there are other reasons why the state should tolerate diversity even with regard to education for citizenship. One reason is fairness, coupled with the recognition that there are many reasonable views about what good citizenship entails. Given that the government has more resources at its disposal than any private individual or corporation, fairness is always a concern when the government favors one particular viewpoint or way of life over others. Perfect government neutrality is impossible, but when the government does use its resources in ways that advantage one particular group or set of beliefs over another (which it constantly does), justification is owed to the disadvantaged group, even when the means used are non-coercive. Deciding which individuals should receive public honor, for example, or what a citizenship education curriculum should include, can be highly controversial. Inevitably, the views of the majority, or at least the most influential even if they are not the numerical majority, are likely to prevail. As long as no fundamental rights are violated, democratic procedures are followed, and reasonable attempts are made to justify the policy even to the disfavored group, this lack of neutrality is not a problem, or at least not a serious one. Those in the minority can organize themselves and try to persuade others to change their views, and in the meantime they are free to lead their own lives according to their own beliefs.

However, when the government acts *coercively* in non-neutral ways that threaten the rights of those in the disfavored groups, a justification beyond "the majority made me do it" or "it serves the common good as we (the legislators) understand it" is necessary. As argued already, coercively preventing others from following the dictates of their consciences in serious matters such as the education of their children or the exercise of their religion can be justified only when the protection of equally fundamental rights of others is at stake, or when there is a serious threat to the public order that is a precondition for the protection of those rights. Rawlsian civic education is necessary neither for the protection of fundamental rights, nor for the preservation of a liberal democratic order even over the long run. To impose it is therefore an unjustifiable infringement of the conscience rights and natural authority of parents.

Gutmann would probably classify my view as another version of the "civic minimalism" that she criticizes in her epilogue to the second edition of *Democratic Education*. As Gutmann describes it, civic minimalism entails that "requiring anything more than the civic minimum constitutes an illegitimate exercise of political authority on the part of citizens, and therefore should be constitutionally prohibited."[116] Gutmann criticizes civic minimalism on the grounds that public funding for education is unjustifiable unless citizens are permitted to ensure that schools teach public values, and that determining the content of a civic minimum is just as controversial as determining the content of a more robust civic education.

Gutmann's first critique of civic minimalism – that "if publicly subsidized schooling cannot have any publicly mandated content, it ceases to make sense as a public good" – simply seems odd, especially because she includes the imposition of values as an essential aspect of the "publicly mandated content" to which she refers.[117] Arguably, the education of children is itself in the public interest, even if that education has no specific connection to civic values. Citizens who can read and write are more likely to be able to contribute to the economy and even to participate more effectively in political life than those who cannot. Education is clearly a public good even when it has no explicitly civic elements.

The central criticism, however, is the second one. Gutmann is right to point out that citizens are likely to disagree regarding educational regulations of any sort, minimal or robust. My point, however, is not that the minimum will be uncontroversial, but that it has to be reasonably defensible *as a minimum* – i.e. as genuinely indispensable for the survival of the political order over time – if we are to enforce it against the conscientious objections of parents. Further, as an empirical matter Gutmann actually concedes that it is relatively easy to achieve a social consensus about basic requirements such as literacy and numeracy. Teaching law-abidingness, industriousness, and the basics regarding the history and government of our nation is also unlikely to raise many eyebrows. What she takes to be actually controversial about civic minimalism is not so much the proposed content, but the fact that "citizens and their accountable representatives must be prevented from mandating

---

[116] Gutmann, *Democratic Education*, 293.   [117] Gutmann, *Democratic Education*, 296.

more than the minimum."[118] In other words, Gutmann sees the minim-
alist approach as a violation of the *democratic community's right* to
determine the content of children's formal education. She is, in other
words, presenting the democratic community (in balance with teaching
professionals) as the primary educational authority with regard to formal
(pre-university) schooling, and arguing that, precisely because that authority is primary, placing strict limits on it would be unjust. Yet if comprehensive authority over children belongs, as I have argued in Chapters 1
and 2, primarily to parents rather than the state, then we have good reason
to limit the authority of citizens and their representatives over other
people's children to that which is minimally necessary for the survival of
society over time (and for the protection of children's basic rights).

This is a point of fundamental disparity between Gutmann's view and
my own. In earlier chapters I have offered an in-depth defense of the
claim that parents have extensive and primary authority over their
children. Gutmann, on the other hand, never seriously considers this
possibility. She quickly mentions and dismisses the view that parents
ought to have *exclusive* authority over the education of their children – a
view she calls "the state of families" – but that position is a straw man,
since almost no one denies that the state should play *some* role in
regulating and supporting education.[119] The difficult question regards
the proper balance of educational authority between parents and the
state. Gutmann thinks this balance should be determined by democratic
deliberation in a way that treats the state (together with professional
educators) as the primary educational authority at least with respect to
formal schooling. That position, however, rests on the undefended
assumption that parental authority is secondary to and derivative
of the authority of the larger community (or at least on the same
plane as the authority of the larger community), rather than primary
and original as I have argued.[120] In other words, Gutmann simply ignores
the possibility that parental rights provide principled limits on the authority of the larger community with regard to the upbringing of children.

Conclusion

In this chapter I have argued that a robust notion of parental rights –
which includes the right to shelter one's children from sympathetic

---

[118] Ibid.   [119] Gutmann, *Democratic Education*, 28–33.
[120] On this point, see also footnote 36.

exposure to diverse ways of life – is compatible with a concern for the education of future citizens capable of living peacefully with those of different creeds and participating meaningfully in civic and political life. Those who dispute this claim do so by arguing that there is a compelling state interest in a specific and controversial type of civic education that is deemed necessary to foster a specific and controversial version of good citizenship. However, that type of civic education, and the version of good citizenship to which it is connected, are highly demanding and hotly contested even among liberals. While agreeing that the state has a serious interest in the education of future citizens, I have tried to show that mandatory Rawlsian civic education– the specific type of civic education advocated by Rawlsians such as Gutmann, Macedo and Callan – serves a state interest (the creation and preservation of a Rawlsian liberal regime) that is, at best, not compelling enough to warrant infringing on the rights of parents, and, at worst, potentially harmful insofar as it would tend toward the elimination or reduction of diverse ways of life that make a positive contribution to the health of our liberal democratic society. Further, even if Rawlsian civic education did serve a compelling state interest, a policy mandating such a curriculum even in private schools and homeschools, and even despite the conscientious objections of parents, seems overly broad. A more narrowly tailored policy that respects the right of parents to exempt their children from offensive aspects of the civic education curriculum would arguably be sufficient, given that only a small minority of parents is likely to object. (If, on the other hand, a majority or a large minority of parents objects, then we might justifiably wonder why a Rawlsian minority has the right to impose its own controversial understanding of liberalism on everyone else.)

By contrast, there *is* a truly compelling state interest in what I call education for minimally decent citizenship, understood roughly as an education that will foster law-abidingness, encourage respect for all persons (though not necessarily for their ideas), enable children to be economically self-supporting as adults, teach them the basics regarding our nation's history and government, and inform them of their civic rights and responsibilities. The state may therefore require parents and schools to include at least these basic aspects of civic education in their curricula, while leaving them free to determine how to do so. The empirical research suggests that many – including many fundamentalist religious parents and schools – are likely to foster civic participation and active democratic engagement above and beyond the minimal requirements of citizenship. But if there are some, like the Amish, whose religion requires relative isolation from political life, the state does not have a sufficiently weighty interest to intervene. The bottom line is that, except where the state has an interest that is *truly* compelling, and where the policy is narrowly tailored to the achievement of that interest, the fundamental rights of individuals – including the rights of parents to raise their children as they think best – ought to be respected.

4

Parental rights and children's autonomy

In the last chapter I argued that mandatory civic education programs of the sort proposed by liberal theorists like Gutmann, Macedo and Callan violate parental rights. By contrast, a mandatory civic minimum (together with more robust optional programs) suffices for the state's interest in educating future citizens, while respecting parental rights and recognizing the ways in which traditional values and ways of life enrich the larger political community, in part by acting as a salutary counter-weight to the individualism, relativism and materialism which typically plague liberal democracies. Yet all of this talk about civic interests may leave one wondering: What about the children themselves? They are, after all, the ones whom education policies impact most directly. Even if, as the Supreme Court determined in *Yoder*, exempting the Amish from compulsory education laws and allowing them to end their children's formal academic education at age fourteen does not pose a serious threat to the civic order, does it not prematurely and drastically restrict Amish children's future possibilities? Or, to take a more common case, what about children of parents like the plaintiffs in *Mozert*, who aim to shelter them from competing conceptions of the good life in order to solidify their adherence to fundamentalist Christian values? Or children whose parents prevent their exposure to diverse ways of life by homeschooling them or sending them to a private school in which everyone shares the same values? Cases like these lead many to worry that granting broad educational authority to parents may prevent children from developing into autonomous adults, or unduly restrict their future possibilities.[1]

---

[1] One of the most influential versions of this claim is made by Joel Feinberg in his land-mark paper, "The Child's Right to an Open Future," in *Whose Child? Children's Rights, Parental Authority, and State Power*, ed. William Aiken and Hugh LaFollette (Totowa, NJ: Rowman & Littlefield, 1980), 124–153. (For a brief but incisive critique of Feinberg's view, see Claudia Mills, "The Child's Rights to an Open Future?" *Journal of Social Philosophy* 34, 4 (Winter 2003): 499–509. Others who express concerns similar to those of Feinberg include: Bruce Ackerman, *Social Justice in the Liberal State* (Binghamton: Yale University

I am sympathetic to these concerns. While I defend the rights of the Amish to educate their children in accordance with their beliefs, I consider their approach to education far from ideal. Likewise, I disagree with any educational program that does not teach children to think critically and enable them to understand and evaluate the reasons for their beliefs. On the other hand, I disagree at least as strongly with the educational approach proposed by some Rawlsian liberal authors who recommend that parents avoid enrolling their children in *any* comprehensive conception of the good life, but rather expose them as even-handedly as possible to a variety of ways of life so that the children can choose for themselves.[2] Yet none of these educational approaches constitutes abuse or neglect. As established in previous chapters, a child's parents are the ones with the authority to make controversial decisions about what is in the best interests of that child. Coercive state intervention *for the sake of children's*

Press, 1980); Harry Brighouse, "Civic Education and Liberal Legitimacy," *Ethics* 108, 4 (July 1998): 719–745; Harry Brighouse, *School Choice and Social Justice* (New York: Oxford University Press, 2000); Eamonn Callan, *Creating Citizens* (New York: Clarendon Press, 1997); James G. Dwyer, *Religious Schools v. Children's Rights* (Ithaca: Cornell University Press, 1998); Walter Feinberg, *Common Schools/Uncommon Identities: National Unity and Cultural Difference* (New Haven: Yale University Press, 1998); Amy Gutmann, *Democratic Education* (Princeton: Princeton University Press, 1999); Kenneth Henley, "The Authority to Educate," in *Having Children: Philosophical and Legal Reflections on Parenthood*, ed. Onora O'Neill and William Ruddick (New York: Oxford University Press, 1979), 254–264; Stephen Macedo, *Diversity and Distrust* (Cambridge: Harvard University Press, 2000); Rob Reich, "Testing the Boundaries of Parental Authority Over Education: The Case of Homeschooling," in *Moral and Political Education*, ed. Stephen Macedo and Yael Tamir (New York: New York University Press, 2002), 275–313; Ian MacMullen, *Faith in Schools? Autonomy, Citizenship, and Religious Education in the Liberal State* (Princeton: Princeton University Press, 2007). These theorists differ from one another on many points. Ackerman, for instance, bases his view on what he considers to be a fundamental liberal commitment to neutrality, and on the belief that non-autonomous lives cannot be good, premises which Gutmann (in *Democratic Education* though not in her earlier work on this topic) and Macedo explicitly reject. Nonetheless, each of these authors would support making some form of education for autonomy mandatory (sometimes as a foreseen and desired side-effect of civic education) even against the objections of parents. Matthew Clayton takes this line of concern even further, arguing that it is a violation of children's autonomy for parents to inculcate *any* comprehensive conception of the good life in their children, even if they also expose their children to alternative views at the same time [Matthew Clayton, *Justice and Legitimacy in Upbringing* (Oxford: Oxford University Press, 2006)]. In this chapter I focus on the more moderate liberal view according to which it is permissible for parents to teach their children a comprehensive conception of the good as long as they also expose them to alternative views, both because this is the dominant view among liberals, and also because I believe that my critique of this view applies *a fortiori* to Clayton's view.

[2] See, for example, Clayton, *Justice and Legitimacy.*

well-being (as distinct from intervention for the sake of the public order), is justified only in cases of abuse and neglect. Therefore it would be wrong for the state to mandate autonomy education *on child-centered grounds* when this is contrary to parents' wishes.

Even Macedo, in defending the *Mozert* decision and criticizing *Yoder*, takes care to do so on *civic* grounds, stating clearly that "the state has no business promoting comprehensive philosophical ideals of individual autonomy."[3] The political liberalism to which Macedo is committed forbids the state from promoting any comprehensive understanding of the good life as such. While Macedo recognizes that the civic education policies he recommends would, as a (desirable) side-effect, promote individual autonomy, he thinks it impermissible to defend such policies on that ground. If my argument in the last chapter was correct, and there are no sufficiently compelling state interests that would justify mandatory Rawlsian civic education, then this "back door" defense of at least a certain degree of autonomy education as a requirement or side-effect of civic education is no longer available.

My defense of parental rights to direct their children's education even when parents' educational choices may hinder children's development of autonomy could stop here. If there are no sufficiently compelling state interests at stake, and if parents' educational decisions do not constitute abuse or neglect, then coercive state interference is simply outside the bounds of state authority. Yet there is nonetheless much more that can and should be said to assuage the concerns of those who, like myself, are sincerely concerned about the well-being of children, and who believe that failing to provide them with an education for autonomy would significantly decrease their chances of leading a good life. Generally speaking, autonomy education includes elements like exposure to diverse worldviews, engagement with criticisms of one's own worldview, and the development of critical thinking skills. It is argued that autonomy education should be required in schools even (or perhaps especially) when parents would prefer to shelter their children from competing conceptions of the good, given autonomy's instrumental (and on some accounts also intrinsic) importance for a good life. In this chapter I will challenge these arguments on the grounds that they tend to overlook or underestimate the potential dangers of such an education for the overall well-being of children (including, ironically, dangers to the development of

---

[3] Macedo, *Diversity and Distrust*, 207.

genuine autonomy). They do so by paying insufficient attention to the importance of moral virtue as a constitutive element of and precondition for genuine autonomy, and by failing to recognize how the development and consolidation of moral virtue may be undermined by autonomy education particularly when such an education leads children to question the values taught at home. I develop my argument through critical engagement with the work of Eamonn Callan, Harry Brighouse and Ian MacMullen. I focus on Callan, Brighouse and MacMullen because they are more moderate and show greater awareness of the potential dangers of autonomy education than most liberal authors, but still, as I will argue below, fail to recognize the full extent of those dangers and thus the full weight of the child-centered arguments against mandatory autonomy education even during adolescence.

Evaluating arguments for mandatory autonomy education

A minimal threshold of autonomy as necessary for a good life

In *Creating Citizens*, Callan argues that while parents do have some discretionary rights over the way that they raise their children, those rights do not include the right to deny their children education for autonomy. In the previous chapter we considered Callan's argument that teaching children to think critically and exposing them sympathetically to diverse ways of life are necessary in order to prepare them for citizenship in a liberal democracy. Here, however, I examine another strand of Callan's account, in which he offers a child-centered justification for mandating educational programs that include these autonomy-promoting elements. It is important to note that Callan is working with a distinctively liberal conception of autonomy. Although Callan does not offer a definition of autonomy, his understanding of it becomes clearer when contrasted with what he calls the value of "simple integrity," in which all of one's roles and actions are harmonized and unified by a set of principles and values that hold a paramount status in moral deliberation. To illustrate what he means by "simple integrity," Callan cites the example of a Presbyterian minister who suggests "that Christians must bring Jesus along on their honeymoon, especially on their honeymoon." Callan remarks that "those of us who do not share his faith may be inclined to smile, but that is only because we share the modern assumption that all roles, whether they be as lover of this person or worshiper of that god, are discrete spheres of engagement among which the autonomous agent freely moves (or aimlessly flits)."[4] This element of detachment from all of one's ethical commitments seems, according to Callan's interpretation, to follow from acceptance of the Rawlsian burdens of judgment,[5] which imply that "the doctrine any reasonable person affirms is but one reasonable possibility among others."[6] It also appears to go hand in hand with "the capacity for and commitment to ongoing rational reflection on all of one's ethical commitments" that Ian MacMullen proposes as a definition of autonomy, a definition which seems consonant with the way Callan views autonomy in *Creating Citizens*.[7] Callan thinks that the liberal autonomous life is better than – indeed, constitutes a liberation from – the life of simple integrity, but nonetheless recognizes that it too is one among many rival conceptions of the good life among which individuals should be free to choose. For this reason he does not want to rest his defense of autonomy education on the value of full-fledged liberal autonomy as such.[8]

Instead, Callan attempts a more subtle argument in favor of autonomy education. This argument is based on the claim that children have an interest in achieving a degree of personal sovereignty which involves "something substantially above a primitive level of agency," and which entails "a degree of autonomous development that takes them beyond the condition [he calls] 'ethical servility.'"[9] What is Callan's notion of ethical servility? First, he explains the general notion of servility, which he characterizes as "a gross failure to understand or appreciate one's equal standing in the moral community as a rights-holder on a par with others."[10] To demonstrate this concept, Callan borrows Thomas Hill's example of the Deferential Wife whose entire life is subordinated to serving her Despotic Husband and obeying his wishes. Callan points out that in this case the wife is servile even if her husband is a benign despot. He then goes on to draw an analogy between Hill's Deferential Wife and a Deferential Child who "believes she has an overriding duty to

---

[4] Eamonn Callan, "Tradition and Integrity in Moral Education," *American Journal of Education* 101, 1 (Nov. 1992): 8.

[5] See Chapter 3, footnote 4.   [6] Callan, *Creating Citizens*, 31.

[7] MacMullen, *Faith in Schools?* 67. As I will discuss below, however, in later work Callan emphasizes the need to include the capacity for reasonable *adherence* to one's commitments within the definition of autonomy, rather than focusing one-sidedly on the capacity for *revision* of commitments (Eamonn Callan, "Autonomy, Childrearing and Good Lives," in *The Moral and Political Status of Children*, ed. David Archard and Colin M. MacLeod (New York: Oxford University Press, 2002), 118–141).

[8] Callan, *Creating Citizens*, 40–41.   [9] Callan, *Creating Citizens*, 152.   [10] Ibid.

serve her parents and acts and feels accordingly."[11] The parental equivalent of the benign Despotic Husband are the parents who think they must control their "child's conduct on all matters of fundamental ethical significance" and, in order to achieve this goal, teach their child that she must always obey them.[12] Callan thinks that the same reasons which should lead us to condemn the vice of servility in the case of the Deferential Wife also hold in the case of the Deferential Child.

Assuming that his reader will concede both of these preliminary points, Callan asks us to imagine a different case, the case of what he calls the "Ethically Servile Child." In this scenario, the parent still aims at ensuring the child will remain faithful to the family's values, but does so by raising the child to have an "ignorant antipathy" toward all competing ways of life and ethical ideals. By "ignorant antipathy," Callan means "a settled affective disposition to refuse to register whatever reason might commend in the objects of one's antipathy, even if, at some later date, one might acquire much knowledge about them."[13] Callan argues that the Ethically Servile Child remains just as subordinate to her parents' will as the Deferential Child, even if she can "enumerate her rights correctly, talk eloquently about their meaning, and prize them as highly as anyone reasonably could."[14] For Callan, the cases are essentially the same because in each of them "the field of deliberation in which the agent operates as an adult has been constrained through childhood experience so as to ensure ongoing compliance with another's will."[15]

Callan believes that education for liberal autonomy, including the development of critical thinking skills and sympathetic exposure to diverse conceptions of the good life, is necessary to prevent children from growing up to be ethically servile. This type of education is not aimed at leading children to adopt a way of life in which autonomy is the highest goal, but at ensuring that the answer each child eventually makes to the question of how to live is not simply a "servile echo of the answers others have given."[16] He concludes that it is beyond the scope of parents' rights to veto an education in which children are exposed sympathetically to diverse ways of life, because to do so would be to prioritize parents' interest in a zone of personal sovereignty, which includes some discretion regarding how to raise their children, over the children's own interest in personal sovereignty.

---

[11] Callan, *Creating Citizens*, 153.   [12] Ibid.   [13] Ibid.   [14] Ibid.
[15] Callan, *Creating Citizens*, 154.   [16] Callan, *Creating Citizens*, 155.

Callan anticipates objections to this argument on the grounds that people whom he would describe as ethically servile may be happy and lead otherwise good lives. Callan agrees that a view of the good life in which autonomy is the paramount value is controversial, and that it would be wrong to impose that view on everyone. However, according to him the reason why it would be wrong to impose autonomy as the highest value is that "people should be free to adjudicate among conceptions of the good for themselves, unless we have decisive moral reason to rule out some conceptions."[17] This sort of argument cannot work as a defense of the right of parents to raise an ethically servile child, because "a necessary assumption in that argument is that human beings have a right to order the diverse possible constituents of the good life in their own way."[18] But "ethical servility denies the individual precisely that freedom."[19] In other words, Callan thinks that parental discretion to choose the values they want to teach their children is based on their own personal sovereignty, understood as their own right to choose and follow their own conception of the good life. Yet to raise an ethically servile child is to prevent that child from having the opportunity to exercise that very same right as he develops into a mature adult. Therefore, to raise an ethically servile child, even with the best of intentions, is at least implicitly to fail to treat the child as a future moral equal.

However, one need not appeal to this autonomy-based conception of parental rights. Rather, as I have argued already, one can conceive of parents' rights as stemming from the primacy of their childrearing authority (as argued in Chapter 1), or, relatedly, as protecting the parents' fundamental moral interest in leading a life of integrity by fulfilling their perceived obligations (as argued in Chapter 2). The fundamental right at stake is therefore not personal sovereignty or autonomy – the "right to order the diverse possible constituents of the good life in their own way" – but integrity, understood as a basic and constitutive aspect of human well-being. Parents' rights provide the necessary moral space to fulfill their perceived parenting obligations, whether or not they have autonomously chosen the conception of the good that shapes those obligations. On this view, therefore, parents would show respect for the moral equality of their children primarily by fostering in them the habits of character that will enable them, as adults, to lead lives of integrity, consistently to overcome weakness of will, social pressures,

---

[17] Ibid.   [18] Callan, *Creating Citizens*, 156.   [19] Ibid.

the promptings of appetite or other barriers to the recognition and
fulfillment of their perceived duties. One might think, as I do, that
teaching children critical thinking skills and exposing them – at the right
time and in the right way – to other ways of life will likewise foster their
integrity by enabling them to have a deeper and firmer commitment to
the values that guide their life, to revise their values in accordance with
the conclusions of rational reflection, and to recognize their obligations
more accurately. Failure to provide such an education, however, would
not deprive them of the ability to lead lives of integrity. If the grounds of
parental rights are understood correctly, there is, therefore, no contradiction or incoherence in defending parents' right to shelter their children
from sympathetic exposure to diverse conceptions of the good life.

A further problem with Callan's argument is his assumption that if
one's autonomy does not surpass that of the Ethically Servile Child, one
lacks all but the most primitive level of agency, and is below the minimal
threshold of autonomy necessary for a good life.[20] According to Callan's
own description, the Ethically Servile Child can "enumerate her rights
correctly, talk eloquently about their meaning, and prize them as highly
as anyone reasonably could."[21] It seems implausible to describe such a
person as lacking all but the most primitive level of moral agency, or to
presume that she cannot lead a good life. Consider the hypothetical case
of two adults, Maggie and Charlie. Both are committed to social justice,
and lead lives of exemplary self-sacrifice in the service of their communities. Both find their lives deeply rewarding and fulfilling. The only
relevant difference between the two is that Maggie was an Ethically
Servile Child whose parents taught her a view of the good life centered
on a comprehensive liberal understanding of social justice, and inculcated in her a settled antipathy to all competing views, while Charlie
received the sort of autonomy education that Callan recommends.
Despite being an adult, according to Callan's characterization Maggie
is still effectively subordinate to her parents' will, since her parents
educated her so as to "pre-empt serious thought at any future date"
about alternative values.[22] I have strong doubts about the psychological
plausibility of this picture, but even granting Callan's characterization, it
seems far-fetched to claim that Maggie lacks all but the most primitive
degree of moral agency, or to deny that she is leading a good life.

[20] Callan, *Creating Citizens*, 152.   [21] Callan, *Creating Citizens*, 153.
[22] Callan, *Creating Citizens*, 154.

Perhaps my objection on this point is largely semantic. When I think of individuals who lack all but the most primitive level of moral agency, I imagine drug addicts or psychologically traumatized victims of severe neglect or abuse in early childhood. Of course, it is clear that this is not what Callan means by the phrase. But the persuasive force of his argument, at least for me, depends to a large extent on the fact that the phrase tends to conjure up images of cases that are incomparably worse than those to which Callan is actually referring. When Callan asserts that parents have no right to raise children in a way that causes them to be deprived of all but the most primitive level of moral agency, or that effectively robs them of the opportunity for a good life, I intuitively agree, but only because, to me, this is equivalent to saying that parents have no right to abuse or neglect their children.

Thus we are basically thrown back to a more fundamental controversy over what constitutes the good life and the role that liberal autonomy plays in the good life. I cannot resolve this controversy here, although my discussion later in the chapter will touch on this topic tangentially. What I hope to have shown in this section is simply (1) that there is no contradiction involved in claiming that parents have rights to deny their children an education for liberal autonomy, since those rights are based not on the value of parental autonomy, but on the value of parental integrity or on respect for pre-political parental authority, and (2) that we cannot circumvent disagreements about the value of liberal autonomy by proposing a "minimal" threshold of autonomy, since agreement on such a threshold is unlikely for those who do not already share a comprehensive liberal conception of the good life.

Autonomy as instrumentally valuable for leading a good life

Other arguments for mandatory autonomy education focus not on the need to achieve a minimal threshold of autonomy as essential to a good life, but rather on the instrumental value of autonomy. Harry Brighouse, for instance, argues that autonomy – which requires one to subject one's morally significant beliefs to rational scrutiny – may "add worth to a life lived according to good values," but is not "a precondition of that life having worth."[23] Rather, living well requires living by genuinely worthy values and endorsing those values 'from the inside,' even if those values

---

[23] Brighouse, *School Choice and Social Justice*, 68.

are not autonomously chosen. However, Brighouse believes that autonomy education – including the development of critical thinking skills
and sympathetic exposure to diverse ways of life – is still necessary
because, especially given the complexities of modern society, "children
will be better able to live well if they are able rationally to compare
different ways of life."[24] Thus Brighouse worries that unless all children
receive an education that facilitates autonomy, many will be deprived of
a significant opportunity to lead a good life.[25]

Ian MacMullen similarly defends mandatory autonomy education
based on autonomy's instrumental value. Drawing on and expanding
the arguments of Brighouse and others, MacMullen makes an impressive
case for the ways in which autonomy, understood as "the capacity for and
commitment to ongoing rational reflection on all of one's ethical commitments"[26] – facilitates a genuinely good life. "Exercising a developed
capacity for ethical autonomy," explains MacMullen, "is the best way for
individuals to detect false or inadequately supported beliefs, root out and
resolve inconsistencies in their ethical doctrine, adjust their goals to suit
their particular character and aspirations, guard against exploitation and
manipulation by others, and prosper in a modern society whose social
and economic institutions require and encourage the exercise of individual choice."[27] Given the important instrumental value of rational reflection for leading a good life, MacMullen claims that mandatory autonomy
education should be no more controversial than other basic educational
requirements like literacy and numeracy: "in each case, there is a sufficient justification that is neutral in the sense that it appeals only to
instrumental value and imposes no substantive constraints on the ethical
positions one may accept as a result of reflection, reading, writing, or
quantitative reasoning."[28]

I agree with Brighouse and MacMullen's claims about the instrumental
value of rational reflection for leading a good life. Yet these claims are
insufficient to justify mandatory autonomy education. First, as I argued
in the last chapter, there are strong civic grounds for literacy and
numeracy requirements, whereas there are insufficient civic grounds
for mandatory Rawlsian liberal civic education (which includes autonomy education). Thus, mandatory educational requirements regarding
literacy and numeracy fall within the boundaries of state authority, while

---

[24] Brighouse, *School Choice and Social Justice*, 69.
[25] Brighouse, *School Choice and Social Justice*, 73.   [26] MacMullen, *Faith in Schools?* 67.
[27] MacMullen, *Faith in Schools?* 112.   [28] MacMullen, *Faith in Schools?* 106.

mandatory autonomy education (which cannot be sufficiently justified on civic grounds alone), does not. Second, in emphasizing the importance of explicit autonomy education for the ability to lead a good life, Brighouse and MacMullen's arguments seem to presume that, absent such an education, children will end up severely handicapped with regard to their capacity for rational reflection. Yet most of the instrumental benefits of autonomy education overlap with the benefits of a solid academic education more generally. It is implausible to claim that children with strong reading, writing and quantitative reasoning skills lack a capacity for rational reflection, or the wherewithal to learn about diverse ways of life if they are dissatisfied with the values being passed on to them by their parents. Children, for instance, who have to read and analyze works of great literature in their high school English classes, or evaluate competing theories of the causes of World War I in a history course, are already receiving an excellent training in critical rational reflection, even if the school does not require them to apply their critical capacities directly to the evaluation of diverse conceptions of the good. Regrettably, as anyone who has taught introductory courses to college freshmen knows, many high school graduates lack the ability to analyze a text or develop a logically coherent argument. But the problem in such cases is usually the lack of rigorous academic preparation, or disciplinary problems that obstruct learning, not the lack of autonomy education as such. Indeed, my experience is that students who were homeschooled or who went to a private (often religious) school that reinforced their parents' values tend to stand out in terms of intellectual curiosity, writing ability, and critical thinking skills, along with overall personal maturity. Perhaps those whose education does not explicitly foster autonomy will be more likely to lack a *commitment* to ongoing rational reflection on their beliefs, but to claim that they will lack the *capacity* goes too far. The lack of *commitment* to ongoing rational evaluation of one's beliefs, however, should bother us much less than the lack of *capacity*, since the key concern here is to ensure that those who are unhappy with their parents' conception of the good have the means by which to find a way of life that is good for them.

Moral virtue, autonomy and the good life

A deeper difficulty with arguments for mandatory liberal autonomy education is that they tend to overlook or underestimate the potential dangers of such an education for the overall well-being of children, including their ability to choose and act on the basis of sound rational reflection rather than on the basis of sub-rational desire. Callan himself criticizes other liberal theorists for focusing on developing children's capacity for autonomous *revision* of their conception of the good, while largely overlooking the equally important capacity for autonomous *adherence* to a conception of the good. As Callan puts it, "if possessing an autonomous character enables and inclines one to make appropriate revision, it must also enable and incline one to resist the pull towards inappropriate revision."[29] Callan goes on to argue that teaching children the steadfastness necessary for adherence to a conception of the good may require, among other things, "shielding children from experiences one believes would confuse or corrupt them, engaging them in activities whose presuppositions they do not yet grasp, instilling beliefs whose grounds remain for some time unexamined."[30] While this type of upbringing "poses risks to the development of autonomy," it also "seems to provide strong insurance against risks to a cluster of dispositions needed to ensure autonomous adherence to conceptions of the good that greater openness would at some point endanger."[31] Education that aims at promoting autonomy may place so much emphasis on the need to be committed to remaining open to rational revision of one's conception of the good that it could end up encouraging children to drift from one conception of the good to another, leading them to develop the habit of abandoning an ideal the moment a more attractive option appears (perhaps more attractive simply because of its novelty). As I will argue in the next section, young children and even adolescents usually lack the moral maturity and life experience to recognize that all that glitters is not gold, or to stick with the gold when sub-rational desire pulls strongly toward the glitter.

Concerns along these lines also lead MacMullen to recognize that there is a positive case for sending a pre-adolescent child to schools that "harmonise with and reinforce the ethical messages she receives at home."[32] One of the reasons against sending children to schools that will undermine the values they are taught at home is that it can result in moral confusion and "disturb the young child's fragile sense of self."[33] MacMullen cites psychological evidence, based on the work of James Marcia, that supports this point. Liberals usually worry about the

---

[29] Callan, "Autonomy, Childrearing and Good Lives," 127.
[30] Callan, "Autonomy, Childrearing and Good Lives," 134.   [31] Ibid.
[32] MacMullen, *Faith in Schools?* 184.   [33] MacMullen, *Faith in Schools?* 186.

situation of children whom Marcia categorizes as "Foreclosures," those whose commitments have been chosen entirely by parents in a way that effectively forecloses a real possibility for revision, due to "strong parental pressure to conform to family values."[34] However, another group that scored equally low in terms of self-directedness was what Marcia called the "Identity Diffusions." Those in this group have a hard time maintaining any set of beliefs over time and are "'easily influenced by others,'" precisely because they have "not developed the ability to make personal commitments."[35] What this research shows, according to MacMullen, is that "our efforts to avoid Foreclosure must not disrupt the coherence of the child's primary culture to the extent that she develops into an Identity Diffusion, lacking an understanding of the nature and value of personal commitments."[36] MacMullen's argument thus echoes and provides further evidence to support Callan's point that we need to be equally concerned about children's development of the capacity for autonomous *adherence* as we are about their development of the capacity for autonomous *revision*. Yet both still believe that, given autonomy's importance for well-being, autonomy education should be required at least at some stage in a child's education.

MacMullen balances concerns about the disruption of a child's primary culture with concerns about the importance of enabling children to become autonomous by recommending that mandatory autonomy education should not involve a challenge to the values taught at home until secondary school. On the basis of Jean Piaget's theory of cognitive development, MacMullen argues that before the age of eleven or twelve "it would be futile to try to move children beyond the limited practice of reason-giving within a fixed ethical framework."[37] Further, when schools reinforce, rather than challenge, the values that young children are taught at home, this provides the "secure grounding in a coherent primary culture" that is important for helping children to grasp "the nature and value of personal commitment" and to avoid "the kind of listlessness that can all too easily inhibit autonomy just as much as lack of critical reflection."[38] In other words, sending children to primary schools in line with parents' values (and thus sheltering them to a considerable extent from competing conceptions of the good) can prevent them from developing into Identity Diffusions or, in Callan's terms, from failing to develop the capacity for autonomous adherence to a conception of the

---

[34] MacMullen, *Faith in Schools?* 187.   [35] Ibid.   [36] Ibid.
[37] MacMullen, *Faith in Schools?* 191.   [38] MacMullen, *Faith in Schools?* 188.

good. Once they have reached the age at which they are intellectually capable of abstract ethical reflection, however, MacMullen believes that respect for children's autonomy interests require that they be sent to schools in which they will be confronted with competing conceptions of the good.

Though correct to recognize the potentially pernicious effects on children of premature exposure to conflicting conceptions of the good life, MacMullen is too quick to dismiss the persistence of those dangers even into the adolescent years. It is true, as Piaget's research has shown, that by early adolescence children typically begin to exhibit a capacity to engage in formal, abstract thought.[39] And MacMullen is right to note that this capacity is a prerequisite for autonomous ethical reflection, which "requires an agent to detach herself from some of her existing beliefs and values to seriously consider the merits of an alternative ethical perspective."[40]

Yet the prerequisites for autonomy (and for leading a good life) are not only cognitive, but also *moral*. Callan hints at the importance of moral virtue in referring to the steadfastness necessary for autonomous adherence to a conception of the good, but still fails to appreciate (or at least articulate) the full extent to which virtue is necessary for genuinely autonomous choice and for leading a good life more generally.[41] Attentiveness to the importance of moral virtue and the conditions for its

---

[39] MacMullen, *Faith in Schools?* 191.   [40] MacMullen, *Faith in Schools?* 192.

[41] Callan does speak about the importance of character education in "Liberal Legitimacy, Justice and Civic Education," but focuses narrowly on inculcating the traits characteristic of a fully autonomous life (in the comprehensive liberal sense), as well as the traits required for citizens to develop "reasonableness" and a sense of justice in the Rawlsian understanding of those terms. An example of the sort of habit that Callan has in mind as necessary for the development of reasonableness and a sense of justice is the following: "a character trait that enables and inclines one to claim what is due to the self and others on the understanding that the self and others are persons of equal intrinsic worth" ["Liberal Legitimacy, Justice and Civic Education," *Ethics* 111, 1 (October 2000): 147]. The following passage gives one a sense of what is meant by character traits characteristic of a fully autonomous life: "To possess an autonomous character is to be someone whose conduct discloses certain values, emotional susceptibilities, and motivational patterns alongside the possession and habitual exercise of critical skills. She is prone to resentment or indignation when others seek to thwart her will on some matter she believes she should decide for herself. She is not merely intellectually capable of questioning traditional practices when these seem unjustified but is positively inclined to do so, and so on" (144). Thus Callan's expressed concern for teaching character does not contradict my claim that his view fails to take the moral prerequisites for autonomy seriously enough, because the moral prerequisites that I have in mind are the traditional moral virtues – justice understood much more broadly than it is on Callan's view, fortitude, temperance

development can help us to see why, even in secondary school, many children may not be prepared to profit from liberal autonomy education, despite their intellectual capacity for abstract thought.

An Aristotelian account of the moral prerequisites for autonomy

An Aristotelian understanding of moral virtue, the conditions for its development, and its relationship to the capacity for sound ethical decision-making, helps to expose some important gaps in the accounts of Callan and MacMullen. In particular, it shows how they (1) fail to give due importance to the ways in which sub-rational desire can undermine the capacity for truly rational revision of and adherence to one's ethical commitments, and (2) do not seriously consider how mandatory autonomy education, even in secondary school, might hinder or undermine the development of a mature moral character in which sub-rational desire is governed by and in harmony with reason.

On Aristotle's view, moral virtue involves the education of sub-rational desire under the guidance of reason. The ability to desire, choose, and act in accordance with reason requires a mature moral character, developed over time through the repeated performance of virtuous actions. Initially, such virtuous actions are non-autonomous, motivated not by a rational grasp of the goodness of one's action, but often by fear of punishment, desire for a reward, or love of one's parents or other educators. But by becoming habituated to act in accordance with virtue "from our very youth,"[42] we train desire to obey reason, even to the extent that, in the fully virtuous person, "it speaks, on all matters, with the same voice as reason."[43] By contrast, Aristotle refers to those without virtue as riddled with profound internal divisions, describing them as inwardly "rent by faction." Those who lack mastery over their sub-rational desires "choose, instead of the things they themselves think good, things that are pleasant but hurtful," and "shrink from doing what they think best for themselves."[44] Such persons are clearly not autonomous and lack the prerequisites for leading a good life. Even if they are capable of and committed to ongoing rational reflection about their conception of the

---

and prudence (also understood more broadly than as a mere facility for determining the most adequate means to one's chosen ends).

[42] Aristotle, *Nicomachean Ethics* II.1, 1103b25.
[43] Aristotle, *Nicomachean Ethics* I.13, 1102b28.
[44] Aristotle, *Nicomachean Ethics*, IX.4, 1166b5–28.

good, and even if they are capable of (cognitive) adherence to their
ethical commitments, they are not consistently able to act in accordance
with those commitments. This is an aspect of autonomy that neither
Callan nor MacMullen emphasize, but it is essential, both as a constitutive aspect of autonomy, and, as I will argue, as a prerequisite for the
cognitive aspects of autonomy.

Lack of moral virtue not only threatens one's ability to act in accordance with one's ethical commitments, but also threatens one's ability to
make sound ethical judgments in the first place. Practical reason – reason
as directed toward acting or making – is, like theoretical reason, a
capacity that needs to be developed and perfected. The perfection of
practical reason as directed toward acting (*praxis*) is what Aristotle calls
phronesis, practical wisdom.[45] Yet practical wisdom is inseparable from
moral virtue, because following the dictates of reason and even being able
to reason correctly about ethical matters requires disciplining one's
desires and appetites. According to Aristotle, "it is impossible to be
practically wise without being good [i.e. morally virtuous]."[46] For, as
Aristotle explains, practical reasoning presupposes a starting-point, a
first principle indicating that which is worthy of pursuit, and such
principles are "not evident except to the good man; for wickedness
perverts us and causes us to be deceived about the starting-points of
action."[47] For instance, a virtuous person's ethical deliberations will
evaluate potential choices and actions with reference to goods that are
inherently choiceworthy, such as friendship or knowledge, while someone who lacks virtue will evaluate choices and actions with reference to
the gratification of sub-rational desires, and may not even be able to
grasp the intrinsic goods that are at stake. Even when it is not a matter
of deciding how to act in a particular circumstance, but of reasoning
more broadly about one's values and commitments, sub-rational desires
can play a powerful, if often sub-conscious, role. A fourteen-year-old,
annoyed by what he perceives as exaggerated parental restrictions
regarding the movies he is allowed to watch, will be all too eager to
criticize the value system that motivates his parents to enforce those

---

[45] Art is the perfection of practical reason as directed toward making. The difference
between acting and making is a complex one that I cannot enter into here. For an
interesting discussion, see Sarah Broadie, *Ethics with Aristotle* (New York: Oxford
University Press, 1993), 202.
[46] Aristotle, *Nicomachean Ethics*, VI.12, 1144a37.
[47] Aristotle, *Nicomachean Ethics*, VI.12, 1144a34–36.

restrictions, and to embrace a competing one, regardless of the genuine merits of each. Every worldview has at least apparent internal contradictions. If one has sub-rational motivations for dismissing that worldview (because, for instance, it condemns conduct in which one desires to engage), one can easily take the presence of such apparent contradictions to be a decisive reason against adhering to it, without undertaking the difficult task of exploring further to see whether or not those contradictions are real or merely apparent.

Unlike the virtue of practical wisdom, which has both moral and intellectual aspects, critical thinking skills are morally neutral, insofar as they can be used both to provide a rational defense of a genuinely good way of life, and to rationalize morally deficient ways of life. While there will be an objectively better argument in favor of the genuinely good way of life, we are all too familiar with the ways in which a person who lacks moral virtue – a person who is in the habit of acting based on sub-rational desires rather than on a reasoned understanding of what is actually good – can be highly skilled at providing rational justifications for actions that are in fact not fully reasonable. For reason to be an effective tool in distinguishing good from bad ways of life, moral virtue is necessary. Even adolescents who have the *cognitive* aspects of the capacity for ethical reflection and choice, therefore, may lack the *moral* aspects of that capacity, insofar as their judgments (as well as their choices and actions) are distorted by sub-rational desire.

Psychological and neurobiological studies likewise indicate that, while intellectually adolescents demonstrate a sophisticated capacity for rational reflection, their decision-making is marred by short-sightedness and a much higher tendency to impulsivity and immediate gratification than adults. In line with Aristotelian theory, this research indicates not simply that adolescents are prone to act against their better judgment, but that their judgment itself is skewed by these sub-rational factors. For instance, "adolescents, in weighing the costs and benefits involved in a decision, tend to weigh proximate benefits more highly and more distal costs lower than do most persons over the age of 21."[48] One factor related to adolescents' tendency toward short-sighted decision-making is that, due to neurobiological changes, sensation-seeking rises to a peak during adolescence, thus "heightening reward salience by making the experience

---

[48] Brian C. Partridge, "The Mature Minor: Some Critical Psychological Reflections on the Empirical Bases," *Journal of Medicine and Philosophy* 38 (2013): 292.

of potentially rewarding stimuli more rewarding."[49] Further, brain imaging has revealed that, in those under eighteen, decision-making predominantly engages the limbic structures (the neurological seat of emotion), while for those over 21, activity of the pre-frontal cortex (involved in reasoning) predominates.[50] Overall, the neurobiological evidence indicates that "the areas of the brain involved in mature executive decisions, that is, those necessary for the realization of reasonable and responsible choices," are still underdeveloped in adolescents, and that this neurobiological immaturity can significantly undermine the reliability of their judgment.[51]

A complementary psychological explanation of the differences between adult and adolescent decision-making focuses not on the more emotional and impulsive nature of adolescents' decisions, but instead on their tendency to lack insight into the "gist" of a situation.[52] Studies show that adolescents tend to make decisions based on a more literal and piecemeal analysis of information, in which they may often miss the forest for the trees, while adults tend to decide based on a "gist representation," an "interpretation that extracts the important nub of information."[53] An adolescent undergoing chemotherapy, for instance, may accurately assess the risks and rewards of drinking at a party, and judge that, for her, the social benefits of drinking outweigh the cost of undermining the effectiveness of her treatment. A mature adult, by contrast, would not even enter into such a cost–benefit analysis, for even to consider a trade-off between minor social benefits and survival would reflect a "fundamental failure of insight," an inaccurate or absent gist representation.[54] This research dovetails nicely with Aristotle's emphasis on the need for experience and moral maturity in order to grasp and order correctly the relevant human goods that are stake in a particular decision, as well as the idea that over time the virtuous person develops the ability simply to "see" what ought to be done without the need for deliberation.[55]

---

[49] Evan Wilhelms and Valerie Reyna, "Fuzzy Trace Theory and Medical Decisions by Minors: Differences in Reasoning between Adolescents and Adults," *Journal of Medicine and Philosophy* 38 (2013): 268–282, at 271.

[50] Partridge, "The Mature Minor," 293.   [51] Ibid.

[52] Wilhelms and Reyna, "Fuzzy Trace Theory," 272.

[53] Wilhelms and Reyna, "Fuzzy Trace Theory," 273–276.

[54] Wilhelms and Reyna, "Fuzzy Trace Theory," 273.

[55] Aristotle, *Nicomachean Ethics* VI.11, 1143b8–13; Louis Groarke, *An Aristotelian Account of Induction: Creating Something from Nothing* (Canada: McGill-Queen's University Press, 2009), 243.

Application of the Aristotelian account to the issue of autonomy education

The Aristotelian account, backed by psychological and neurobiological research, gives us several reasons to be wary of the claim that most adolescents will benefit, on balance, from criticism of their family's values and exposure to competing points of view. First of all, a cafeteria-style offering of different conceptions of the good life, in which none is presented as inherently superior to any of the others, can simply be an invitation to pick and choose elements of different conceptions insofar as they enable one to justify the indulgence of sub-rational desires. This can be a temptation for someone at any stage of life. For the person of mature moral character, however, the long-standing habits of self-governance in accordance with reason afford an ability to think critically about different conceptions of the good life, and to revise views in accordance with reason and moral experience, rather than having the reasoning process distorted by sub-rational desire or lack of moral insight. A child who has not yet achieved a stable self-dominion with reference to some conception of the good, or an adolescent who is only beginning to achieve that dominion, does not have the inner moral resources – the moral virtues – that are prerequisites for the ability to make fully reasonable judgments about conceptions of the good life. It seems to be precisely for these reasons that Aristotle thinks that ethics can be taught only to people of mature moral character, with sufficient life experience, for only "those who desire and act in accordance with a rational principle" will benefit from the study of ethics.[56]

Secondly, the fact that adolescents' reasoning tends to be distorted by sub-rational factors and lack of moral insight – and that they themselves generally do not recognize this – implies that adolescents still need authoritative parental guidance, including clear and consistently-enforced rules of conduct. Since practical wisdom depends on the prior acquisition of moral virtue, but moral virtue is developed through the education of desire by habitually acting as the practically wise person would act, the development and consolidation of moral virtue involves obedience to authority – relying on the practical reason of others who are more practically wise than oneself. Of course adolescents should be given more freedom to make their own decisions than younger children, as this

---

[56] Aristotle, *Nicomachean Ethics* I.3, 1095a10.

experience is necessary for the development of their own practical reasoning capacity, but clear boundaries are still necessary to protect them from the impulsivity, short-sightedness and inexperience that tend to cloud their judgment.

Studies on parenting styles corroborate this claim, indicating that authoritative parenting – characterized by a blend of responsiveness and demandingness, with clear and firm standards of behavior but also respect for children's individuality and encouragement of dialogue – produces the best outcomes not only in early childhood but in adolescence as well. According to the typology that developed out of the work of Diana Baumrind, authoritative parenting is contrasted with three other parenting types: (1) authoritarian parenting, which is high on demandingness but low on warmth and responsiveness, imposing strict standards with little or no room for dialogue, (2) indulgent or permissive parenting, which is high on warmth and responsiveness but low on demandingness, allowing "children to regulate their own activities as much as possible," and not insisting that children "obey externally defined standards" and (3) neglectful or disengaged parenting, low on both responsiveness and demandingness.[57] Studies have found that adolescents from authoritative homes report "significantly higher academic competence, significantly lower levels of problem behavior, and significantly higher levels of psychosocial development than adolescents from authoritarian, indulgent or neglectful households."[58] Further, while authoritarian parenting is less effective than authoritative parenting, and both authoritarian and indulgent parenting are better than neglectful parenting, authoritarian parenting tends to produce better outcomes overall than indulgent parenting. Adolescent children of authoritarian parents "report less school misconduct, less drug use, fewer somatic symptoms, and a more positive orientation toward school than their

[57] Diana Baumrind, "Rearing Competent Children," in *Child Development Today and Tomorrow*, ed. William Damon (San Francisco: Jossey-Bass, Inc., 1989), 353–354; L. J. Crockett and R. Hayes, "Parenting Practices and Styles," *Encyclopedia of Adolescence*, Vol. 2 (Elsevier, 2011), 241–248, www.sciencedirect.com/science/article/pii/B978 0123739513000776. Last accessed on January 7, 2016.

[58] Susie D. Lamborn et al., "Patterns of Competence and Adjustment among Adolescents from Authoritative, Authoritarian, Indulgent, and Neglectful Families," *Child Development* 62, 5 (October 1991): 1057. See also Patrick C. L. Heaven and Joseph Ciarrochi, "Parental Styles, Conscientiousness, and Academic Performance in High School: A Three-Wave Longitudinal Study," *Personality and Social Psychology Bulletin* 34, 5 (April 2008): 451–461.

indulgently reared peers."[59] Adolescents with indulgent parents scored better than those with authoritarian parents only on measures related to positive self-perception.[60] It is also interesting to note that among Asian and African American adolescents, authoritarian parenting produces outcomes almost as positive as authoritative parenting, and that some minority children may actually benefit from a more authoritarian parenting style.[61] This could be due to cultural differences in the way that children interpret parenting behaviors. For instance, one study showed that "parental control behaviors were linked to adolescents' perceptions of parental hostility and rejection in German and North American samples, whereas in Japan, Korea and China the same behaviors were associated with perceptions of parental warmth and acceptance."[62] Likewise, "among Latinos and African Americans, parenting strategies that appear restrictive and controlling to outsiders" were interpreted "positively, as being motivated by parental concern," among ethnic group members.[63] It seems, therefore, that while the best parenting includes high levels of both discipline and responsiveness (including respect for children's autonomy), lack of discipline tends to be more harmful than lack of responsiveness even in the adolescent years.

The second potential danger of autonomy education can therefore be summarized as follows. The firm and consistent exercise of parental authority is important for the well-being of children all the way until adulthood. Autonomy education, by its very nature, encourages children to be critical of ethical claims or standards based on authority, and to trust their own reasoning instead. Education for autonomy could therefore be detrimental even to adolescent children – who often lack moral insight and whose reasoning is often still coopted by the influence of sub-rational desire – to the extent that it undermines the moral authority of parents by encouraging children to criticize their parents'

---

[59] Lamborn et al., "Patterns of Competence and Adjustment," 1059. See also Sigrun Adalbjarnardottir and Leifur G. Hafsteinsson, "Adolescents' Perceived Parenting Styles and Their Substance Use: Concurrent and Longitudinal Analyses," *Journal of Research on Adolescence* 11, 4 (2001): 401–423.
[60] Lamborn et al., "Patterns of Competence and Adjustment," 1059.
[61] Crockett and Hayes, "Parenting Practices and Styles," 241–248; Laurence Steinberg et al., "Over-Time Changes in Adjustment and Competence among Adolescents from Authoritative, Authoritarian, Indulgent, and Neglectful Families," *Child Development* 65, 3 (June 1994): 754–770.
[62] Crockett and Hayes, "Parenting Practices and Styles," 247.   [63] Ibid.

values and offering sympathetic portrayals of ways of life that the parents have taught their children to view as bad.

This brings me to my third concern about autonomy education, which is that the weakening of parental moral authority can also undermine parents' efforts to foster moral virtue in their children, to teach habits of self-mastery, courage, fairness, generosity, and so forth. To introduce children to the complexity of the moral life and to competing conceptions of the good life, before they have learned any one coherent moral view and have developed a strong moral character by habitually governing their actions in accordance with that view, may thwart the process of developing a rational dominion over sub-rational desire. Even in adolescence, children's habits of self-dominion are likely in many cases to be too fragile to survive a critique of the conception of the good that grounded them. Exposure to the merits of conflicting moral views and to criticisms of the moral views that parents are trying to inculcate endangers the morally immature person's still precarious rational dominion over sub-rational desire. This is especially the case when such exposure occurs in school – as opposed to inevitable contact with other viewpoints in the larger culture through the Internet, television, billboards, magazines, social interactions, and so forth – given that children are taught to view school teachers as trustworthy authorities. Such exposure would be analogous to fomenting opposition to legitimate authorities in a fledgling political community that is just beginning to achieve a minimal level of social order and stability.

The renowned psychologist and sociologist Francis Ianni conducted some noteworthy empirical research that supports this concern. Ianni and his associates observed and interviewed thousands of adolescents in a variety of communities across the United States in order to explore the causes of both success and failure in the delicate transition from adolescence to adulthood. Ianni's conclusion is that "the most important determinant of how adolescence will be experienced and with what results" is "how the various social contexts of a community are integrated in terms of the continuity and congruence of their values, norms and rules."[64] In other words, Ianni found that adolescents fare best – in terms of outcomes like academic and professional achievement, overall psychosocial development, and avoidance of

---

[64] Francis Ianni, *The Search for Structure: A Report on American Youth Today* (New York: The Free Press, 1989), 15.

delinquency, substance abuse, and other problem behaviors – when family, school, church and peer groups offer a coherent set of values and standards, rather than presenting conflicting messages. This research suggests that the construction of a mature and stable moral identity in adolescence relies heavily on the scaffolding of a harmonious external structure of values.

It could be objected that it might be better to prevent the consolidation of self-dominion, rather than attain self-dominion based on a false or inferior conception of the good. However, just as in the political realm one might opt to support a decent though imperfect government to avoid a descent into civil war or a power vacuum that paves the way for tyranny, in the *polis* of the soul consolidation of stable rational rule by a decent though imperfect conception of the good is better than paving the way for the tyranny of sub-rational desire. Further, as has already been argued, just as peace and relative civil order is a precondition for reasonable public deliberation and critical reflection on ways to make the government more just, for an individual person a relatively stable rational ordering of desires is a prerequisite for critical rational reflection on the principles by which those desires are currently ordered. Therefore, children's development of the capacity for ethical reflection, and their well-being more generally, require that they achieve self-dominion – i.e. that they attain moral maturity based on some decent even if imperfect conception of the good. After one has sufficient self-mastery to engage critically with other views in a dispassionate way, that original conception of the good can then be revised.

Of course, the risk of turmoil and violence may be better than the consolidation of a tyrannical or otherwise grossly unjust regime. Likewise, it might be better to risk moral instability than to allow a child to develop into a terrorist or a highly-disciplined criminal. Yet here we are talking not about such extreme cases, in which state intervention would be justifiable on civic grounds, and which at any rate are likely to be tantamount to abuse or neglect. Here we are talking about cases in which conscientious parents, even if perhaps overprotective or somewhat authoritarian in their educational methods, want to shelter their children from exposure to diverse ways of life.

As noted in the last chapter, creating a "hothouse" environment in which children can build the foundations of moral character while sheltered from the sorts of temptations that would be present in the public schools is, in fact, one of the primary aims of the Christian schools that James Dwyer vehemently criticizes (along much the same lines as Brighouse and Callan) in *Religious Schools v. Children's Rights*. It is also particularly interesting to note, especially given the criticism that such schools fail to respect children's autonomy, that many of these schools will only accept children who want to attend. As Paul Parsons observes in *Inside America's Christian Schools*, "Before accepting a student, many principals interview both the parents and the child – separately. If the child doesn't want to go to that school, that's usually an automatic rejection slip to the parents."[65] Sometimes the students themselves want to attend Christian schools precisely because they do not think they are ready to face the difficult moral environment in the public school. Parsons recounts the following anecdote from Michael Healan, principal of Hartford Christian Academy in Connecticut, regarding his admissions interview with an eighth grader: "'The boy said he was facing lots of temptations at his public school. . . He said kids were constantly pressuring him to take drugs and do things he didn't want to do. At that age, some don't have a character strong enough to withstand peer pressure. They are tender young plants who can't take the storms of life yet."[66]

There are, in sum, a number of reasons to support the claim that parents' decision to shelter their children from sympathetic exposure to alternative ways of life does not necessarily prevent children from achieving genuine autonomy or, more importantly, from enabling them to lead a good life. Particularly in cases where it conflicts most starkly with the values children are learning at home, autonomy education may be more harmful than helpful to children (even in secondary school) by (1) tempting children to abandon a good way of life without sufficient reason due to the sway of sub-rational desire (thus weakening their capacity for autonomous adherence to a conception of the good), (2) undermining the parental authority that even adolescent children need to guide their still-immature practical reasoning, and (3) threatening the consolidation of moral virtue in children by leading them to question the value system that grounds those virtues. Further, on the Aristotelian account one could argue that a person who is not autonomous in the liberal sense but who possesses moral virtue is better off than the person who possesses *only* the cognitive conditions of autonomy but whose actions are effectively ruled by sub-rational desire. This account is in line

[65] Paul F. Parsons, *Inside America's Christian Schools* (Macon, GA: Mercer University Press, 1987), 14.
[66] Parsons, *Inside America's Christian Schools*, 15.

with the conclusions of sociological and psychological research which indicate that, even in adolescence, children tend to fare best when parents set and enforce clear and consistent standards, and when those standards are reinforced by schools and other social institutions. Thus we should be *more* concerned about dangers to the development and consolidation of the moral virtues than about dangers to the development of the cognitive conditions of autonomy, since the former are preconditions for the latter, and the former are more indispensable to overall human well-being.

Finally, it is also worth noting that the cognitive conditions of autonomy are arguably easier to attain on one's own as an adult than are the moral conditions, because the moral conditions are habits that require a long period of time to develop, and good moral habits become more difficult to develop as one grows older (because of longstanding bad habits that need to be uprooted), while the cognitive conditions can be acquired relatively quickly and are not time sensitive to the same degree. It is true that someone whose education does not promote autonomy may lack a *commitment* to critical rational reflection, and not merely sufficient exposure to diverse ways of life. (I have argued already that a solid academic education in itself enables children to develop at least a basic *capacity* for critical rational reflection.) Yet if our primary concern is autonomy's *instrumental* value for leading a good life, the lack of commitment to ongoing rational evaluation of one's beliefs is less important than the lack of capacity, given that unhappiness or dissatisfaction with a particular way of life is itself an impetus for reflecting critically on one's conception of the good. It is also true that one can become attached to long-held beliefs, and thus more hesitant to revise such beliefs even when new evidence comes to light that would warrant such a revision. Nonetheless, attachment to beliefs simply because one has held them for a long time is the result of sub-rational influences, the remedy for which is *moral* virtue, not primarily more knowledge or improved critical thinking skills.

The autobiographical essays in *Religious Upbringing and the Costs of Freedom: Personal and Philosophical Essays* are instructive in this regard. The book consists of philosophers' reflections on their own experiences as children raised in traditional religious families whose parents attempted to shelter them to varying degrees from sympathetic exposure to conflicting ways of life. In many cases, their upbringing seems to have been of the sort that Callan believes would lead to "ethical servility." These philosophers have since rejected their parents' beliefs in whole or in part, and they have mixed opinions regarding whether or not it should be considered within the bounds of parental rights (moral and/or legal) to deny their children broader and more sympathetic exposure to diverse ways of life. Nonetheless, even the accounts of the authors who take a strong stance in favor of mandatory autonomy education seem to confirm my point that one can attain the cognitive conditions of autonomy with relative ease as an adult – in the cases of the book's authors, the distancing from parents' beliefs usually occurred in college. Further, though it is impossible to prove, because the authors themselves do not distinguish the inculcation of moral virtue from other aspects of their upbringing, one might conjecture that the development of a strong moral character due at least partially to the way in which they were raised may have been an important factor in enabling them to break away from the beliefs of their parents despite the emotional difficulties that such a choice always involves. It is also worth noting that the biggest complaint of the authors most critical of their upbringing was the psychological cost involved in rejecting their parents' beliefs. Such a cost, however, is not specific to situations in which children reject the beliefs of their traditional religious families in favor of a more liberal worldview. Rather, such a cost is always involved when children reject their parents' beliefs in a radical way, regardless of whether the children reject traditional beliefs in favor of more liberal ones, or reject their parents' liberal beliefs in order to embrace a totalistic faith or some other more conservative conception of the good.[67]

Conclusion

In this chapter I have offered several lines of response to those who argue that the promotion of children's well-being requires mandatory autonomy education even against the objections of conscientious parents who believe that it is in the best interests of their children to shelter them from competing conceptions of the good life. First, I have pointed out that, as implied by my argument in the last chapter, mandatory autonomy education cannot be justified on civic grounds alone. Given the account of parental authority and parental rights defended in the first two chapters, child-centered coercive state interference with parents' child-rearing decisions (as distinct from interference on civic grounds) is

[67] Peter Caws and Stefani Jones, ed., *Religious Upbringing and the Costs of Freedom: Personal and Philosophical Essays* (University Park, PA: Pennsylvania State University Press, 2010).

justified only in cases of abuse and neglect. But – unless we stretch the definition of abuse and neglect so far that it includes any serious parental decision with which the state disagrees – to shelter one's children from diverse conceptions of the good life is neither abusive nor neglectful. In fact, as I have argued, it may even be beneficial.

Second, I argued, in dialogue with Callan, that denying children an education that takes them beyond what he considers to be a "minimal threshold of autonomy" is not a failure to respect their equal moral worth, since parental childrearing authority protects parents' right to fulfill their perceived obligations, not (even minimally) their autonomy. I pointed out, further, that Callan's claims about the minimal threshold of autonomy necessary to lead a good life are implausible, or at least inseparable from his controversial Rawlsian liberal conception of the good life.

Finally, I argued that while advocates of mandatory autonomy education are right to note the instrumental value of autonomy for leading a good life, their arguments are insufficient to show that those who receive an explicitly autonomy-promoting education are, on balance, better prepared to lead a good life than those whose parents shelter them from competing conceptions of the good life. For while the latter are more likely to end up without a commitment to ongoing rational revision of their values, and to lack sympathetic understanding of diverse ways of life, the former (particularly if the values taught in school conflict sharply with those taught at home), are more likely to end up morally confused, incapable of the steadfastness and commitment required for autonomous adherence to a conception of the good, lacking moral virtue more generally, or succumbing to the ever-present temptations to substance abuse, irresponsible sexual conduct, and other problem behaviors that can have long-lasting negative consequences. In addition, I argued that MacMullen overstates his case for the *distinctive* value of autonomy education, given that many of its instrumental benefits are also attainable through a strong academic education more generally.

However, my account does *not* imply that there is no place at all for autonomy education in schools. Indeed, the Aristotelian view that I have presented itself speaks in favor of teaching critical thinking skills and encouraging rational reflection on one's beliefs, in part by engaging with conflicting points of view. Yet this has to be done at the right times and in the right ways so as to avoid the dangers of undermining parental moral authority and/or producing moral confusion in those too immature to benefit from a critical approach to their own values and exposure to alternative worldviews. Thus my view would support, or at least be compatible with, *non*-mandatory autonomy education programs – programs with an "opt-out" option, or programs offered in situations where even poor parents have feasible alternatives to public schools – with an emphasis on character education especially (but not only) in elementary and middle school. Such programs should be non-mandatory, even if they correctly prioritize the moral conditions of autonomy, both out of respect for the rights of conscientious parents who believe that the programs may be harmful to their children, and out of a concern that, precisely in cases where parents and the school have rival approaches to moral education, the lack of coherence in moral education may be more harmful to children than the lack of exposure to alternative views. Further, worries about the inability of standardized autonomy curricula to consider differences in the moral maturity of children at the same grade level, or about the possibly deleterious effects of exposing children to contradictory views too early or in the wrong way, would be mitigated if parents were more involved in designing and implementing such curricula, had the effective ability to choose a school in line with their values, and could exempt their children from classes that they judged to be potentially harmful.

My aims in this chapter have been, first, to show that concern for the development of children's autonomy need not be incompatible with robust parental discretionary rights over education – including the right to deny children sympathetic exposure to alternative ways of life – and, second, to call attention more generally to the importance of the moral prerequisites for autonomy, and for leading a good life more generally, which the discussion on this issue has thus far largely ignored. Even for those not fully convinced by my view in its entirety, this second consideration is one that anyone concerned about children's well-being should take into account when trying to determine which educational methods and policies would best promote that goal.

5

Policy implications

Overview

In the preceding chapters I have argued for a robust notion of parental rights to direct the education of their children with minimal coercive state interference. At the heart of debates about the scope and limits of parental educational authority as against state educational authority is the question: To whom do children "belong"? Some, like Amy Gutmann, believe that children "belong" to the larger political community at least as directly as to their families, in the sense that the educational authority of the political community is on the same plane as the educational authority of parents. Indeed, on this view, the state even has a certain primacy, since it is the political community that determines how educational authority is divided among parents, the state and (for Gutmann) professional educators. Such a view would be compatible with laws against homeschooling, with laws requiring all children to attend state-run schools, with compulsory comprehensive sex education, civic education or autonomy education in all schools, and with a denial of exemptions from educational regulations for objecting parents like the plaintiffs in *Wisconsin v. Yoder* and *Mozert v. Hawkins*.

By contrast, I have defended the claim that children "belong" primarily to their parents. In other words, children are *primarily* and *directly* members of families, and only *secondarily* and *indirectly* members of the larger political community, because the intimate relationship between parent and child gives parents the most direct and immediate special obligation to care for and exercise paternalistic authority over their children. Further, on my view, because parental authority is based on intrinsic features of the parent–child relationship, the authority of parents is *natural* and *original*, not *conventional* or *derivative* of the authority of the state or larger community. Thus the childrearing authority of parents and the state are on different planes, with paternalistic state authority over children ordinarily exercised only via the mediation of parental authority, and aimed at helping rather than replacing parents in their educational task.

Since, on my account, parents' authority is grounded on parents' special obligations to their children, parental rights can be conceived of not only as protecting parental authority, but also as protecting parents' conscience rights, their right to integrity understood as a negative right to fulfill one's perceived obligations.[1] Because parental obligations are personal, and therefore non-transferable, the state cannot absolve parents of their educational obligations by stepping in to educate children in their stead. In this sense, parental rights are much like free exercise rights that protect individuals' ability to fulfill their perceived religious obligations – many of which must be carried out personally. While parents often rightfully seek the assistance of others in raising and educating their children, the primary responsibility to direct and oversee their children's upbringing belongs personally to *them*, and fulfilling that responsibility conscientiously is central to their own overall flourishing as persons. Thus when educational regulations require parents to allow their children to be exposed to certain ideas or a particular educational environment which they believe is potentially harmful, they face a situation in which fulfilling their perceived parental obligations becomes nearly impossible. Either they must break the law (and risk having their child taken from their custody as a result), or they must knowingly place their child in harm's way. Given the primacy of parental educational authority, the fundamental importance of conscience rights, and the central role of childrearing in the personal fulfillment of parents,[2] it is unjust to place parents in such a situation unless there is no less burden some way to achieve a compelling state interest.

Some argue that one such compelling interest is the education of future citizens. I considered this concern in Chapter 3, in dialogue with Rawlsian liberal theorists who believe that mandatory education for

---

[1] Note that for many parents, childrearing obligations are not only moral but also religious, and thus the good of religion – of harmony with God understood as the transcendent source of existence and meaning – is at stake in addition to the good of integrity. In such cases, parents' claim is arguably even weightier, due to the distinctive and uniquely important role that the good of religion plays in the life of someone fully aware of its demands. On this point, see my "Beyond Equal Liberty": Religion as a Distinct Human Good and the Implications for Religious Freedom," *Journal of Law and Religion* (forthcoming, 2016).

[2] On the natural law view, fulfilling one's parental responsibilities well is a central aspect of human flourishing with respect to marriage and family life.

Rawlsian liberal citizenship is essential for the preservation of a liberal democratic society. In response, I argued that the claims of these theorists rest on a specifically Rawlsian understanding of liberalism and of the virtues essential to good liberal citizenship, an understanding which is highly controversial even among liberals. I also pointed out, following William Galston, that there are other elements within liberalism that would speak in favor of a more pluralistic approach to civic education that is more accommodating to non-liberal ways of life, and that non-liberal ways of life actually make an important contribution to the health of a liberal society. On these grounds I argued that the state lacks a clear compelling interest in mandatory Rawlsian civic education.

I then offered a more general framework for determining the scope and limits of state authority with regard to citizenship education. While citizenship education is an important state interest, I argued that there are limits on the means by which the state can pursue that interest. The conscience rights of parents, and their natural authority over their children, are among those limits. In general, when a state interest is in conflict with a fundamental right of individual citizens, the state is justified in pursuing that interest by coercive means only if the interest is truly compelling, and only if there are no less burden some means of achieving that interest. Applying this general normative framework to the issue of civic education, I claimed that the state ought to tolerate forms of citizenship education which it considers imperfect, within the bounds of certain minimal requirements which the state has a compelling interest to enforce even against the conscientious objections of parents. Based on these criteria, I concluded that a policy of mandatory Rawlsian civic education would be unjust because it infringes on the conscience rights and authority of some parents and does not promote a state interest that is compelling enough to justify such infringement.

Finally, in the last chapter I addressed the concern that granting overly broad educational authority to parents may be harmful to children. Specifically, many liberal theorists worry that allowing parents to shelter their children from competing conceptions of the good life may constitute a failure to respect children's interest in becoming autonomous adults. These theorists, such as Eamonn Callan, Harry Brighouse and Ian MacMullen, argue that the state should ensure that all children receive an education that facilitates their future autonomy, even if elements of such an education may conflict with the values that parents believe they are obligated to pass on to their children. I responded to these concerns by pointing out, first of all, that child-centered coercive state intervention in childrearing (as opposed to intervention on civic grounds) is justified only in cases of abuse and neglect, and that the failure to provide autonomy education does not meet that justificatory bar. Secondly, I argued that an Aristotelian account of moral development, which emphasizes the importance of the *moral* prerequisites for autonomy, rather than just the cognitive or intellectual prerequisites, gives reasons to believe that those who lack moral maturity are not prepared to reasonably assess the relative merits of different worldviews. To be capable of choosing rationally among rival visions of the good life, without such a choice being dictated effectively by sub-rational desire, moral virtue is essential. Sympathetic exposure in school to values in conflict with those that parents teach at home, together with encouragement to adopt a critical attitude toward one's parents' values, is likely to undermine children's still fragile self-mastery by calling into question the moral authority of parents and the principles that have undergirded their early moral education. Empirical evidence further supports this perspective by indicating the neurobiological limitations on adolescent decision-making, and shows that positive childrearing outcomes are associated with clear and consistent parental discipline as well as coherence in the expectations and values of parents, school and community groups.

The claim that parents have rights to raise their children free from all but the most minimal coercive state interference is ultimately a claim about authority. Working out the scope and limits of parental rights requires determining the proper sphere of parental authority as against state authority, and also determining how to adjudicate the competing claims of parents and the state where those spheres of authority overlap. In the preceding chapters I have argued that parental authority derives from the very nature of the parent–child relationship.[3] That authority extends in scope over the whole sphere of decisions and actions regarding the provision of children's developmental needs at all levels, and extends in time until the point at which children become competent to provide for their own needs and direct their own process of personal development.[4]

---

[3] Although I have not emphasized this aspect of the argument, parental authority also derives from respect for the basic human good of marriage, which includes the right and responsibility to raise the children which may result from one's marital union.

[4] From a moral (rather than legal) perspective, parental authority admits of degrees because it exists in virtue of children's needs. Thus while legally it is necessary to establish an age at which children are granted full legal rights to direct their own lives, at which point parents cease to hold legal authority over and responsibility for their children, from a moral

It is true, of course, that aside from being members of families, children are also members of the larger political community.[5] That political community, via the authorities which govern it, has certain responsibilities and related rights with regard to children. Charged with the promotion of the common good, which includes the individual good of all members of the community, the political authority has a responsibility to concern itself with the well-being of children, and also to take measures to facilitate the ordered reproduction of society over time. However, if I am correct that parents are the ones with primary paternalistic authority over children, and that parental authority is original rather than derivative of the state's authority over children, the state's responsibility for children's well-being is a subsidiary one which ought to be carried out in a subsidiary way – i.e. by facilitating the task of parents and helping children through the mediation of their parents, rather than attempting to help children in ways that usurp, oppose or simply bypass parental authority. Only in situations of genuine abuse and neglect may the state step in to exercise paternalistic authority over children in a direct and immediate way, because in those cases parental authority has lost its legitimacy.

The state's responsibility to facilitate the ordered reproduction of society over time (which includes concern for the education of future citizens) is limited for different, though related reasons. In establishing

perspective parental authority gradually recedes as children mature to the point at which they are capable of governing themselves. Parental responsibility to provide for children's material needs, as well as parental moral authority, usually extend beyond the legal age of majority, but also usually begin to diminish before legal adulthood. As children mature – here I mean genuine maturity, not simply a physical passing of years – parental authority takes on more of an advisory than obligatory nature, and parents can also rightfully expect that children begin at least helping to provide for their own needs and contribute to the family economy. Further, in extreme cases of conflict between parents and legal minors who are in fact mature enough to govern themselves, the children can seek legal emancipation before they reach age eighteen. In such cases the state is not intervening in an internal family dispute, but deciding whether or not to grant the status of legal majority (with its attendant rights and responsibilities) to someone who has not yet reached the normal age of legal majority. Such a decision is of a fundamentally different character than a decision in which the state, while leaving a child under parental authority, steps in to overrule parents' judgment regarding what would be in the child's best interests.

[5] In some cases, they may also be members of other authoritative communities, such as churches. To the extent that this is the case, those other communities may also have certain responsibilities toward and authority over children, but, like the responsibilities and authority of the political community, they are subsidiary to those of the parents and should generally function in a mediate way through and in cooperation with the authority of parents (rather than in opposition to or in place of parental authority).

policies in pursuit of this important aspect of the common good – just as in the establishment of policies aimed at the pursuit of any aspect of the common good – the state ought to avoid infringements on individual rights whenever possible. This is, moreover, not simply an ad hoc constraint on the pursuit of the common good. For since the good of each individual is a constitutive part of the common good of the community, the protection of individual rights is, to the extent to which those rights are serious and fundamental, at the very core of the common good itself. A policy aimed at maintaining the public order either in the short run or over time therefore simply fails to promote the common good if it does so at the unnecessary cost of infringing individual rights. The word "unnecessary" is an important qualification, however. Where the state seeks a good that is genuinely compelling, such that failure to achieve it will result, either immediately or over the long term, in societal breakdown or grave violation of the fundamental rights of others, and where there are no less burden some means of achieving that good, it may justifiably infringe on some individual rights. I say "some" individual rights because, in the case of a genuinely inviolable right – a right that protects a basic and fundamental aspect of human well-being, such as the right to life – there will be no case in which infringement is justified. Other rights, such as the right to freedom of speech, or the right to vote, may justifiably be infringed in some circumstances because these rights protect goods that are only instrumentally important to human well-being.

One right which is unique in this regard is the right to moral integrity, often referred to as the right to freedom of conscience. This right does protect a basic and fundamental aspect of human well-being, because to flourish as a human person is, centrally, to flourish morally. However, conscience rights are unique by comparison with other fundamental rights because they protect a right to act on one's *subjective* understanding of the requirements of morality, and thus they sometimes protect a right to do what is wrong insofar as the agent sincerely believes it to be morally obligatory. In such cases, the state may at times pursue a policy that infringes on conscience rights when what individuals believe themselves to be obligated to do conflicts with equally important rights of others or seriously undermines a compelling state interest.[6] For example,

---

[6] When the individual's subjective understanding of his moral obligations is objectively correct, I believe that in principle there can never be a genuine conflict with a correct assessment of the requirements of the political common good. Whenever such a conflict

the state can protect children's rights by forbidding physical abuse, even though this may infringe on the conscience rights of some parents who believe that they have a moral obligation to discipline their children through the use of severe and health-threatening corporal punishment. Likewise, the state can seek to promote the ordered reproduction of society over time (and also foster the well-being of children) by enforcing certain minimal educational requirements that will enable children to be self-supporting and law-abiding as adults, and that will ensure that all citizens have at least a basic knowledge of their civic rights and duties. However, both because the state is fallible in its assessment of the requirements of the common good, and because of the fundamental importance of conscience rights, even when promoting compelling state interests the state should seek to design policies in such a way that they are as narrowly tailored as possible to the promotion of that interest in order to avoid conflict with the conscience rights of citizens, and the state should also be generous in granting exemptions from general laws to protect conscience rights insofar as it is feasible and does not significantly undermine the goal of the policy.

Policy implications

In order to illustrate what my account of parental rights in education might imply in practice, in this section I will briefly discuss some of the policy implications of my view. Some of these implications have already been mentioned in passing in earlier chapters, but a more complete discussion of them requires bringing together the various aspects of my argument for parental rights. Note that, even when discussing court cases, I will be assessing policies from a *moral* perspective, not a constitutional one. The constitutionality of the policies is a separate question, and I do not deal with it here. Thus it is possible, for instance, to agree in principle that the Amish families in *Wisconsin v. Yoder* had a moral right to an exemption, even if one thinks that granting such an exemption is

---

seems to arise it is either because the individual has wrongly judged his moral obligation or the state has wrongly judged the requirements of the common good. Nonetheless, since in practice the state will sometimes err with regard to judgments about the requirements of the common good, there may be cases in which the state legitimately (based on beliefs about the requirements of the common good) infringes on the conscience rights of those who are correct in their assessment of their own moral obligations. The fallibility of the state in this regard is one more reason to err on the side of protection for individual conscience rights in borderline cases.

outside the scope of judicial authority. Political and economic feasibility are also important considerations that I leave to the side in my discussion, because my aim here is simply to clarify in broad terms the moral boundaries of state educational authority, not to make detailed, positive policy recommendations.

Exemptions and accommodations

The two most widely-discussed court cases in the literature on parental rights – *Wisconsin v. Yoder* and *Mozert v. Hawkins* – deal with the question of whether or not the state has an obligation to accommodate parents who object to some aspect of the education laws or curricular requirements. In *Yoder*, Old Order Amish parents sought an exemption from Wisconsin's compulsory education statute in order to school their children at home and teach them a non-standard curriculum that would prepare them for life in the Amish community. In *Mozert*, by contrast, the parents had not been accused of violating education laws. In this case the parents are not defendants but plaintiffs, seeking to force an uncompromising school board to grant them an accommodation. Because they objected to the content of the school's reading curriculum – which, in addition to teaching the relevant academic skills, also sought to expose children to diverse ways of life in conflict with the plaintiffs' values – the parents sought the right to teach their children an alternative reading curriculum in line with their beliefs while keeping them in the public school. Do the parents in these cases have a right to the accommodations that they seek, and, more generally, what are the principled limits on such accommodations?

Wisconsin v. Yoder

First, let us consider *Yoder*. As mentioned in Chapter 3, Wisconsin's compulsory education law, and the minimal curricular requirements it established for compliance with that law, seem just in principle. Those laws provide reasonable regulations to ensure that all children receive an education for minimally decent citizenship. In principle, therefore, those laws are within the state's proper sphere of authority and do not unduly limit parental discretionary authority. Yet the overall environment of the public schools was infused with worldly values to which the Amish did not want their children to be exposed, especially in the impressionable years of early adolescence. Further, having their children engaged full time in academic learning even at home would make it impossible for the parents to provide their children with the vocational training they considered essential. The real problem, therefore, was that the parents believed themselves to have a serious religious and moral obligation to prepare their children for the Amish way of life, and that the state's requirements made that impossible as a practical matter.

It is interesting to note that the decision to prosecute in this case did not seem to be motivated either by a concern that the education the Amish were providing for their children would insufficiently prepare them to be law-abiding and productive citizens, or that it unduly limited the children's future life options. Rather, Superintendent Kenneth Glewen would have been happy to let the Amish do as they wished on the condition that they send their children to the public high school for the first couple of weeks, which would be sufficient for the children to be counted among the school's pupils for the purpose of funding allocation. When the Amish refused to comply with such an unprincipled scheme, Glewen retaliated by filing a complaint with the district attorney.[7]

Nonetheless, let us imagine for the sake of argument that the state had legitimate motivations in prosecuting the Amish parents for failing to comply with the compulsory education statutes. According to the standard I have defended, laws that burden conscience rights are justified only if they are necessary to achieve a compelling state interest, and are narrowly tailored to the achievement of that interest. There are two possible compelling state interests at stake in *Yoder*: (1) educating children to be law-abiding and productive citizens and (2) protecting children from abuse and neglect. If exempting the Amish is compatible with these two interests, then the government can and should tailor the compulsory education law more narrowly (by exempting the Amish) in order to avoid the burden on conscience rights.

First, therefore, we need to ask whether or not the Amish method of education will prepare their children to be law-abiding and productive citizens. Given that the Amish community has been exemplary throughout the nation's history in terms of producing law-abiding, peace-loving, self-supporting citizens, there is clearly no case to be made that the

---

[7] See Shawn Francis Peters, *The Yoder Case* (Lawrenceville, KS: University Press of Kansas, 2003), 32. Peters points out that Glewen's decision to prosecute was also "influenced by legitimate concerns over maintaining discipline in the local schools" (33). Nonetheless, the fact that Glewen was willing to let the Amish do as they wished, provided that their doing so would not lead to a reduction of state funding, seems to indicate that those legitimate concerns alone would not have led him to prosecute.

education they have traditionally provided to their children will fail to prepare them for at least minimally decent citizenship. One might argue that if the Amish community were to become a sizable portion of the population we might effectively cease to live in a democracy, because the Amish eschew political participation on principle. As an empirical matter, this seems highly unlikely to happen. Yet even if it did, that would simply mean that a minority of non-Amish would effectively govern the majority Amish population. As long as the rights of the Amish (as well as all other citizens) are respected, there would be nothing wrong in principle with such an arrangement. Given that allowing the Amish to educate their children in accordance with their beliefs would pose no clear threat to the survival of a just public order even in the long run, there is no justification in this case for overriding the presumption in favor of accommodation when just laws conflict with parental rights.

What about the rights of the children? Perhaps, by denying their children two additional years of conventional schooling, Amish parents are effectively guilty of abuse or neglect. From a non-Amish perspective, the vocational education that the Amish parents offer to their high-school-age children does not sufficiently foster the development of the child's intellectual capacities, and is therefore defective in that regard. Yet the education offered in many of America's public high schools is academically defective as well, with a recent assessment indicating that only 26% of high school seniors are performing at or above grade level in math, and only 38% in reading.[8] Another study found that the top twenty books assigned in high schools have an average reading level of 5.3 (just beyond fifth-grade level).[9] Moreover, even when it is successful academically, conventional high school education often fails to help children mature with regard to technical knowledge and abilities, or with regard to work ethic, responsibility and other values that the Amish emphasize. From an Amish perspective, excessive intellectual development is harmful to one's prospects for eternal salvation, and it is important to immerse children in the Amish way of life particularly during the impressionable years of adolescence. Based on their beliefs, therefore, the Amish are acting in the best interests of their children. Given that the moral and

---

[8] 2013 National Assessment of Educational Progress. Available at: www.nationsreportcard .gov/reading_math_g12_2013/#/. Last accessed on January 12, 2015.

[9] *What Kids are Reading*, Renaissance Learning, 2015. Available at: www.doc.renlearn.com/ KMNet/R004101202GH426A.pdf. Last accessed on January 12, 2015.

religious education of children is at the very center of parents' rightful
sphere of authority, on a controversial question about what constitutes
the best interests of the child the parents' judgments should be respected.
As the Court recognizes, there is nothing in the Amish parents' conduct
that comes even close to counting as abuse or neglect: "The record
strongly indicates that accommodating the religious objections of the
Amish by forgoing one, or at most two, additional years of compulsory
education will not impair the physical or mental health of the child."[10]
The state, therefore, has no warrant to interfere on the children's behalf.

A slightly different concern is raised by Justice Douglas in his partial
dissent. Douglas argues that, given the age of the children, their own
views about the matter should have been consulted. As Justices Stewart
and Brennan point out in their concurrence, one of the children, Frieda
Yoder, did testify to the effect that she does not want to attend the public
high school because it would be contrary to her own religious beliefs.
Douglas argues that the other two children in the case should have been
given the opportunity to state their views as well. Whether or not
Douglas is right about his claim that, as a constitutional matter, the
Court ought not to have decided the case without hearing from all of
the children involved, as a moral matter his point is worth considering.
As a matter of moral principle, as children mature to the point of being
able to make reasoned moral judgments for themselves, parents ought to
respect those judgments. However, as the psychological and neurobiological evidence cited in the previous chapter indicates, it is also the case
that a child mature enough to make reasoned moral judgments may still
lack the requisite experience and insight to be able to judge well in many
situations, as well as the self-mastery necessary to consider what would
be truly best in a cool-headed way, rather than devising sophisticated
rationalizations to justify the gratification of sub-rational desires. Parents
are the ones in the best position to know the difference between a child's
sincere and mature moral convictions, on the one hand, and, on the other
hand, spurious rationalizations or judgments reflecting a lack of experience and insight regarding what really matters. The state, lacking knowledge of the child that comes anywhere near that of parents, is not well-
equipped to make such judgments. Further, given that even a child's
sincere judgment about what is in his or her own best interests may still
be wrong due to lack of experience or the limitations of an immature

[10] 406 U.S. 234.

brain (see Chapter 4), parents are still the ones obligated to make the final decision (though they should take the child's own judgment of the matter into account). Parents are the ones with the authority to decide whether or not the child's wishes on any particular matter should be followed or not. To give the courts that authority would therefore be an unjust intrusion on parents' sphere of authority (except, as always, in cases where parents are exercising that authority in ways that are tantamount to genuine abuse or neglect).

For the sake of argument, let us suppose that Barbara Miller, the high-school-age child of another plaintiff in the case, had thought carefully about the matter and desired to continue her formal academic education by attending the public high school. Did the Court do Barbara an injustice by failing to consider her perspective on the matter? No, because neither the Court, nor any other organ of the state, possesses the authority to intervene in this dispute between Barbara and her parents. The parents' educational decisions in this case neither threaten the public order nor constitute abuse or neglect; there is therefore no justification for coercive state action. It is true that from a moral perspective, Barbara's parents ought to listen carefully to Barbara's request for further conventional schooling. If after a sincere dialogue with Barbara they deem her views to be the result of mature and thoughtful judgment, and do not think that there are important countervailing factors she has failed to consider or is too inexperienced to understand, they should allow her to attend the public high school. They might disagree with the decision and try to persuade her to change her mind, but if they think her decision is a mature one they should not prevent her from following it.

However, even if – because of an erroneous judgment on their part, or simply because they do not take Barbara's views as seriously as they should – they fail to honor Barbara's desire to attend high school, that educational decision is still within their sphere of authority and the state has no right to intervene.[11] Parents are the ones with the authority to make controversial decisions about what type of education is in the best interests of their children. That means that the state needs to honor

---

[11] If, hypothetically, Barbara's disagreements with her parents in this regard were serious enough, she could also seek legal emancipation. Barring such action on Barbara's part, however, Barbara remains within her parents' sphere of authority until the age of legal majority, and coercive intervention on the part of the state without sufficient justification – i.e. except in cases of abuse, neglect, or threat to the public order – would amount to an unjust usurpation of that authority.

parents' decisions in this regard even when it disagrees with the parents' judgment, excluding cases of abuse and neglect, and within the limits set by the requirements of public order. If the parents are convinced that the Amish way of life is truly the best one, and that Barbara needs further education in Amish values before she can truly make a well-informed decision that effectively involves rejecting that way of life, they may reasonably consider themselves obligated to deny or delay Barbara's request. The age of maturity in the Amish community is 16. If, at that point, Barbara still wants to attend high school in order to prepare herself for a life outside of the Amish community, she will be free to do so. Being one or two years behind her peers in academic learning is not a difficult obstacle to overcome in the long run, especially considering that the education she receives in her community will likely put her ahead of most of her peers in self-discipline, work ethic and the acquisition of many practical skills.

The bottom line is that Douglas was wrong to think that the Court should not have decided the case without listening to the views of each of the children involved. All that the Court needed to determine was that the parents' decision did not constitute abuse or neglect, and that it was compatible with the requirements of public order. Beyond that, the state has no right to interfere with the parents' childrearing methods.

Mozert v. Hawkins

As I have already dealt at some length with *Mozert* in Chapter 3, and devoted Chapter 4 to the issue of autonomy education, here I will only consider the case briefly, bringing together the various strands of argument.

Although in *Mozert* the parents were not being prosecuted but were themselves the ones initiating a lawsuit against the state, as in *Yoder* the case effectively deals with a situation in which parents are seeking relief from unjust state incursions into their rightful sphere of authority, and thus threatening their conscience rights by preventing them from fulfilling their perceived childrearing obligations. The coercive aspect of the state's power is less obvious in *Mozert* because it operates indirectly by effectively penalizing parents financially if they must pay to send their children to alternative schools when the public school curriculum is offensive to their beliefs. *Mozert* presents an example of unjust state coercion only because the public schools have a monopoly on public funding. Given that monopoly, the *Mozert* parents had the right to an accommodation allowing them to exempt their children from the offensive aspects of the reading curriculum and provide alternative instruction, because the state lacks the legitimate authority to enforce that curriculum coercively against the objections of parents.

As I argued in the Chapter 3, the state's interest in exposing children to diverse ways of life is not compelling enough to warrant overriding parents' conscientious objections to the content of the curriculum. Further, in Chapter 4 I made the case that sheltering children from exposure to diverse ways of life is not tantamount to abuse or neglect, and is therefore within the bounds of parental discretionary authority. While I agree that an ideal education would involve teaching critical thinking skills and exposing students to the best arguments in favor of competing views (at the right time and in the right way), the state lacks the authority to enforce this educational ideal on those who disagree with it because such an education is not necessary for the preservation of the public order, and the failure to provide such an education is far from constituting abuse or neglect. Moreover, as I also argued in Chapter 4, exposure to diverse ways of life may be more harmful than helpful to children who have not yet achieved a sufficient level of moral maturity, and parents are the ones who are in the best position to know when children have reached that point.

These conclusions about the *Mozert* case can be generalized to apply to any case in which parents have an objection to some aspect of the public school curriculum. The primacy of parental educational authority means not only, as I argued with regard to *Yoder*, that there should be a presumption in favor of exempting parents even from just educational regulations. It also means a presumption in favor of accommodating parents who want to exempt their children from particular aspects of a public school curriculum that are offensive to their beliefs. Of course, the usual limitations on that presumption – the requirements of public order, and the protection of children from abuse and neglect – apply here as well. Some might object that an overly generous accommodation policy would lead to a flood of exemption requests, creating an administrative nightmare and siphoning resources away from actual educational programs. If this turned out to be the case, that would provide a reason to make the accommodation policy more restrictive – though it would also make the need for effective school choice programs all the more pressing. However, there is no reason to think that parents will abuse a lenient accommodation policy or that such a policy will be unworkable in practice. The state of Minnesota, for example, already has such a policy on the books. The state's education law includes a section on parental curriculum review which reads as follows:

> Each school district shall have a procedure for a parent, guardian, or an adult student, 18 years of age or older, to review the content of the instructional materials to be provided to a minor child or to an adult student and, if the parent, guardian, or adult student objects to the content, to make reasonable arrangements with school personnel for alternative instruction. Alternative instruction may be provided by the parent, guardian, or adult student if the alternative instruction, if any, offered by the school board does not meet the concerns of the parent, guardian, or adult student. The school board is not required to pay for the costs of alternative instruction provided by a parent, guardian, or adult student. School personnel may not impose an academic or other penalty upon a student merely for arranging alternative instruction under this section. School personnel may evaluate and assess the quality of the student's work.[12]

The Minnesota policy is exemplary from the parental rights perspective,[13] and its continued existence (the statute was enacted in 1993) is evidence that such a generous accommodation policy is indeed feasible in practice.

Are exemptions unfair?

Others object to granting exemptions or accommodations not on practical grounds, but as a matter of principle.[14] Brian Barry, for instance,

---

[12] Minnesota Statutes 2014, Section 120B.20.

[13] It is true that the Minnesota policy explicitly denies the state's obligation to pay for alternative instruction, but this is only in cases where school personnel have attempted to make arrangements for alternative instruction but even these arrangements fail to satisfy the parents or students. Perhaps, since public schools enjoy a monopoly on public funding, the state ought at least partially to fund alternative instruction in these instances. Full respect for parental rights in education would, as I argue below, require an end to the public school's monopoly on public educational funding. Nonetheless, given the current situation, Minnesota's policy seems to strike a reasonable balance between protection of parental rights and prudential safeguards for the sake of economic and administrative feasibility, since the state is required to offer acceptable alternative instruction, and in cases where parents deem the alternative still objectionable, seeking a private tutor or buying their own educational materials for a specific subject poses a relatively small financial burden (as opposed to the financial burden involved in paying for a complete education at a private school).

[14] I have incorporated much of the argument in this section into a lengthier defense of robust legal protections for religious freedom and conscience rights in "Beyond Equal Liberty." Here I do not distinguish between claims of conscience and specifically religious claims, but in "Beyond Equal Liberty" I explain the distinction and its implications.

argues that justice does not require making exemptions to general laws when those laws impose a special burden on some individuals due to their religious, cultural or moral beliefs. In fact, granting exemptions could even be considered a form of unfair special treatment. Rather, on Barry's view justice requires equal opportunity, understood as the situation in which everyone has an equal choice set. Neither the fact that some "will make different choices from these identical choice sets, depending on their preferences for outcomes and their beliefs about the relation of actions to the satisfaction of their preferences," nor the fact that for some these preferences and beliefs will be the result of religious, cultural or moral commitments, is any way relevant to claims of justice.[15] All laws, argues Barry, burden some individuals more than others – namely, those individuals who have a strong preference to do what the law forbids. In fact, according to Barry "the essence of law is the protection of some interests at the expense of others when they come into conflict."[16] Barry cites the example of laws against rape, in which "the interests of women who do not want to be raped are given priority over the interests of potential rapists."[17] Likewise, laws against pedophilia prioritize the interests of children over the interests of potential pedophiles. Although "these laws clearly have a much more severe impact on those who are strongly attracted to rape and pedophilia than on those who would not wish to engage in them even if there were no law against them," Barry states quite sensibly that "it is absurd to suggest that this makes the laws prohibiting them unfair."[18] Similarly, claims Barry, those with expensive tastes will receive less satisfaction from their income, but this does not mean that justice requires allocating additional resources to them.[19] Barry argues that costs arising from beliefs should be treated no differently than costs arising from preferences. If, for example, humane slaughter laws require that Jews and Muslims either act against their religious beliefs or forego eating meat altogether, then so be it.[20] There is nothing special about religious or moral convictions, according to Barry, that warrants treating them differently. Both convictions and preferences can be influenced through conscious cultivation, and neither convictions nor preferences are simply a matter of choice. There is no difference between the two, concludes Barry, that is relevant to claims of justice. While exemptions might be granted out of prudence or generosity,

---

[15] Brian Barry, *Culture and Equality* (Cambridge: Harvard University Press, 2001), 32.
[16] Barry, *Culture and Equality*, 34.   [17] Ibid.   [18] Ibid.
[19] Barry, *Culture and Equality*, 35.   [20] Ibid.

justice does not require them. The upshot of Barry's account is that except in rare instances, "either the case for the law (or some version of it) is strong enough to rule out exemptions, or the case that can be made for exemptions is strong enough to suggest that there should be no law anyway."[21]

Barry's argument is powerful, but ultimately unsatisfying because it rests on a problematic understanding of law and a failure to recognize the important difference between preferences and claims of conscience. Law is not, as Barry claims, fundamentally about protecting the interests of some at the expense of others. Indeed, Barry himself seems to assume that we have good reason to protect the interests of those who do not want to be raped against the "interests" of potential rapists. Yet his position does not offer any basis for explaining why this is the case. On my view, law is about promoting the common good, of which the good of each individual is a constitutive aspect. Freedom from sexual violation is an important condition for individual well-being, and engaging in rape is incompatible with the genuine well-being of the rapist himself. My understanding of law explains why we have no reason to take preferences to commit rape (or other immoral acts) into account in making the law (except as a prudential matter), and also explains why laws against rape do not fail to respect the equality of the person inclined to commit rape. For in my view laws against rape protect the genuine interests (the overall human well-being) of both potential rape victims and potential rapists. Preferences to commit rape are unreasonable, and therefore the law is not unjust to those who hold those preferences when it forbids them from acting upon such preferences.[22]

Reasonable preferences – by which I mean preferences to act in a way that is compatible with but not required by practical reasonableness – should be treated in the law as Barry suggests. In other words, when it is a matter of limiting individuals' ability to act in accordance with reasonable preferences, if there is a good enough reason to have the law, then there is usually also a good enough reason to preclude granting exemptions when that law burdens individuals unequally as a result of their preferences. Forbidding individuals from acting in accordance with some of their reasonable preferences is perfectly compatible with the respect

---

[21] Barry, *Culture and Equality*, 39.

[22] In many cases, of course, the common good may require that laws tolerate actions based on unreasonable preferences when prohibition of them would do more harm than good. The grounds and limits of toleration are discussed at greater length in Chapter 3.

for individual well-being that the common good requires, as long as individuals have sufficient liberty to make and pursue a reasonable plan of life. Overall human well-being does not require acting upon all of one's reasonable preferences – indeed, to do so would be impossible. Further, cooperating with others at various levels of association for the pursuit of common goods – which is itself required for human well-being – always involves certain limitations on one's ability to act in accordance with reasonable preferences. Acceptance of such limitations is therefore not only compatible with individual human well-being, but is in fact required by it. There is, then, no injustice involved per se in the legal restriction of actions in accordance with reasonable preferences, because such restrictions are perfectly compatible with the well-being of those burdened by them.

This does not mean that justice places no limits on the extent to which, or the manner in which, law restricts the pursuit of reasonable preferences. In order to serve its function of promoting the common good, the law should avoid unnecessarily restricting individual liberty with regard to the pursuit of reasonable preferences, and should also try to avoid unfairness in distributing the benefits and burdens (among which are the inevitable restrictions on individual liberty) of common life. If a law fails to meet the first requirement, it should be repealed in its entirety. The second requirement applies not to any one law in isolation, but to the body of law as a whole.[23] Failure to meet the second requirement can be remedied only by sweeping changes, not just isolated exemptions. The fact that a particular law disproportionately burdens some individuals by preventing them from acting in accordance with their reasonable preferences is therefore not usually grounds for an exemption. My account of what justice requires when it comes to laws that limit the pursuit of reasonable preferences is thus complementary to, but ultimately in agreement with Barry's, at least in its conclusions.

[23] This is true for laws that burden individuals with regard to the pursuit of reasonable preferences because there is no difference in kind between the sort of burden involved in restricting one type of reasonable preference-satisfaction or another. Determining unfairness in this regard, therefore, requires considering the body of laws as a whole to see if one group's pursuit of reasonable preferences is significantly more burdened overall than that of other groups. When, as I argue below, what is at stake are not reasonable preferences but claims of conscience, the situation is different, because a burden on conscience is more serious in kind, and not only in degree, than a burden on preferences.

Claims of conscience, however, differ importantly from reasonable preferences in a way that Barry's account fails to recognize. Acting on reasonable preferences is compatible with, but not required by, practical reasonableness. It is therefore compatible with, but not a requirement of, human well-being. By contrast, following one's conscience (understood as a dictate of practical reason) is a *requirement* of practical reasonableness. Acting against the dictates of conscience directly damages one's integrity – the harmony among one's feelings, beliefs, judgments, and actions – which is a basic and constitutive aspect of human well-being. There is a crucial difference, therefore, between courses of action that are compatible with practical reasonableness, and courses of action that are required or forbidden by practical reasonableness. Omitting the former is not necessarily harmful to human well-being – indeed, given the variegated nature of the human good, pursuing one aspect of human well-being in any given moment will almost always involve foregoing an opportunity to pursue other aspects of human well-being, the pursuit of which might all be practically reasonable. However, failing to do what reason requires, or doing what reason forbids, always damages human well-being. Laws which forbid individuals from acting in accordance with the dictates of their consciences, therefore, place a burden on those individuals that differs not only in degree, but in kind, from the sort of burden involved in forbidding someone to act in accordance with a reasonable preference. For this reason, a law that requires one to act against a requirement or prohibition of reason is more burdensome in kind, and not only in degree, than a law that limits the pursuit of reasonable preferences. Laws that require one to act against an absolute moral prohibition present the weightiest burden, insofar as positive moral obligations can sometimes be overridden in extenuating circumstances (like the threat of legal punishment),[24] while absolute moral prohibitions admit of no exceptions. There is therefore at least a *prima facie* claim of justice to an exemption from laws that burden conscience by requiring what reason forbids or forbidding what reason requires, although that claim may be defeated in cases where granting it would be incompatible with the protection of others' fundamental rights or the preservation of the public order.

---

[24] For more on this point, see Christopher Tollefsen, "Conscience, Religion and the State," *American Journal of Jurisprudence* 54 (2009): 103ss.

Even with regard to laws that burden conscience rights, however, a further distinction needs to be made between laws that make it very difficult for individuals to follow their consciences, and laws that make it impossible to do so. In the first category we could include Barry's example of humane slaughter laws that may leave many Jews and Muslims with the option of either violating their integrity by acting against their consciences, or refraining from eating meat.[25] Assuming that the plaintiffs in *Mozert* did have the financial means to send their children to a private school more in line with their values, the *Mozert* case is also one in which the lack of an accommodation, combined with the public schools' monopoly on pubic educational funding, makes it difficult but not impossible for the burdened individuals to fulfill their perceived obligations. Given that favoring the common good as I understand it means avoiding the creation of serious legal disincentives to individuals' maintenance of integrity, there seems to be a strong reason to grant an exemption in such cases, even aside from considerations regarding the primacy of parental educational authority. Fairness would also speak in favor of an exemption in cases of this sort, given that the burden on individuals with conscientious objections to a law differs in kind from the burden imposed on those who simply have a reasonable preference to act in a way that the law forbids, but whose consciences do not require them to do so.

The argument for an exemption is even stronger, however, in a second category of cases, in which the law makes it literally impossible for individuals to follow their consciences by fulfilling their perceived obligations, even if they are willing to make considerable sacrifices in order to do so. Barry overlooks the existence of laws in this category, yet some laws that violate parental rights in education would fit this description – for instance, cases like *Mozert* in which the parents object

---

[25] It is important to clarify that, in this case, the conscience rights of those in favor of humane slaughter laws (even those who believe the practice of humane slaughter to be morally required) are in no way violated by exempting some Jews and Muslims from the laws. Conscience rights protect one's ability to direct one's *own* actions in accordance with one's perceived obligations, not to force others to act in accordance with what one believes *their* obligations to be. If some Jews and Muslims engage in slaughter practices that I believe are inhumane, that does not violate *my* conscience, or disproportionately burden my conscience rights unless there are attempts to outlaw humane slaughter entirely, or attempts to require me to cooperate in some way with inhumane slaughter practices (as would be the case, for example, if laws mandated that I serve kosher meat in my restaurant).

to some aspect of the public school curriculum or environment but lack the means to pay for private education or to homeschool their children. *Wisconsin v. Yoder* seems to provide a real-life example of this situation, since the parents had to choose between failing to fulfill their perceived obligations to educate their children at home in the Amish way of life, or risk having their children removed from their care for failure to comply with education laws (in which case they would be even more severely prevented from fulfilling their parenting obligations). Although the state did not actually get to the point of threatening to take the children away from their parents, it might have come to that if the Amish had lost the case and had persisted in their refusal to comply with the compulsory education statutes.

A proper understanding of the relationship among law, the common good and the good of individuals, together with an understanding of the crucial difference between preferences (even reasonable preferences) and moral obligations or claims of conscience, therefore helps us to see why respect for parental rights, understood as a subset of conscience rights, will sometimes require, among other measures, the granting of exemptions from otherwise reasonable educational regulations.

Sexual education

Debates about sexual education in the public schools involve not only claims about the rights of parents to exempt their children, but also concerns about whether the inclusion of sexual education in the curriculum is itself an overreach of state educational authority. Currently, most states mandate or permit some form of sexual education in the public schools. The government claims that it needs to take an active role in educating children about sexuality for two reasons: concern with public health and concern with children's well-being. Both of these are legitimate concerns. However, the state ought to pursue its public health goals without infringing on individual rights (including parents' conscience rights) insofar as this is possible, and the state's responsibility for children's well-being is subsidiary to that of parents, who are the primary educators of children particularly in moral and religious matters. Indeed, almost all state education statutes explicitly affirm this point, not only in general terms but specifically with reference to sexual education. Given that sexual education deals with particularly sensitive issues about which many parents have deeply-held moral and religious convictions, that complete moral neutrality is impossible in the presentation of these issues,[26] and that the nature of the subject would speak in favor of teaching children about it in the intimate and trusting environment of the home, ideally it would be best to avoid teaching about this subject in the public schools altogether. However, since unfortunately many parents fail to fulfill their responsibilities in this regard, and the rate of sexually transmitted infections and teenage pregnancies presents a serious threat to the common good, it may be justified in these circumstances for the government to take a more proactive role by, for example, offering sexual education in public schools (although what the content of those classes ought to be is another issue). Still, given the primacy of parental educational authority particularly on moral and religious matters, schools should consult and inform parents regarding the content of their sexual education curriculum, and, for responsible parents who disagree with the school's approach or simply think it is best to teach their children about these matters at home, there ought to be a relatively easy way to exempt children from the curriculum. Even better, it should arguably be the case that children can only attend the sexual education classes if parents provide explicit permission. This is the usual *modus operandi* in several states, and it seems to be most in line with parental rights given that teaching about sexuality is an extremely sensitive and morally charged task which can be carried out best in an intimate and trusting home environment, and which falls squarely within the most impermeable area of the parents' sphere of authority – the area of moral and religious education. Schools can also indirectly facilitate the sexual education of children by impressing on parents the importance of speaking with their children about these matters, and also by offering classes or educational materials for parents in order to help them fulfill their responsibility in this regard.

Some may argue that the children of parents who want to pass on conservative sexual values might be psychologically harmed by the failure to learn about sex in an open and liberal way, or that, if parents only teach about abstinence and do not inform their children about birth control methods, the children will be more vulnerable to pregnancy and

---

[26] To teach children about how to make responsible decisions in the area of sexuality without making any reference to moral considerations is, in itself, a failure of neutrality, because, for those who believe that decisions about sex are irreducibly moral, to teach about sex in an amoral way is already a distortion of the truth. Obviously, this applies only to classes about sexual decision-making and behavior, not to science classes about human reproductive biology.

sexually transmitted infections in the case that they do not live up to their parents' expectations. These objections, however, are based on controversial moral views and empirical predictions which are not borne out by the research.[27] Further, it is important to distinguish between two different types of claims in support of mandatory comprehensive sex

---

[27] There is significant debate about the relative effectiveness of abstinence-only sexual education versus comprehensive or "abstinence-plus" sexual education. While some studies claim that abstinence-only programs are ineffective or less effective than comprehensive or abstinence-plus programs, others have found them to be more effective, and none has found them to have a *negative* impact. For instance, a study conducted by Jemmott et al., which was a randomized controlled experimental study, found after a two-year follow-up that the abstinence-only program reduced the rate of sexual initiation by one-third in comparison with the control group, and those who did become sexually active were not less likely to use contraception. Jemmott et al. also evaluated two other programs, one contraception-only program, and one comprehensive sexual education program, finding that neither program delayed nor reduced teen sexual activity, or increased contraceptive use [J. B. Jemmott et al., "Efficacy of a Theory-Based Abstinence-Only Intervention Over 24 Months," *Archives of Pediatrics and Adolescent Medicine* 164, 2 (2010): 152–159]. We cannot really draw fully-informed conclusions about the relative effectiveness of abstinence-only versus comprehensive sexual education until more randomized controlled experimental studies on the effectiveness of abstinence-only sexual education programs are conducted. There are, however, already a number of quasi-experimental studies indicating that abstinence-only programs can be effective. See, for example, Stan Weed, Irene H. Ericksen, Allen Lewis, Gale E. Grant and Kathy H. Wibberly, "An Abstinence Program's Impact on Cognitive Mediators and Sexual Initiation," *American Journal of Health Behavior* 31, 1 (2008): 60–73; Stan E. Weed, Irene H. Ericksen and Paul James Birch, "An Evaluation of the Heritage Keepers Abstinence Education Program," Institute for Research and Evaluation (Salt Lake City), November 2005, at www.heritageservices.org/Stan%20Weed's%20HHS%20Conference%20article .pdf ; Robert Lerner, "Can Abstinence Work? An Analysis of the Best Friends Program," *Adolescent & Family Health* 3, 4 (April 2005): 185–192; Robert Rector and Christine Kim, "Abstinence Education Works: A Review of 15 Evaluations on the Effectiveness of Abstinence Programs," The Heritage Foundation, April 2007, www.abstinence.net/pdf/contentmgmt/Abstinence_Works__15_Evaluations.pdf; Christine Kim and Robert Rector, "Evidence on the Effectiveness of Abstinence Education: An Update," The Heritage Foundation, February 2010, www.heritage.org/research/reports/2010/02/evidence-on-the-effectiveness-of-abstinence-education-an-update#_ftnref36; G. Denny and M. Young, "An Evaluation of an Abstinence-Only Sex Education Curriculum: An 18-month Follow-Up," *Journal of School Health* 76, 8 (2006): 414–422; Andrew S. Doniger, "Impact Evaluation of the 'Not Me, Not Now' Abstinence-Oriented, Adolescent Pregnancy Prevention Communications Program, Monroe County, New York," *Journal of Health Communications* 6 (2001): 45–60; Elaine Borawski et al., "Evaluation of the Teen Pregnancy Prevention Programs Funded through the Wellness Block Grant (1999–2000)," Center for Health Promotion Research, Department of Epidemiology and Biostatistics, Case Western Reserve University, School of Medicine, March 23, 2001; Stan E. Weed, "Title V Abstinence Education Programs: Phase I Interim Evaluation Report to Arkansas Department of Health," Institute for Research and Evaluation, October 15, 2001.

education. The first is a claim that providing comprehensive sexual education in schools is important for children's well-being both psychologically and physically. The second is the public health concern regarding teenage pregnancy and the spread of sexually transmitted diseases. Let us consider these two claims by applying the following principles that I have defended in earlier chapters: (1) Parents have a conscience right to direct their children's education especially in moral and religious matters. (2) The state is only justified in infringing on the conscience rights of parents in cases where what parents think they are obligated to do is tantamount to abuse or neglect, or in cases where the state has a compelling interest that cannot be achieved without such infringement. The first claim is effectively that failing to provide comprehensive sexual education to children is tantamount to abuse or neglect. Yet this is clearly implausible. Ideal parenting would require educating one's children about sexuality, as a proper understanding of sexuality is important for overall personal maturity (though parents may reasonably judge that comprehensive sexual education as it is usually taught in schools actually does not convey a proper understanding of sexuality). But if the failure to provide an adequate sexual education to one's children counts as abuse or neglect, then so do things like the failure to teach children self-mastery by allowing them habitually to indulge their whims. Such a broad definition of abuse or neglect would effectively obliterate all parental discretionary authority and create a warrant for constant state surveillance of and intrusion into family life that would clearly violate parental rights and be harmful for the well-being of parents and children alike. Further, if such were the case, the definition of abuse or neglect would change depending on who is in power, since a liberal government might consider it neglectful to deprive children of comprehensive sexual education, while a conservative one might deem that same education to be harmful and therefore abusive.

What about the claim that mandatory sexual education is necessary for the preservation of public health? Teenage pregnancy and the spread of sexually transmitted infections do constitute important public health concerns, but a policy that mandates sexual education in schools without allowing parents to exempt their children if they have moral or religious objections is unnecessarily broad, particularly given the highly controversial nature of the content of sexual education curricula. In 2011, for instance, New York City adopted a mandatory sexual education policy which allows parents to exempt their children only from specific classes on birth control methods, not from the whole sexual education curriculum.

Even if the public health interest at stake were compelling enough to warrant coercive government action, that interest could be pursued in a way that is much less burden some to the conscience rights of parents. For example, the city could require that all parents provide sexual education to their children either by allowing them to attend classes at school or through instruction provided at home or by churches or other community organizations. They could also consult parents about the content of the school curriculum, thereby making conscientious objections much less likely. In the case where children do not attend the classes at school, parents could be required to offer some proof that their children have received alternative instruction, perhaps in the form of an examination or a written statement from the children summarizing what they learned.

Even such an alternative plan could be problematic especially if the state has detailed and controversial requirements about the content that must be covered in such instruction. For instance, *HealthSmart*, the recommended curriculum for the New York City public schools at the time when the mandatory sexual education policy was adopted, includes discussion of sexual behaviors such as oral sex, anal sex and the use of lubricants as early as sixth grade. Requiring that parents or other community organizations likewise cover such topics in the alternative sexual health instruction that they provide for children would violate the conscience rights of those parents who, for example, think they have an obligation to preserve the innocence of their pre-adolescent children, or who simply believe that a different approach to sexual education would be healthier and more effective. To avoid running foul of parental rights, the minimal content requirements for alternate sexual education would have to be narrowly tailored to the purported compelling state interest – in this case, the prevention of sexually transmitted infections and teenage pregnancy – and would also have to leave room for parental discretion regarding the appropriate age at which to provide such instruction, within certain boundaries. A narrowly tailored policy would also have to allow for legitimate differences of opinion regarding what kind of curriculum best advances the compelling interest in question. Given the evidence that programs focusing exclusively on abstinence can indeed be highly effective, the views of parents who believe that such an abstinence-only approach to sexual education is better for their children should be respected.[28] An alternative plan that meets these requirements would be

---

[28] See footnote 27.

much more in line with parental rights than the New York City policy, while still fulfilling the aims of that policy.

Even such a modified plan could be objectionable, however, given that it still gives the state the power to define and enforce the minimal content requirements for adequate sexual education, a task which in principle falls within the parents' sphere of authority. An even better option, therefore, would be one which eschews coercion entirely. The government could take active measures to inform parents regarding statistics about sexual activity, sexually transmitted infections and pregnancy among middle-school and high-school age children in the community, urge parents to speak with their children about these matters, offer information sessions for parents, and tell parents that optional classes will be offered at the public schools which children can only attend with explicit parental permission. Only if such non-coercive measures fail to ameliorate the public health concerns might the state be justified (if we grant the assumption that there is a compelling interest at stake) in moving to a narrowly tailored coercive plan such as the one I outlined above.

Public schools and school funding

Many of the concerns mentioned in the previous two sections would be greatly ameliorated if the public schools did not have a monopoly on public funding. Ending the selective funding of state-run schools through, for example, charter school and voucher programs, is crucial for bringing current policies into line with the requirements of parental rights. Two guiding principles ought to be kept in mind in this regard. The first is that educational authority and responsibility belong primarily to parents. The second is that the larger political community has an indirect responsibility for the well-being of children, and a direct responsibility for the education of future citizens, though both goals ought to be pursued in ways that respect the primary authority and the conscience rights of parents. A wide variety of educational policies would be in accordance with these principles. A number of prudential (and therefore also morally relevant) considerations would have to be taken into account when determining which particular policies are best for a given community. However, these principles do rule out some policies as unjust. For example, any policy that effectively denies the primacy of parental educational authority is out of bounds. This would include policies according to which compulsory education laws can be fulfilled *only* through public school attendance, or *only* by attending schools that teach a state-approved curriculum (where standards for approval are beyond the civic minimum, as outlined in Chapter 3.) It would also include a policy that would make homeschooling illegal (as it used to be in most of the United States until almost the end of the twentieth century, and as it is in some European countries, such as Sweden and Germany), or which would make homeschooling or private schooling extremely difficult because of excessively burdensome regulations.

Likewise, policies that grant public schools a monopoly on public funding are inherently problematic because they make state-run schools the default option for educating one's children, sending the false message that the state, rather than the parents, has primary responsibility and authority for children's formal education. Such policies also fail to respect the conscience rights and primary educational authority of parents by making it impossible for some, and significantly burdensome for most, to place their children in an educational environment that they consider best-suited to their children's needs and most in line with their values. In other words, public schools' monopoly on public funding skews parents' decision-making about the best environment in which to educate their children, effectively makes public schooling compulsory for those who cannot afford the alternatives, and financially penalizes many other conscientious parents by forcing them to pay for public schools through their taxes, and also, if they choose to send their children to a private school or educate them at home, to pay for private education or homeschooling.[29]

Such is the case, as we have already seen, with the plaintiffs in *Mozert v. Hawkins*. Because the district court denied them the right to exempt their children from the offensive diversity-oriented reading curriculum, and because the public schools have a monopoly on public funding, the parents either had to allow their children to be exposed to beliefs they considered harmful, or face the significant cost (which for some might have been beyond their means) of sending their children to private schools or homeschooling them. If there were effective school choice programs, conflicts like the *Mozert* case could be avoided almost entirely because parents could choose to send their children to the schools that best match their own values. Further, on a school choice model, schools have an incentive to be attentive to and accommodating of concerns like

---

[29] It seems reasonable that parents should be able to use vouchers not only to pay for private school tuition, but also to help pay for homeschooling expenses if they choose to educate their children at home.

those of the *Mozert* parents, because when parents pull their children out of a school in opposition to the curriculum, they take at least part of their funding with them. Providing such financial incentives to school boards that will push them to treat parents as primary educators would itself be a positive development to bring the school system further in line with parental rights.

On principle, therefore, some form of school choice policy seems to be a requirement of respecting the primacy of parental authority and the conscience rights of parents. There are, of course, other important considerations, such as the promotion of racial integration, a concern for the most disadvantaged children, and the promotion of academic excellence. Such considerations can and should certainly be taken into account in the design of school choice programs, but it is important to remember that the means by which we seek to achieve such important policy goals are limited by individual rights. Education policies that fail to respect the primary authority and conscience rights of parents are morally out of bounds.

Some critics of school choice programs in which the state gives parents a voucher that can be used to pay for tuition at a participating private or religious school argue that these programs may run afoul of the First Amendment's prohibition on government establishment of religion by allowing public funds to flow to religious schools if (as is often the case) parents use the voucher to send their children to a religious school.[30] The Supreme Court took up this question in *Zelman v. Simmons-Harris*,[31] ruling that Cleveland, Ohio's voucher program does not run afoul of the First Amendment's Establishment Clause, even though many parents choose to use the vouchers to send their children to a religious school. Chief Justice Rehnquist, writing for the majority, argued that the voucher program involves no government endorsement of religion or direct contribution to religious education, since it makes the funds available to individuals who may then "exercise genuine choice among options public and private, secular and religious."[32] The four dissenting justices, however, were skeptical of this rationale. Justice Stevens, for instance,

---

[30] See for instance, Paul Finkelman, "School Vouchers, Thomas Jefferson, Roger Williams and Protecting the Faithful: Warnings from the Eighteenth and the Seventeenth Century on the Danger of Establishments to Religious Communities," *Brigham Young University Law Review* 2008, 2 (2008): 525–566, as well as the dissenting opinions in *Zelman v. Simmons-Harris* (536 U.S. 639, 2002).

[31] 536 U.S. 639 (2002).   [32] 536 U.S. 662.

argues that "the fact that the vast majority of the voucher recipients who have entirely rejected public education receive religious indoctrination at state expense does . . . support the claim that the law is one 'respecting an establishment of religion.'"[33]

Reframing the issue from a parental rights perspective can help to uncover the flaws in Justice Stevens' reasoning. For if we think of voucher programs as a way in which the state properly exercises its *subsidiary* role in education by providing resources with which *parents* can exercise *their* educational responsibilities, then we should applaud the fact that vouchers make it more feasible for *both* religious and non-religious parents to send their children to a school in line with the values they want to pass on to their children. Since in the United States public schools (including charter schools) are necessarily non-religious due to constitutional restrictions, without vouchers religious parents are actually at a relative disadvantage in comparison with non-religious parents. Thus, granting public schools a monopoly on public funding actually favors non-religion over religion in a way that is arguably unfair to religious parents (and could in itself be seen as an unconstitutional lack of religious neutrality on the part of the state, though making that case would require much further argumentation).

The main reason (at least historically) why public funds have been used for educational purposes is not the state's indirect interest in the well-being of children per se, but rather the state's direct interest in ensuring the ordered reproduction of society over time through the education of children to be law-abiding and productive citizens. This brings us to a second concern voiced in Stevens' dissent and shared by the other minority justices, which is that even an indirect flow of public funds to religious schools will "increase the risk of religious strife and weaken the foundation of our democracy." Justice Souter's dissenting opinion presents some powerful examples of the ways in which vouchers could cause religious strife:

> Religious teaching at taxpayer expense simply cannot be cordoned from taxpayer politics, and every major religion currently espouses social positions that provoke intense opposition. Not all taxpaying Protestant citizens, for example, will be content to underwrite the teaching of the Roman Catholic Church condemning the death penalty. Nor will all of America's Muslims acquiesce in paying for the endorsement of the religious Zionism taught in many religious Jewish schools, which combines

---

[33] 536 U.S. 685.

"a nationalistic sentiment" in support of Israel with a "deeply religious" element. Nor will every secular taxpayer be content to support Muslim views on differential treatment of the sexes, or, for that matter, to fund the espousal of a wife's obligation of obedience to her husband, presumably taught in any schools adopting the articles of faith of the Southern Baptist Convention. Views like these, and innumerable others, have been safe in the sectarian pulpits and classrooms of this Nation not only because the Free Exercise Clause protects them directly, but because the ban on supporting religious establishment has protected free exercise, by keeping it relatively private. With the arrival of vouchers in religious schools, that privacy will go, and along with it will go confidence that religious disagreement will stay moderate.[34]

Justice Souter's observations do provide important reasons for caution, but these concerns are not fatal to a well-designed voucher program. First, there are many things currently taught in the public schools – just think of battles regarding sexual education or the teaching of evolution – to which taxpayers with a variety of religious beliefs or with no religion at all have serious conscientious objections. Forcing all taxpayers to support the secularism and liberal attitude toward sexuality dominant in many public schools seems actually *more* likely to spark religious strife than a situation in which schools that teach a diversity of views (including, at least potentially, one's own views) all have indirect access to public funds through the mediation of parental choice.

Second, Souter's reasonable concern that voucher programs may actually undermine the ability of religious schools to pursue their mission by subjecting them to additional regulations can be avoided if the voucher program is properly designed. In Chapter 3 I argued that the state's legitimate interest in education for citizenship would justify the coercive enforcement of a civic minimum, requiring that all children learn core academic skills and acquire basic knowledge of their civic rights and duties along with a basic understanding of the nation's history and government. I also argued there that concerns about teaching values like tolerance and respect for diversity can be met in a way that accommodates the wide variety of approaches to these values that exist among both religious and non-religious citizens. The tolerance that a pluralistic democracy requires does not imply believing that those with different moral and religious views are equally correct or even that they are good people. Rather, it only implies a commitment to respect others' rights and

[34] 436 U.S. 715.

live in peace with them despite religious, moral and political disagreements, and there are elements in all of the major faith traditions that can be drawn on to support such a commitment. Following the conclusions of my argument in Chapter 3, therefore, there seems to be no compelling reason to burden voucher schools with any requirements beyond a civic minimum. A voucher program designed in line with these principles would not run the risk of interfering with or corrupting the mission of religious schools.

Nor does empirical evidence give any ground to think that the public function of education will be undermined if vouchers lead to an overall shift in educational provision such that fewer children are educated in public schools and more are educated in private and religious schools. On the contrary, the evidence indicates that private and religious schools often do a better job of civic education (and education overall) than public schools, particularly (in the case of religious schools) among the most disadvantaged.[35] And they do so without the sorts of burden some regulations that Souter envisions as needing to accompany a voucher program. A widespread voucher program (or tax rebate program for families with higher incomes) – even one that does not involve new regulations that could undermine the mission and identity of voucher schools – therefore seems at least as likely to fulfill the civic purposes of education than a system in which government-run schools have a monopoly on public educational funding.

Further, the evidence thus far does not support the skeptics' predictions that ending the public schools' monopoly on public educational funding through charter schools and voucher programs will create racial/ethnic stratification or negatively impact those who are worst off by

---

[35] David E. Campbell, "The Civic Side of School Choice: An Empirical Analysis of Civic Education in Public and Private Schools," *Brigham Young University Law Review 2008*, 2 (2008): 487–524; Margaret Brinig and Nicole Garnett, Lost Classroom, *Lost Community: Catholic Schools' Importance in Urban America* (Chicago: University of Chicago Press, 2014); Patrick J. Wolf et al., "Private Schooling and Political Tolerance," in *Charters, Vouchers and Public Education*, ed. Paul E. Peterson & David E. Campbell (Washington, DC: Brookings Institution, 2001), 268, 281; Jay P. Greene, "Civic Values in Public and Private Schools," in *Learning from School Choice*, ed. Paul E. Peterson & Bryan Hassel (Washington, DC: Brookings Institution, 1998): 83, 100–102; Terry Moe, "The Two Democratic Purposes of Education," in *Rediscovering the Democratic Purposes of Education*, ed. L. M. McDonnell, P. M. Timpane and R. Benjamin (Lawrence: University Press of Kansas, 2000), 127; James Coleman and Thomas Hoffer, *Public and Private High Schools: The Impact of Communities* (New York: Basic Books, 1987), 60–79.

siphoning away resources from struggling public schools.[36] In fact, it seems that some of the most disadvantaged groups gain most from school choice programs. A 2013 study found that, while in the aggregate charter schools do not yield consistent academic gains relative to the traditional public schools (although they do show a clear trend toward improvement over time), charter schools had significant positive impacts in both reading and math scores for students in poverty, English language learners, and special education students.[37] Further, some charter schools specifically target the most disadvantaged students,[38] and both charter schools and vouchers at least in principle provide disadvantaged students with school choice opportunities that they otherwise would not have. The positive impact of voucher programs on the academic achievement of voucher users tends to be especially high for African American students,[39] and in some instances vouchers can promote desegregation by providing the means by which African American families can send their children to predominantly-white private schools.[40]

There is also evidence to indicate that vouchers and charter schools will improve academic performance overall through the incentivizing effects of increased competition among schools.[41] A study of the Milwaukee voucher program found that the increased competition from vouchers correlated with statistically significant improvements on test scores in the public schools most affected by the vouchers.[42] Only the Milwaukee program was studied, because, at least at the time, it was the only program widespread and longstanding enough to create significant

---

[36] Ron Zimmerman et al., *Charter Schools in Eight States: Effects on Achievement, Attainment, Integration and Competition* (Santa Monica, CA: The RAND Corporation, 2009).

[37] Edward Cremata et al., *National Charter School Study*, Center for Research on Education Outcomes, Stanford University (2013), http://credo.stanford.edu/documents/NCSS%202013%20Final%20Draft.pdf

[38] For an account of one highly successful charter school that targets the most disadvantaged students in San Jose, California, see Joanne Jacobs, *Our School* (New York: Palgrave MacMillan, 2007).

[39] Patrick J. Wolf, "School Voucher Programs: What the Research Says about Parental School Choice," *Brigham Young University Law Review* 2008, 2 (2008): 415–446.

[40] Deborah E. Beck, "Jenkins v. Missouri: School Choice as a Method for Desegregating an Inner-City School District," *California Law Review* 81, 4 (July 1993): 1029–1057

[41] Cremata et al., *National Charter School Study*.

[42] Caroline Minter Hoxby, "Rising Tide," *Education Next* 1, 4 (Winger 2001): 69–74, www.educationnext.org/rising-tide/. Last accessed on January 14, 2015. See also Clive R. Belfield & Henry M. Levin, "The Effects of Competition Between Schools on Educational Outcomes: A Review for the United States," *Review of Education Research* 72 (2002): 279.

increases in the fluidity of the education market. Studies of charter school programs in Arizona and Michigan also showed significant improvements in the affected public schools as a result (it is hypothesized) of the increased competition.[43]

There may be mixed (though hopeful and never conclusively negative) reports regarding the academic impact of school choice programs overall, but one finding is consistent: parents and students who participate in these programs report significantly higher levels of school satisfaction in comparison with control groups.[44] Although school choice is not a panacea that will magically cure all of the ills of the American education system, empowering parents to choose the school that they believe is best-suited to the needs of their children is, in and of itself, a significant gain insofar as it brings policies more into line with the primacy of parental educational authority. Further, laws and policies affect behavior not only directly through what they require, allow or forbid, but also indirectly by shaping attitudes and beliefs.[45] Educational policies are no exception. In addition to their direct effects, policies that increase effective school choice also have the indirect positive effect of sending the (true) message that parents, not the state, are the ones with the primary authority and responsibility for the education of children, thus helping to facilitate an ethos of greater parental involvement in and attentiveness to their children's education.

Conclusion

Much more fundamental than the policy recommendations discussed above are the general principles regarding the nature, content and scope of parental rights that I have developed in the preceding chapters. Parents, not the state, have primary and original childrearing authority, because they are the ones with the most direct and immediate obligation to care for their children, and because children directly and primarily "belong" to – i.e. are members of and under the care of – their families,

---

[43] Caroline Minter Hoxby, "Rising Tide," *Education Next* (Winger 2001), www.educationnext.org/rising-tide/. Last accessed on January 14, 2015.

[44] Philip Gleason, et al., *The Evaluation of Charter School Impacts: Final Report* (NCEE 2010–4029). Washington, DC: National Center for Education Evaluation and Regional Assistance, Institute of Education Sciences, U.S. Department of Education, www.ies.ed.gov/ncee/pubs/20104029/pdf/20104029.pdf and Wolf, "School Voucher Programs," 415–446.

[45] See Robert George, *Making Men Moral* (New York: Oxford, 2002).

and only indirectly and secondarily "belong" to the larger political community. The negative right of parents to raise their children as they think best, free from undue coercive state intervention, protects parents' sphere of authority and the goods that authority exists to promote – especially the well-being of children, in whose development parents play an irreplaceable role, and also the well-being of the family as a whole. Policies that unjustly usurp this authority – i.e. that intervene coercively in childrearing except in cases that involve abuse, neglect or a significant threat to the public order – are therefore seriously contrary to the common good. Strong protections for parental rights are a central component of any just political order whose laws and institutions aim to foster the well-being of its members in both present and future generations.

BIBLIOGRAPHY

2013 National Assessment of Educational Progress. Accessed on January 12, 2015. www.nationsreportcard.gov/reading_math_g12_2013/#/.

Abowitz, Kathleen Knight and Jason Harrish. "Contemporary Discourses of Citizenship." *Review of Educational Research* 76, 4 (2006): 653–690.

Ackerman, Bruce. *Social Justice in the Liberal State*. Binghamton: Yale University Press, 1980.

Adalbjarnardottir, Sigrun and Leifur G. Hafsteinsson, "Adolescents' Perceived Parenting Styles and Their Substance Use: Concurrent and Longitudinal Analyses." *Journal of Research on Adolescence* 11, 4 (2001): 401–423.

Allen, Douglas. "High School Graduation Rates Among Children of Same-Sex Households." *Review of Economics of the Household* 11, 4 (December 2013): 635–658.

Aquinas, Thomas. *Summa Theologiae, translated by the Fathers of the English Dominican Province*. New York: Benziger Brothers, 1948.

Archard, David. "The Obligations and Responsibilities of Parenthood." In *Procreation and Parenthood*, edited by David Archard and David Benatar, 103–127. Oxford: Oxford University Press, 2010.

Aristotle. *The Complete Works of Aristotle*, edited by Jonathan Barnes. Princeton: Princeton University Press, 1984.

Arons, Stephen. *Compelling Belief: The Culture of American Schooling*. New York: McGraw-Hill Book Company, 1983.

Austin, Michael. *Conceptions of Parenthood*. Burlington, Vermont: Ashgate, 2007.

Baker, Catherine. *Behavioral Genetics: An Introduction to How Genes and Environments Interact Through Development to Shape Differences in Mood, Personality, and Intelligence*. Washington, DC: American Association for the Advancement of Science, 2004.

Barry, Brian. *Culture and Equality*. Cambridge: Harvard University Press, 2001.

Baumrind, Diana. "Rearing Competent Children." In *Child Development Today and Tomorrow*, edited by William Damon, 349–378. San Francisco: Jossey-Bass, Inc., 1989.

Bayne, Tim. "Gamete Donation and Parental Responsibility." *Journal of Applied Philosophy* 20, 1 (2003): 77–87.

Beck, Deborah E. "Jenkins v. Missouri: School Choice as a Method for Desegregating an Inner-City School District." *California Law Review* 81, 4 (July 1993): 1029–1057.

Belfield, Clive R. and Henry M. Levin. "The Effects of Competition Between Schools on Educational Outcomes: A Review for the United States." *Review of Education Research* 72, 2 (2002): 279–341.

Belliotti, Raymond, "Honor Thy Father and Mother and to Thine Own Self Be True." *The Southern Journal of Philosophy* 24, 2 (1986): 149–162.

Berlin, Isaiah. *The Crooked Timber of Humanity: Chapters in the History of Ideas.* New York: Alfred A. Knopf, 1991.

Bohman, James. "Deliberative Toleration." *Political Theory* 31, 6 (December 2003): 757–779.

Bohman, James and Henry Richardson. "Liberalism, Deliberative Democracy, and 'Reasons that All Can Accept.'" *The Journal of Political Philosophy* 17, 3 (2009): 253–274.

Borawski, Elaine et al. Evaluation of the Teen Pregnancy Prevention Programs Funded through the Wellness Block Grant (1999–2000), Center for Health Promotion Research, Department of Epidemiology and Biostatistics, Case Western Reserve University, School of Medicine, March 23, 2001.

Bou-Habib, Paul. "A Theory of Religious Accommodation." *Journal of Applied Philosophy* 23, 1 (2006): 109–126.

Bowlby, John. *A Secure Base.* New York: Basic Book Publishers, 1988.

Boyle, Joseph. "The Place of Religion in the Practical Reasoning of Individuals and Groups." *American Journal of Jurisprudence* 43 (1998): 1–24.

Brennan, Samantha and Robert Noggle. "The Moral Status of Children: Children's Rights, Parents' Rights, and Family Justice." *Social Theory and Practice* 23 (1997): 1–25.

Brighouse, Harry. "Civic Education and Liberal Legitimacy." *Ethics* 108, 4 (July 1998): 719–745.

School Choice and Social Justice. New York: Oxford University Press, 2000.

Brighouse, Harry and Adam Swift. "Parents' Rights and the Value of the Family." *Ethics* 17, 1 (October 2006): 80–108.

Brinig, Margaret and Nicole Garnett. *Lost Classroom, Lost Community: Catholic Schools' Importance in Urban America.* Chicago: University of Chicago Press, 2014.

Broadie, Sarah. *Ethics With Aristotle.* New York: Oxford University Press, 1993.

Burtt, Shelley. "Religious Parents, Secular Schools: A Liberal Defense of an Illiberal Education." *The Review of Politics* 56, 1 (Winter 1994): 51–70.

Callan, Eamonn. "Autonomy, Childrearing and Good Lives." In *The Moral and Political Status of Children*, edited by David Archard and Colin M. MacLeod, 118–141. New York: Oxford University Press, 2002.

Creating Citizens: Political Education and Liberal Democracy. New York: Oxford University Press, 1997.

"Liberal Legitimacy, Justice and Civic Education." *Ethics* 111, 1 (October 2000): 141–155.

"Tradition and Integrity in Moral Education." *American Journal of Education* 101, 1 (November 1992): 1–28.

Campbell, David E. "The Civic Side of School Choice: An Empirical Analysis of Civic Education in Public and Private Schools." *Brigham Young University Law Review* 2008, 2 (2008): 487–524.

Caws, Peter and Stefani Jones, editors. *Religious Upbringing and the Costs of Freedom: Personal and Philosophical Essays*. University Park, PA: Pennsylvania State University Press, 2010.

Chubb, John E. and Terry M. Moe. *Politics, Markets and America's Schools*. Washington, DC: The Brookings Institution, 1990.

Clayton, Matthew. *Justice and Legitimacy in Upbringing*. Oxford: Oxford University Press, 2006.

Coleman, James and Thomas Hoffer. *Public and Private High Schools: The Impact of Communities*. New York: Basic Books, 1987.

Conger, Kimberly and Bryan McGraw. "Religious Conservatives and the Requirements of Citizenship: Political Autonomy." *Perspectives on Politics* 6, 2 (June 2008): 253–266.

Coons, John E. and Stephen D. Sugarman. *Education by Choice: The Case for Family Control*. Berkeley: University of California Press, 1978.

Cowden, Mhairi. "What's Love Got to Do With It? Why a Child Does Not Have a Right to be Loved." *Critical Review of International Social and Political Philosophy* 15, 3 (2012): 325–245.

Cremata, Edward et al. *National Charter School Study*, Center for Research on Education Outcomes: Stanford University (2013). www.credo.stanford.edu/documents/NCSS%202013%20Final%20Draft.pdf. Accessed on July 8, 2014.

Cristillo, Louis. "The Case for the Muslim School as a Civil Society Actor." In *Educating the Muslims of America*, edited by Yvonne Haddad, Farid Senzai and Jane I. Smith, 67–84. New York: Oxford University Press 2009.

Crockett, L.J. and R. Hayes. "Parenting Practices and Styles." *Encyclopedia of Adolescence*, Vol. 2 (Elsevier, 2011): 241–248. DOI:10.1016/B978-0-12-373915-5.00077-2

Curren, Randall. *Aristotle on the Necessity of Public Education*. Lanham, MD: Rowman and Littlefield, 2000.

de Tocqueville, Alexis. *Democracy in America*. Translated by Harvey C. Mansfield and Delba Winthrop. Chicago: University of Chicago Press, 2000.

Denny, G. and M. Young. "An Evaluation of an Abstinence-Only Sex Education Curriculum: An 18-month Follow-Up." *Journal of School Health* 76, 8 (2006): 414–422.

Dewalt, Mark. *Amish Education in the United States and Canada*. Lanham, MD: Rowman and Littlefield Publishers, Inc., 2006.

Doniger, Andrew S. "Impact Evaluation of the 'Not Me, Not Now' Abstinence-Oriented, Adolescent Pregnancy Prevention Communications Program, Monroe County, New York." *Journal of Health Communications* 6 (2001): 45–60.

Dozier, Mary et al. "Lessons from the Longitudinal Studies of Attachment." In *Attachment from Infancy to Adulthood*, edited by Klaus Grossman et al., 305–319. New York: The Guilford Press, 2005.

Dworkin, Ronald. *Taking Rights Seriously*. Cambridge: Harvard University Press, 1978.

Dwyer, James. *Religious Schools v. Children's Rights*. Ithaca: Cornell University Press, 1998.

Eberle, Christopher. *Religious Conviction in Liberal Politics*. New York: Cambridge University Press, 2002.

Feinberg, Joel. "The Child's Right to an Open Future" in *Whose Child? Children's Rights, Parental Authority, and State Power*, edited by William Aiken and Hugh LaFollette (Totowa, NJ: Rowman & Littlefield, 1980), 124–153.

Feinberg, Walter. *Common Schools/Uncommon Identities: National Unity and Cultural Difference*. New Haven: Yale University Press, 1998.

Finkelman, Paul. "School Vouchers, Thomas Jefferson, Roger Williams and Protecting the Faithful: Warnings from the Eighteenth and the Seventeenth Century on the Danger of Establishments to Religious Communities." *Brigham Young University Law Review* 2008, 2 (2008): 525–566.

Finnis, John. *Natural Law and Natural Rights*, Second Edition. New York: Oxford University Press, 2011.

Finnis, John, Joseph Boyle and Germain Grisez. *Nuclear Deterrence, Morality and Realism*. Oxford: Oxford University Press, 1987.

Fried, Charles. *Right and Wrong*. Cambridge: Harvard University Press, 1978.

Galston, William. *Liberal Pluralism*. New York: Cambridge University Press, 2002.
    Liberal Purposes. New York: Cambridge University Press, 1991.
    "Parents, Government and Children." In *Child Family and State*, edited by Stephen Macedo and Iris Marion Young, 211–233. New York: New York University Press, 2003.
    "Two Concepts of Liberalism." *Ethics* 105, 3 (April 1995): 516–534.

Gaus, Gerald. *Justificatory Liberalism*. New York: Oxford University Press, 1996.

Gaus, Gerald and Kevin Vallier. "The Roles of Religious Conviction in a Publicly Justified Polity: The Implications of Convergence, Asymmetry and Political Institutions." *Philosophy and Social Criticism* 35 (2009): 51–57.

George, Robert. *Making Men Moral*. New York: Oxford University Press, 1993.
    "The Concept of Public Morality." *American Journal of Jurisprudence* 45, 1 (2000): 17–31.

George, Robert and Christopher Wolfe. "Natural Law and Public Reason." In *Natural Law and Public Reason*, edited by Robert George and Christopher Wolfe, 51–74. Washington, DC: Georgetown University Press, 2000.

Gheaus, Anca. "The Right to Parent One's Biological Baby." *The Journal of Political Philosophy* 20, 4 (Dec. 2012): 432–455.

Gilles, Stephen. "On Educating Children: A Parentalist Manifesto." *The University of Chicago Law Review* 63, 3 (1996): 937-1064.

Gleason, Philip et al. *The Evaluation of Charter School Impacts: Final Report* (NCEE 2010–4029). Washington, DC: National Center for Education Evaluation and Regional Assistance, Institute of Education Sciences, U.S. Department of Education. Accessed on July 12, 2015. www.//ies.ed.gov/ncee/pubs/20104029/pdf/20104029.pdf

Greene, Jay P. "Civic Values in Public and Private Schools." In *Learning from School Choice*, edited by Paul E. Peterson and Bryan Hassel, 83–106. Washington, DC: Brookings Institution Press, 1998.

Grim, Brian and Roger Finke. *The Price of Freedom Denied: Religious Persecution and Conflict in the 21st Century*. New York: Cambridge University Press, 2011.

Grisez, Germain. *The Way of the Lord Jesus, Volume 2: Living a Christian Life*. Quincy, IL: Franciscan Press, 1993.

Grisez, Germain, Joseph Boyle and John Finnis. "Practical Principles, Moral Truth and Ultimate Ends." *American Journal of Jurisprudence* 32 (1987): 99–151.

Groarke, Louis. *An Aristotelian Account of Induction: Creating Something from Nothing*. Canada: McGill-Queen's University Press, 2009.

Gutmann, Amy. "Civic Education and Social Diversity," *Ethics*, Vol. 105, 3 (April, 1995): 557–579.

"Children, Paternalism, and Education: A Liberal Argument," *Philosophy and Public Affairs* 9, No. 4 (Summer, 1980): 338–358.

Democratic Education. Princeton: Princeton University Press, 1999.

Gutmann, Amy and Dennis Thompson. *Democracy and Disageement*. Cambridge, MA: Belknap Press, 1996.

Why Deliberative Democracy? Princeton: Princeton University Press, 2004.

Haslanger, Sally. "Family, Ancestry and Self: What is the Moral Significance of Biological Ties?" *Adoption and Culture* 2 (2009): 91–122.

Heaven, Patrick C. L. and Joseph Ciarrochi. "Parental Styles, Conscientiousness, and Academic Performance in High School: A Three-Wave Longitudinal Study." *Personality and Social Psychology Bulletin* 34, 5 (April 2008): 451–461.

Henley, Kenneth, "The Authority to Educate," In *Having Children: Philosophical and Legal Reflections on Parenthood*, edited by Onora O'Neill and William Ruddick, 254–264. New York: Oxford University Press, 1979.

Hough, Cassandra. "Learning About Love: How Sex Ed Programs Undermine Healthy Marriage." The Public Discourse, October 20, 2014. Accessed on August 14, 2015. www.thepublicdiscourse.com/2014/10/13831/.

Hoxby, Caroline Minter. "Rising Tide." *Education Next* (Winter 2001). Accessed on January 14, 2015. www.educationnext.org/rising-tide/.

Ianni, Francis. *The Search for Structure: A Report on American Youth Today.* New York: The Free Press, 1989.

Jacobs, Joanne. *Our School.* New York: Palgrave MacMillan, 2007.

Jemmott, J.B. et al. "Efficacy of a Theory-Based Abstinence-Only Intervention Over 24 Months." *Archives of Pediatrics and Adolescent Medicine* 164, 2 (2010): 152–159.

Kahane, David. "Liberal Virtues and Citizen Education." In *Citizenship After Liberalism*, edited by Karen Slawner and Mark Denham, 103–145. New York: Peter Lang Publishing, 1998.

Kant, Immanuel. *Grounding for the Metaphysics of Morals.* Indianapolis: Hackett Publishing Company, Inc. 1993.

Kim, Christine and Robert Rector. "Evidence on the Effectiveness of Abstinence Education: An Update." The Heritage Foundation, February 2010. Accessed on August 14, 2015. www.heritage.org/research/reports/2010/02/evidence-on-the-effectiveness-of-abstinence-education-an-update#_ftnref36

Kolodny, Niko. "Why Relationships Justify Partiality? The Case of Parents and Children." *Philosophy and Public Affairs* 38, 1 (2010): 37–75.

LaFollette, Hugh, "Licensing Parents Revisited," *Journal of Applied Philosophy*, 27 (2010): 327–343

    Personal Relationships: Love, Identity and Morality. Cambridge: Blackwell, 1996.

Lamborn, Susie D. et al. "Patterns of Competence and Adjustment among Adolescents from Authoritative, Authoritarian, Indulgent, and Neglectful Families." *Child Development* 62, 5 (Oct. 1991): 1049–1065.

Lee, Patrick and Robert George. *Conjugal Union: What It Is and Why It Matters.* New York: Cambridge University Press, 2014.

Lee, Patrick and Robert George. *Body–Self Dualism in Contemporary Ethics and Politics.* New York: Cambridge University Press, 2008.

Lerner, Robert. "Can Abstinence Work? An Analysis of the Best Friends Program." *Adolescent & Family Health* 3, 4 (April 2005): 185–192.

Liao, S. Matthew. "The Right of Children to be Loved." *The Journal of Political Philosophy* 14, 4 (2006): 420–440.

    "Why Children Need to be Loved." *Critical Review of International Social and Political Philosophy*, 15, 3 (2012): 347–358.

Macedo, Stephen. *Diversity and Distrust.* Cambridge: Harvard University Press, 2003.

    Liberal Virtues. New York: Oxford University Press, 1990.

"Multiculturalism for the Religious Right? Defending Liberal Civic Education." In *Democratic Education in a Multicultural State*, ed. Yael Tamir, 65–80. Oxford: Blackwell Publishers, 1995.

"Transformative Constitutionalism and the Case of Religion: Defending the Moderate Hegemony of Liberalism." *Political Theory* 26, 1 (Feb, 1998): 56–80.

MacIntyre, Alasdair. *Dependent Rational Animals*. Chicago: Open Court, 1999.

MacMullen, Ian. *Faith in Schools? Autonomy, Citizenship, and Religious Education in the Liberal State*. Princeton: Princeton University Press, 2007.

Marquardt, Elizabeth, Norval D. Glenn and Karen Clark. *My Daddy's Name is Donor: A New Study of Young Adults Conceived Through Sperm Donation*. New York: Institute for American Values, 2010.

Mertes, Heidi and Guido Pennings. "Embryonic Stem Cell-Derived Gametes and Genetic Parenthood: A Problematic Relationship." *Cambridge Quarterly of Healthcare Ethics* 17, 1 (January 2008): 7–14.

Mill, J.S. *On Liberty*. Cambridge: Cambridge University Press, 1997.

Mills, Claudia. "The Child's Rights to an Open Future?" *Journal of Social Philosophy* 34, 4 (Winter 2003): 499-509.

Moe, Terry. "The Two Democratic Purposes of Education." In *Rediscovering the Democratic Purposes of Education*, edited by L. M. McDonnell, P. M. Timpane and R. Benjamin, 127–147. Lawrence, KS: University Press of Kansas, 2000.

Moore, Kristin Anderson et al. *Marriage from a Child's Perspective: How Does Family Structure Affect Children, and What Can We Do About It?* Child Trends Research Brief, June 2002. Accessed on August 14, 2015. www.childtrends.org/wp-content/uploads/2002/06/MarriageRB602.pdf.

Moschella, Melissa. "Rethinking the Moral Permissibility of Gamete Donation." *Theoretical Medicine and Bioethics* 35, 6 (2014): 421–440.

"The Wrongness of Third-Party Assisted Reproduction: A Natural Law Account," *Christian Bioethics* (forthcoming).

"Beyond Equal Liberty: Religion as a Distinct Human Good and the Implications for Religious Freedom." *Journal of Law and Religion* (forthcoming).

Moschella, Melissa and Robert George. "Does Sex Ed Undermine Parental Rights?" *New York Times*, October 19, 2011. Accessed on June 15, 2015. www.nytimes.com/2011/10/19/opinion/does-sex-ed-undermine-parental-rights.html.

"Natural Law." In *International Encyclopedia of the Social and Behavioral Sciences*, Second Edition, edited by James D. Wright, 320–324. (Oxford: Elsevier, 2015). Accessed on August 14, 2015. www.sciencedirect.com/science/article/pii/B9780080970868860845.

Mozert v. Hawkins County Public Schools 827 F.2d. 1058 (6th Cir. 1987).

Nozick, Robert. *The Examined Life*. New York: Simon and Schuster, 1989.

Parsons, Paul F. *Inside America's Christian Schools*. Macon, GA: Mercer University Press, 1987.

Partridge, Brian C. "The Mature Minor: Some Critical Psychological Reflections on the Empirical Bases." *Journal of Medicine and Philosophy* 38 (2013): 283–299.

Perry, Michael. *Love and Power: The Role of Religion and Morality in American Politics*. New York: Oxford University Press, 1991.

Peters, Shawn Francis. *The Yoder Case*. Lawrenceville, KS: University Press of Kansas, 2003.

Pierce v. Society of Sisters, 268 US 510 (1925).

Putnam, Robert. *American Grace*. New York: Simon and Schuster, 2010.

   Bowling Alone. New York: Simon and Schuster, 2000.

Rawls, John. *Political Liberalism*. New York: Columbia University Press, 1993.

   "The Idea of Public Reason Revisited." In *The Law of Peoples*. Cambridge, MA: Harvard University Press, 2001.

Raz, Joseph. *Practical Reason and Norms*. London: Hutchinson, 1975.

Rector, Robert and Christine Kim, "Abstinence Education Works: A Review of 15 Evaluations on the Effectiveness of Abstinence Programs," The Heritage Foundation, April 2007. Accessed on April 10, 2015. www.abstinence.net/pdf/contentmgmt/Abstinence_Works__15_Evaluations.pdf.

Regnerus, Mark. "How Different are the Adult Children of Parents Who Have Same-Sex Relationships? Findings from the New Family Structures Study." *Social Science Research* 41, 4 (July 2012): 752–770.

Reich, Rob. "Testing the Boundaries of Parental Authority Over Education: The Case of Homeschooling." In *Moral and Political Education*, edited by Stephen Macedo and Yael Tamir, 275–313. New York: New York University Press, 2002.

Richards, Norvin. *The Ethics of Parenthood*. New York: Oxford University Press, 2010.

Romeike v. Holder, 718 F.3d 518 (6th Cir. 2013).

Schoeman, Ferdinand. "Rights of Children, Rights of Parents, and the Moral Basis of the Family." *Ethics* 91, 1 (October 1980): 6–19.

Shields, Jon. "Between Passion and Deliberation: The Christian Right and Democratic Ideals." *Political Science Quarterly* 122, 1 (2007): 89–113.

Siegel, Deborah H. and Susan Livingston Smith. "Openness in Adoption." March 2012, The Evan B. Donaldson Adoption Institute. Accessed on August 14, 2015. www.adoptioninstitute.org/old/publications/2012_03_OpennessInAdoption.pdf.

Simon, Yves. *Philosophy of Democratic Government*. Notre Dame: University of Notre Dame Press, 1993.

Steinberg, Laurence et al. "Over-Time Changes in Adjustment and Competence among Adolescents from Authoritative, Authoritarian, Indulgent, and Neglectful Families." *Child Development* 65, 3 (June 1994): 754–770.

Stout, Jeffrey. *Democracy and Tradition*. Princeton: Princeton University Press, 2004.

Strike, Kenneth. "Must Liberal Citizens Be Reasonable?" *The Review of Politics* 58, 1 (Winter 1996): 41–48.

Sullins, D. Paul. "Emotional Problems among Children with Same-Sex Parents: Difference by Definition," *British Journal of Education, Society and Behavioural Science* 7, 2 (2015): 99–120.

Thompson, R. A. "The Legacy of Early Attachments." *Child Development* 71, 1 (2000): 145–152.

Tollefsen, Christopher. "Conscience, Religion and the State." *American Journal of Jurisprudence* 54 (2009): 93–115.

"Is a Purely First Person Account of Human Action Defensible?" *Ethical Theory and Moral Practice* 9 (2006): 441–460.

Tolo, Kenneth W. *The Civic Education of American Youth: From State Policies to School District Practices*, Lyndon B. Johnson School of Public Affairs Policy Research Project Report, Volume 133. Austin: Lyndon B. Johnson School of Public Affairs, 1999.

Velleman, David. "Persons in Prospect." *Philosophy & Public Affairs* 36 (2008): 221–288.

Verba, Sidney, Kay Lehman Schlozman and Henry E. Brady. *Voice and Equality: Civic Volunteerism in American Politics*. Cambridge: Harvard University Press, 1995.

Waldron, Jeremy. "Public Reason and 'Justification." *Journal of Law, Philosophy and Culture* 119 (2007): 107–134.

Waldron, Jeremy and Melissa Williams, "Introduction," In *Toleration and its Limits*, edited by Jeremy Walrdron and Melissa Walsh, 1–27. New York: New York University Press, 2008.

Walsh, Moira. *Freedom and the Legitimacy of Moral Education: Philosophical Reflections on Aristotle and Rousseau*. Dissertation, University of Notre Dame, 1998.

Walzer, Michael. *Just and Unjust Wars*. New York: Basic Books, 2000.

Weed, Stan E. Title V Abstinence Education Programs: Phase I Interim Evaluation Report to Arkansas Department of Health, Institute for Research and Evaluation, October 15, 2001.

Weed, Stan E., Irene H. Ericksen, Allen Lewis, Gale E. Grant and Kathy H. Wibberly. "An Abstinence Program's Impact on Cognitive Mediators and Sexual Initiation." *American Journal of Health Behavior* 31, 1 (2008): 60–73.

Weed, Stan E., Irene H. Ericksen and Paul James Birch, "An Evaluation of the Heritage Keepers Abstinence Education Program." Institute for Research and Evaluation (Salt Lake City), November 2005. Accessed on May 14, 2015. www.heritageservices.org/Stan%20Weed's%20HHS%20Conference%20article.pdf.

Westheimer, Joel and Joseph Kahne. "What Kind of Citizen? The Politics of Educating for Democracy." *American Educational Research Journal* 41, 2 (Summer 2004): 237–269.

What Kids are Reading. Renaissance Learning, 2015. Accessed on January 12, 2015. www.doc.renlearn.com/KMNet/R004101202GH426A.pdf.

Wilhelms, Evan and Valerie Reyna. "Fuzzy Trace Theory and Medical Decisions by Minors: Differences in Reasoning between Adolescents and Adults." *Journal of Medicine and Philosophy* 38 (2013): 268–282.

Williams, Melissa. "Citizenship as Identity, Citizenship as Shared Fate, and the Functions of Multicultural Education." In *Citizenship and Education in Liberal Democratic Societies,* edited by Kevin McDonough and Walter Feinberg, 209–249. New York: Oxford University Press, 2003.

Wolf, Patrick J. et al. "Private Schooling and Political Tolerance." In *Charters, Vouchers and Public Education,* edited by Paul E. Peterson and David E. Campbell, 268–290. Washington, DC: Brookings Institution Press, 2001.

Wolf, Patrick J. "School Voucher Programs: What the Research Says about Parental School Choice." *Brigham Young University Law Review* 2008, 2 (2008): 415–446.

Wolfe, Alan. *One Nation, After All.* New York: Viking, 1998.

Zelman v. Simmons-Harris, 536 U.S. 639 (2002).

Zimmerman, Ron et al. *Charter Schools in Eight States: Effects on Achievement, Attainment, Integration and Competition.* Santa Monica, CA: The RAND Corporation, 2009.

INDEX

abstinence-only education, 72, 168–169, 171–172
abstinence-plus education, 169
abuse, 68–69, 120–121, 141, 144–145, 149–150, 152–153, 170
academic defectiveness, 156–157
accommodation, 92–93, 111–112, 154–167
Ackerman, Bruce, 120
adolescents, 121–122, 132, 137–141
  decision-making by, 68, 135–136, 150
adopted children, 41–43
adoptive parents, 28–29, 44–45, 63
African Americans, 139, 178
agency, moral, 126–127
Allen, Douglas, 38–39
American political system, 96–97
Amish. *See Wisconsin v. Yoder*
Aquinas, Thomas, 9, 26–28, 54, 109–110
  Gutmann and, 25
  spiritual womb and, 25–26, 28
Aristotle, 9, 25–28, 64, 68–69
  autonomy and, 137–144
  laws and, 26
  moral prerequisites for autonomy and, 133–136
Arons, Stephen, 95
Association of Christian Schools International, 104–105
authenticity, 51
authoritarian parenting, 138–139
authoritative communities, 151
authoritative parenting, 138
authority, 5, 14, 18–19
  common good and, 19, 47

legitimate, 101
natural parental, 25, 34–35
paternalistic, 19–20, 63–64
political, 19–20, 47–48, 66–67, 75
rights as spheres of, 61–63
autonomy, 18, 83, 104, 121, 130, 147, 149–150
  Aristotle and, 137–144
  of children, 119
  cognitive conditions of, 142–143
  ethical servility and, 123–125
  explicit education for, 128–129
  genuine, 121–122, 142
  instrumental value of, 127–128
  integrity and, 125–126
  liberalism and, 85–86, 122
  mandatory education for, 122–127
  minimal threshold of, 127, 145
  moral conditions of, 143
  moral prerequisites for, 133–136
  moral virtues and, 121–122, 129–133
  non-mandatory education programs, 145–146
  rational reflection and, 128–129
  simple integrity and, 122–123
  standardized curricula, 146

Barry, Brian, 52, 161–164, 166–167
basic goods, 10, 13–15, 57
Baumrind, Diana, 138
Berlin, Isaiah, 9, 78
biological cause, 35–38
biological parent–child relationship, 34–35, 44–45
  adoptive parents and, 44–45
  benefits of, 39, 41, 43–44
  bodily relationship and, 35–36

biological parent–child relationship
(cont.)
    identity and, 36, 39–40
    love and, 39, 41
    moral relevance of, 45
    non-transferable obligations and,
        34–35, 41
    open adoption and, 42–43
    parental obligations as personal
        obligations and, 38–39
    as personal relationship, 37
    race and, 43
biological parenthood, 6, 20, 34–35,
    38–39
bodily relationship, 35–36
Boggs (Judge), 91
Bohman, James, 98–99
Bou-Habib, Paul, 6–7, 52–53, 55–56
Boyle, Joseph, 9–10
brain imaging, 135–136
Brennan (Justice), 157
Brighouse, Harry, 121–122, 127–129,
    141–142, 149–150
burdens of judgment, 77–78, 81–82, 90,
    95, 104, 122–123
    Callan, Eamonn, and, 80–81
    good citizenship and, 77
    Macedo and, 76
    reasonable pluralism and, 77–78
    tolerance and, 79–80
Burtt, Shelley, 104–106

Callan, Eamonn, 4, 6, 24, 98–99,
    121–122, 130, 141–142, 149–150
    burdens of judgment and, 80–81, 95
    citizenship and, 7–8
    ethical servility and, 143–144
    freedom of conscience and, 24
    mandatory autonomy education and,
        122–124, 126
    mandatory Rawlsian civic education
        and, 74, 80–82
    reasonableness and, 132–133
    rights and, 110
Catholicism, 25, 57, 82, 87, 93–94,
    175–176
causality, 35
central tradition of western thought, 9

charter schools, 175, 177–179
Child Trends Research Institute, 38–39
Christian Coalition, 96–97
Christian Right, 96–97
Christian school movement, 104–105,
    141–142
churches, 151
citizenship, 7–8, 89–90, 93, 101. *See also*
    good citizenship; minimally
    decent citizenship
    conscience rights and, 149
    diverse understanding of, 103
    diversity and, 86, 114
    liberal democratic, 74–76
    participatory, 103
    prerequisites of, 94–95
    requirements of, 90
civic education, 100–102, 106–107,
    113–114, 147, 149, 177. *See also*
    mandatory Rawlsian civic
    education
    autonomy and, 121
    conscience rights and, 75
    liberalism and, 74–75
    Mozert v. Hawkins and, 90–91
    political virtues and, 104
civic liberalism, 79–80
civic minimalism, 115–116
civic participation, 117–118
Clayton, Matthew, 120
cloning, 43
coercion, 76–77, 107–108, 114–115
coercive force, 109–111, 113–114
coercive interference, 67–68, 72,
    144–145, 149–150
cognitive development, 131–132
colonization effects, 86–87
common good, 47–48, 66–67, 147–153,
    166
    authority and, 19, 47
    political authority and, 19–20
    sexual education and, 167–168
communal childrearing, 23–24, 46
competition, increased (among
    schools), 178
comprehensive liberalism, 76, 80, 87, 99
comprehensive sexual education,
    mandatory, 169–171

conceptual thought, 36
Conger, Kimberly, 96–97
conjoined biological parenthood, 38–39
conjugal union, 25–26, 28
conscience, 14–15, 59–60
    freedom of, 24, 95, 110–112, 152
    reasonable preferences and, 165
conscience rights, 15, 17, 50, 61, 148, 152
    citizenship and, 149
    civic education and, 75
    free exercise and, 16
    humane slaughter laws and, 166
    physical abuse and, 152–153
    practical reason and, 15–16
    right to integrity and, 50–51
    sexual education and, 169–170
conscious social reproduction, 82–84
conservative religious activists, 96–97
corporal punishment, 152–153
Cowden, Mhairi, 39
Creating Citizens (Callan), 122–123
critical thinking skills, 83, 121–122, 124, 135, 145–146, 160
Culture and Equality (Barry), 52

decision-making
    by adolescents, 68, 135–136, 150
    democratic, 83–84
deliberative democracy, 76
democratic community, rights of, 115–116
democratic decision-making, 83–84
democratic deliberation, 116
Democratic Education (Guttmann), 5, 115, 120
democratic engagement, 117–118
dependency, 32–33, 38, 44
Dependent Rational Animals (MacIntyre), 31–32
Dewey, John, 91–92
disengaged parenting, 138
dishonesty, 109–110
disintegrity, 54–55
diversity, 84–87, 89, 92–93
    citizenship and, 86, 114
    education, 8, 104, 173

    exposure to, 90–91, 93
    tolerance of, 103
diversity state, 86
donor-conceived persons, 41–42
Douglas (Justice), 157, 159
drugs, 16–17, 86–87
duty of civility, 77–80, 88–89, 97, 103
Dwyer, James, 69–71, 141–142

ECHR. See European Court of Human Rights
educational funding, 8, 172–179
educational policies, 8
effective school choice, 58
Ellis, Tom, 42
emancipation, 151, 158
embryo switch, 22–23
Employment Division v. Smith, 16–17
Establishment Clause, of First Amendment, 174–175
ethical reflection, 132, 135, 141
ethical servility, 123–125, 143–144
Ethically Servile Child, 124–125
European Court of Human Rights (ECHR), 3
exclusionary reasons for action, 61–63
exemptions, 58, 154–167
explicit autonomy education, 128–129
expressive liberty, 6–7, 24, 51–52, 109–110

fair terms of cooperation, 77
fairness, 114, 166
family
    Romeike family, 1–2
    as sovereign community, 66–67, 70
    structure of, 38–39
family community, 47–48
Family Research Council, 96–97
financial structures, 61
Finnis, John, 9–10, 15, 51, 54–55
First Amendment, 174–175
first-person judgments, 53
formative influences, 59
foundational premises, 9
fraternal twins, 40–41
Free Exercise Clause, 175–176

CPSIA information can be obtained
at www.ICGtesting.com
Printed in the USA
LVHW082028200720
661090LV00008B/88